Ordinary People and Everyday Life

Ordinary People and Everyday Life

Perspectives on the New Social History

Edited by

James B. Gardner

and

George Rollie Adams

The American Association for State and Local History
Nashville, Tennessee

Funding provided by the National Endowment for the Humanities made possible the series of seminars on which this book is based and supported editorial work on the book itself.

Library of Congress Cataloging in Publication Data

Main entry under title:
Ordinary people and everyday life.

   Includes bibliographies and index.
   1. United States—Social conditions—1960–   —Addresses, essays,
lectures.   2. United States—Historiography—Addresses, essays, lectures.
I. Gardner, James B., 1950–   .   II. Adams, George Rollie.
III. American Association for State and Local History.
HN59. 2.072   1983   973   83–3707
ISBN 0–910050–66–X

Contents

Preface

Over the past two decades, the new social history has challenged dramatically the way we look at our past. Historians no longer value only great men and great events; now, the ordinary people and everyday activities basic to the American experience are prized, as well. This fundamental reorientation has expanded substantially the boundaries of historical inquiry and inspired significant new departures in research and analysis.

Convinced of the importance of disseminating this work as broadly as possible, the American Association for State and Local History sponsored in 1980 and 1981 a series of five seminars on current historical scholarship and its implications for interpretive activities in museums and historical agencies. The National Endowment for the Humanities provided funding for the series, which was entitled "Re-examining America's Past." Participants were chosen through competitive application and came from museums and historical agencies across the nation. Instructors included distinguished scholars in American history and material culture and leading historical society and museum professionals expert in recent interpretive developments.

The nine essays that follow are based on presentations that the authors made in the seminar series. The goal of this volume is not to provide a detailed "state of the art" anthology, but rather, as the subtitle indicates, to present various perspectives on what the new social history is all about and where it seems to be going. We hope the volume will broaden awareness of this new scholarship and convey something of the excitement and vitality that these fresh perspectives can bring to the study and understanding of America's past. Among those who should find the essays helpful are museum and historical agency professionals who are respon-

sible for conducting research and for designing and implementing interpretive programs, scholars who are considering new research approaches, teachers and students who are seeking an overview of recent
developments in the field, and others who are interested in current trends
in American historical scholarship.

    We are indebted to the instructors and the participants who helped to
make the seminar series successful; to the National Endowment for the
Humanities, for further support for publication of the essays; and to the
American Association for State and Local History, for sponsoring both
the seminar series and this volume.

James B. Gardner
George Rollie Adams

Ordinary People and Everyday Life

Seeking relief from the pressures of daily life, vacationers stroll along the boardwalk at Connecticut's Hammonassett Beach in this photograph taken about 1920 by T. S. Bronson.

New Haven Colony Historical Society

1

The New Social History: An Overview

Peter N. Stearns

THE RISE OF SOCIAL HISTORY has been the most dramatic development in American historical research over the past two decades. One reviewer, commenting on a recent survey of American history today, indeed asserts that every branch of historical writing has become "social," with political historians charting the link between social groupings and voting behavior, and intellectual historians studying such arcane fields as book publishing, to discover, not what the leading ideas of the past were, but how widely and by what means they spread[1] Certainly the ramifications of social history have spilled over into many other areas. Even in its own right, social history has become a major facet of the discipline of history, with at least four specialist journals[2] and a growing array of monographs to support its claim.[3]

This dramatic change in the way historians define what history is—for the rise in social history involves no less—can of course be assessed in narrowly academic terms. Written mainly for a scholarly audience, much of the new research seems particularly remote—partly because it is novel, but partly because many social historians have been trying to impress not only other historians but also a wider array of social scientists, which can induce some very technical presentations indeed.

The field has significance beyond the confines of the academy, however. For one thing, the rise of social history runs partially counter to recent laments about the decline of history in this country. It has obviously not stemmed many of the symptoms of decline, but it stands as dramatic evidence that major sources of vitality remain. Furthermore, social history has remarkable implications for popular attention to history. In Britain, a new journal, *History Workshop*, which specializes in one

3

kind of social history, has drawn a large "amateur" audience and considerable direct participation in research and writing. Much of the flowering of adult historical interest in the United States, such as the current concern with family and community roots, although not caused by academic social history, relates to it quite directly. The dissemination of social history approaches and findings in the schools is gaining momentum.[4] And even beyond what has already occurred, the potential interaction between social history and a broad audience is immensely exciting.

Simply put: social history can interest people in the past in new ways. Many social historians, presenting their main findings to an adult audience, have encountered the "I-didn't-know-that-was-history" reaction. That statement is a sad comment on the inability of more traditional history to spill over into adult intellectual concerns, but it also presents the challenging prospect that social history can forge new links.

Many social historians would argue that their specialty provides not only new insights into the past but also a new and dynamic sense of how the past has forged the present. This is not a unique claim. Any good history contributes to this kind of understanding, and social history most definitely is history. For some, however, social history gets closer to the stuff of life than other kinds of history do and thus contributes more directly to a grasp of the patterns of contemporary society as they continue or as they contrast with past trends and sometimes to a sense of personal values.

Social history is exciting, in a period when history more generally has receded a bit. It can link with popular historical interest in a dynamic fashion. It can be a particularly meaningful kind of history, at least to some. These are fairly sweeping claims, and the fact that they issue from a committed social historian hardly argues for their objectivity. It is time to turn to a fuller definition of social history—if not definitively to prove the claims, at least to show why they are possible.

Social history must be seen both as a set of topics and as an approach to history. The topical definition is simplest and carries us a good way into the field, but by itself it remains incomplete.

Social history involves two broad subject areas that conventional history has largely ignored. First, it deals with ordinary people, rather than the elite. The first excitement surrounding the surge of social history over the past two decades centered on the claim that the common folk—not just the movers and shakers of politics or intellectual life—have a vibrant past and contribute to larger historical processes. "History from the bottom up" was an early slogan that retains great validity.[5] The people studied were relatively inarticulate, in that few of them spoke or wrote as a matter of public record, but social historians working imaginatively with new sources have found that few if any groups are really inarticulate. Records of protest, demographic data, diaries and anonymous writings, and artistic and artifactual evidence have filled in the gaps left by more conventional materials. The result has been rapid advance in historical knowledge of the working class, of blacks and ethnic groups, of women. The list of groupings steadily multiplies, with a concern for age categories the most recent general addition. Children, youth, and the elderly all have solid histories,[6] though—perhaps revealingly—the middle-aged have yet to be captured as a category. Increasingly, a given individual in the past, though perhaps never noted by name, is brought into a whole series of group analyses, by class, gender, ethnicity, or region.

While the development of categories for the historical study of ordinary people proceeds, a second topical approach moves to greater prominence: the history of ordinary activities, institutions, and modes of thought. Thus, age categories can be seen as groupings of people but also as stages of life that have histories of their own. The study of workers or the lower middle class edges into an examination of work and leisure as historical phenomena. Sexual behavior; social mobility; family roles and functions; attitudes and practices relating to death; popular health and medicine, including mental illness; crime and law enforcement—all these areas have rich and growing histories, in some cases with specialist journals attached. At their best, the histories deal both with behavior and with values and attitudes (what French social histories call *mentalités*).[7] Thus we know the evolution of courtship behavior, but are also moving into some assessment of changes in the emotional experience and expectations that courtship entailed.[8] In principle, there is no area of human behavior not purely and simply determined by biology, and thus unchanging, that cannot be illuminated by historical analysis. A few have not yet been tackled—we have no history of sleep habits, and only some hints about the history of boredom—but the goal is now clear. Social historians intend to bring into the historical record not only all kinds of people, but all aspects of behavior and value systems, as well.

The social historians' ability to generate a wide array of new historical topics explains much of the excitement in the field. The emphasis on ordinary people often related closely to political changes in American society. Concern for blacks, women, or youth derived important inspiration from contemporary developments, though the concern has now outstripped purely political impetus. The interest in ordinary aspects of life, though less obviously political, stems from growing concern about problems of crime or the stability of the family. It ties history to the ways we measure life, today, in our own society.

Many conventional historians, convinced that politics is the begin-

ning and end of what is important in the past, were appalled at this
effervescence of new historical topics, and some remain so. Social historians undeniably complicate our sense of what the past was, beyond the
simple framework of constitutional changes and the ebb and flow of
political parties. But social historians—nothing if not brash—do more
than that, and that is why social history is not just a topical branch of
history, such as political, economic, or intellectual history, but also a
distinctive approach to the past. Obviously, social historians alter
priorities in the historical record. They are saying, at least implicitly, that
the great and famous cause less than we used to think, while ordinary
people cause more. They are saying that political actions are not necessarily more important than changes in demographic behavior, that the history of great ideas must often yield to changes in the way people treat
children.

As a result of their distinctive interests, social historians develop, as
well, a particular approach to time. Again, they are historians, which
means that they are centrally concerned with change and therefore with
making chronology intelligible; but they normally proceed in terms of
relatively large sweeps, rarely by year-to-year analysis. Major change is
identified in terms of a decade or two, not a specific year. Relatedly, as
social historians gain increasing command of their field, they develop
alternative periodizations. Presidential administrations and even major
wars may demarcate relatively little in social history, compared to the
implications of changes in rates of illegitimate births. The main periods in
the modern history of illegitimacy run from 1780 to 1870, from 1870 to 1960,
and from 1960 to the present, which means that conventional units like
the Age of Jackson, despite whatever some of Jackson's opponents may
have thought, have had relatively little to do with the phenomenon.

Compared to conventional historians, social historians are uncom-
fortable with events. They deal instead with processes, with distinctive
trends within the periods they mark out. Single events like battles or
individual cases of epidemic diseases rarely cause major or durable
changes in the way ordinary people behave or in the ordinary activities of
life—or, at least, so most social historians assume. When they do cause
major changes—such as, for example, the impact of the Black Plague on
the history of death or the role of World War II in altering women's work
patterns—events must of course be included in discussions of periodization and causation. But social historians rarely explore events for their
own sake. Their narrative is more in terms of the unfolding of a process—
such as the way Irish immigrants accommodated to the American mobility ethic[9]—than in terms of one event leading to another. Obviously also,

social historians tend to treat individuals as illustrations of large group-ings or trends.

Those characteristics make reading social history not only rather dif-ferent from reading other kinds of history, but also, for some, a more difficult or less rewarding experience. They mean, as well, that historians cannot easily move back and forth between conventional and social his-tory. The social historian's approach to names, dates, and events is more than just a reflection of the kinds of subjects he or she is interested in; it constitutes a distinctive new way of viewing the past.

And some social historians go one step further: they claim that their approach will ideally yield a total history, in which politics, military de-velopments, and seminal ideas merge with farmers' behavior, child-rearing habits, and recreational patterns into an integrated picture of what society was like.[10] Claims to total history have rarely been realized, least as yet. In the United States, they have been most clearly approxi-mated in a variety of exciting local studies, rather than in a larger regional or national frame.[11] Even when incompletely realized, however, the claim is important. Social historians, in their most honest and imperialis-tic moods, mean to leave nothing out in their remaking of our map of the past.

Social history is often bedecked with the adjective *new*, on the appar-ent assumption that the basic label alone is not sufficiently descriptive. The adjective is slightly amiss, even with the skeptical quotation marks that are often attached to it. Some social history topics have long been studied. Thus, immigrant history easily precedes the interest in the lower classes of the past few years. Going back even further, the great historians of the nineteenth century commented elaborately on various aspects of life and began focusing on politics as the stuff of history only toward the end of the century. Even the contemporary rise of social history is two decades old, which mutes its novelty somewhat. Of course, Americans love the newness label, and historians package their product only a little more subtly than do the devisers of deodorant ads. The label is not nec-essarily meaningful. But despite some real hesitations, including the very definite note that some good social history has long been done, the new-ness label does offer some advantages in completing a definition of the field.

Some historians find social history new simply because its gains are novel. Some mean to imply, through novelty, a recognition of the ways social history differs from conventional history in approach as well as in topical range. Some are also expressing their sense of discomfort that social history lacks some of the familiar benchmarks of mainstream politi-

cal history. But the adjective *new* also leads to some confusion, in particular to the erroneous identification made with quantitative history. Historians' recent enthusiasm for numerical evidence, and relatively sophisticated manipulation thereof, developed at about the same time that social
history began its upswing. Several subfields in social history have de-
pended heavily on quantitative materials; key cases in point are demographic behavior, structural aspects of family history, crime, social protest, and social mobility.[12] But while there is overlap, social history should
not be confused with quantitative methods. Some of the most sophisticated quantitative work has applied to roll call and voting behavior
analysis, in the—you guessed it—*new* political history. Social historians
are becoming increasingly skeptical of the adequacy of quantitative evidence in their field. Some exciting topics, such as the history of emotions,
simply have no significant quantitative aspect at all; they must be handled
through qualitative evidence. Family structure, in the sense of measurable household size, is less meaningful to most social historians than the
functions families serve.[13] Social mobility depends on a qualitative estimate of the prestige ranking of occupations, in addition to the numerical
data. Crime rates must similarly be combined with perceptions of crime.
Even changes in birth rates involve issues of motivation, for which numbers are inadequate beyond setting up the topic.

So social history is not quantitative history, and vice versa.[14] That is
important to keep in mind, for the confusion with quantitative methods
could limit social history's accessibility. It is true that good social historians need a quantitative *sense*—that is, a willingness to try to test the
representativeness of their evidence even when it is not strictly numerical. Thus, wills are sampled, for what they contribute in understanding
family relationships among rather large groups of people. Diaries are
utilized, to understand how at least middle-class people thought and
behaved regarding ordinary aspects of life like disease or religion. This
concern for the extent of behavior patterns, or the social resonance of key
attitudes, often cannot be formally quantitative, and it certainly need not
be highly technical or arcane; but it does suggest some relatively novel
problems that social historians face in contrast to, for example, biog-
raphers or the narrators of past battles—problems that may, after all,
justify a *newness* label.

The clearest way that contemporary social history is new, and not just
different from conventional history, lies in its departure from an older
strand of social history popular since the 1920s. Contemporary social
historians are at pains to distinguish their research from "pots-and-
pans" history. Those who sought to define the field afresh in the 1960s

had to fight against an older definition of social history, which they saw as too narrow and often too antiquarian. The charting of changes in fashions or eating utensils is obviously a part of social history as now defined, but not when conducted without much reference to wider social significance or developments outside the realm of purely material culture. Like a good bit of the history of art or of manufacturing technology, a kind of history of fashions persists that moves rather descriptively from one set of styles to another. The fact that historians of dress and similar artifacts once seemed to sum up the field of social history made it understandable, if not entirely desirable, that social historians whose purposes were considerably wider enjoyed the term *new* as a means of setting themselves off from a tradition that they felt they had surpassed. This battle, largely implicit all along, in any event, has long since been won. In fact, it is now clear that social historians moved too far away from material culture. It is only recently that eating, including utensils as well as foods, and—more tentatively— dressing have re-entered the list of "ordinary activities" that social historians seek to chart.[15] Here, too, the *new* label, understandable as a way- station, may now confuse more than it illuminates.

Few social historians in fact now think of themselves as new. Differ- ent, yes, but not new. The continued use of the adjective largely serves to indicate how distinctive social history is from the kind of history that most of us, professional social historians included, were taught in school. Many historians, not to mention a wider public, have yet to assimilate the social-history way of looking at the past, and the persistence of the novelty label reflects that very real distinction. Within their own ranks, social historians evolve. They extrude new topics, and they switch em- phases, as in the extent of their reliance on quantification or in some renewed attention to material culture;[16] but their basic approach and self-definition are novel no more.

Indeed it is the solidity of the field's advance, not its novelty, that really demands attention. When social history really did seem new, in contrast to antiquarian material culture history or conventional political history, it was possible to see it as a fad. First, after World War II, Ameri- can historians reached out to intellectual history as a supplement to con- ventional interests; then the generation of scholars that entered profes- sional ranks in the 1960s reached out to the social; what would the next generation do? The question remains valid, and no one can contend that social history will rise forever. But it seems fairly certain that at least the next generation is going to be doing social history, too, as has been the case in countries like France, where the field developed somewhat ear- lier. We must therefore inquire not only into what caused the field's new definition but even more into what continues to sustain it. Such inquiry, too, furthers an understanding of what social history is all about and of what it can accomplish.

Three sources contributed to social history's advance in the 1960s and therefore to the impression of novelty it began to create:

1. *Foreign example.* French historical scholarship started its conversion to a dominant emphasis on social history between the wars; and after World War II, its prominence became increasingly visible. The journal *Annales*[17] still serves as centerpiece to a sophisticated approach to social history. Growing numbers of Americans, starting with specialists in French history itself, were affected by the French work. Social history in Britain, though less spectacular in certain respects, was even more influential. E. P. Thompson, whose example has incited much of the recent effort in working-class history, is probably more widely cited by Americans than is any other single historian.[18]

2. *The social science influence.* Social history also constitutes the most recent effort by historians to bridge the gap between their work and that of social scientists. Thus social history is in part an effort to deal historically with topical areas that sociologists first examined, often inadequately, because of their characteristic lack of concern for past dimensions. The social science influence correspondingly marks American social history off from French and particularly British examples.

3. *The political climate.* The initial emphasis on "inarticulate" groups derived considerably, as we have already noted, from the effervescence of the 1960s, in which conventional history seemed largely irrelevant. More broadly, American social history has been stimulated by concern about major features of contemporary American life, which again lie outside clear political realms. Most obviously, the fascination of American social historians with the family—and family history has been far more imaginatively and extensively developed in this country than elsewhere—has something to do with the distinctively problematic quality of contemporary family life in this country.

Social history continues to reflect these three initial influences. American work has had its own impact on social history elsewhere—the rise of social history in Germany is particularly indebted to American example—but some sense of involvement with European initiative remains. The social science example is still more active. Social historians have freed themselves, however, from the most deferential approach to sociological models and are even to be found arguing that it is from social history, not social science, that creative theories about human behavior must spring.[19] Fruitful interchange has certainly been maintained with

political sociology, in particular, but also with specialties such as gerontology and family sociology.[20] Finally, while the leftist orientation of
social history, never as dominant here as in Great Britain, has yielded
somewhat to changes in political climate—and possibly to middle-aged
success—a sense of involvement with contemporary problem areas de-
cidedly remains.

Additional factors now feed the ongoing excitement of the field,
though they link with the initial sources of strength. The ability to generate a steady stream of new topics, in terms of both new groups to analyze
and new aspects of the human experience to subject to historical assessment, marks the dynamism of the premise of social history. New topics
promote younger scholars, but also, interestingly, reinvigorate more established social historians. Thus, while leadership in uncovering a fascinating evolution of the functions surrounding household activity has
fallen to relatively new researchers,[21] the related inquiry into changes in
the emotional intensity of the family has been shared by social historians
who initially made their marks in other areas.[22] But more than scholarly
promotion is involved: new topics and the expansion of social history into
its second-generation exploration of social behavior and outlook maintain the field's promise to a wider public, in opening every aspect of
society to the perspective of the past.

Related to topical expansion is the explosion of source materials, as
inarticulate people and private activities literally speak volumes. Census
data, police records, wills, a surprising array of heretofore neglected
worker autobiographies, diaries of unheralded middle-class women, and
some limited re-entry into the evidence provided by material artifacts—
these records as well as some re-use of more conventional sources have
easily supported the range of social-historical interests. Important questions remain incompletely answered, from past crime rates to the inner
satisfactions men gained from the rise of sports in the latter nineteenth
century; but few cannot at least be approached with substantial evidence.

As topics and sources expand, major discoveries, some of them significantly modifying established wisdom, feed excitement in the field.

Item: It used to be commonplace for psychiatrists and psychohisto-
rians to claim that a child's witnessing parental sexual intercourse was a
traumatic experience (thus were both Hitler and Luther partially explained).[23] In fact, any social historian (or anyone else who has considered the implications of most preindustrial housing) knows that such
witnessing must have been relatively common. Social historians have
been working imaginatively in exploring new ideas of privacy, including
new housing arrangements,[24] that may have altered the nature of that

experience, and certainly its frequency, in contemporary society. Psychiatrists, learning relatively readily, have now dropped their insistence on inherent trauma in inadvertent infant voyeurism.

Item: The common impression of a clear evolution, with modernity, from an extended to a nuclear family is inaccurate. Also inaccurate are related beliefs, such as the notion of a warm supportive atmosphere for older family members before the blight of modern familial collapse.[25] Both preindustrial and industrial societies, and the evolution from one to the other, require more complex analysis. In this instance, sociologists and gerontologists have been somewhat slow to learn, but as they do, not only will the historical picture be modified but our impression of some basic trends in contemporary life will change, as well.

Item: Crime does not invariably rise with urbanization. Particular kinds of city conditions cause crime—notably, newness to the city—but not cities themselves. Many rural areas have high crime rates.[26] The best predictor of crime rates turns out to be past crime rates, not urbanization, youth percentage, or other of the more common targets. Modern society has almost certainly reduced disorder while greatly increasing sensitivity to violence; at least part of the contemporary crime problem, then, results from differential rates of change between perceptions and actual crime.

Item: The basic sexual revolution in modern history began in the later eighteenth century. Our understanding of more recent changes in sexual standards is enhanced by a grasp of that initial shift.[27]

Item: Mobility patterns in the United States prove considerably less impressive than rhetoric suggests. More of the American experience, contemporary as well as historical, needs interpretation in light of the rhetoric-reality gap.[28]

In sum: Social history maintains vitality by providing new insights into a variety of areas in which a historical sense has long been used to suggest perspective on the present. The social historians' efforts are by no means confined to refutations of oversimplifications. Generalizations have emerged that add significantly to any existing framework. Thus the growing interest in the gradual rise of a modern sense of home, as a center for meals, conversation, and the like, from the seventeenth century until its current partial decline. Thus the growing literature on familial emotional intensity as a modern invention. Thus the interesting notion of a crisis in male identity in the United States around the end of the nineteenth century, which helps give context for more recent developments in the male world.[29] Thus, finally, the impressive charting of the attacks on traditional leisure forms as part of industrialization, and the effort to assess the resultant impact on the nature of contemporary leisure.[30] In most of the areas they have touched, social historians provide not only a topical expansion of history and historical sources, but also a framework of generalizations, a sense of trends. That framework in turn embellishes the interpretation of the past—adding depth, for example, to a statement of basic stages or periods in American history, while placing present trends in vibrant context.

At its best, and for those people for whom a historical approach aids understanding, social history's continuing vitality depends above all on its contribution to some sense of why our lives and our society are the way they are. An understanding of the history of the work experience thus helps us grasp the nature of work choices people make today and characteristic limitations on those choices. Realization that family emotions we regard as normal are in fact rather recent and unusual historical artifacts may or may not help us grapple better with the problems our emotional expectations engender, but they at least allow us to think about them, to stand back a bit. Thus the kinds of contemporary concerns that quite appropriately fed social history at its recent outset have broadened into a reliance on social history for recurrent insight into the way people, societies, even we ourselves function.

The reader may by now have gathered that many social historians believe, with some passion, that their field is the best thing that has happened to the discipline of history since the invention of academic salaries. That impression is one legitimate aspect of explaining what the new field is about: it does carry with it a zeal that, at the least, contrasts with the fatigued resignation that has recently characterized other aspects of the discipline. Logic might then suggest that the only remaining step is to convert all aspects of history—research, teaching, public programs— into some form of social history, and light will again shine upon us all.

Such may ultimately be the case; but the rise of social history has also brought with it some problems—some inherent, some significant but remediable—that must be mentioned before my final exordium.

Social history can unquestionably seem confusing to some accustomed to more conventional modes. The playing down of specific dates and biographical focus robs history of some familiar landmarks. Some will like the result; some will not care particularly; but others will be a bit put off. "When do we get to the history?" is not an uncommon reaction to too rarified a social history diet. Social historians' concern for process also leads to tension with those who have long enjoyed some social history topics, but in the more antiquarian style of artifacts for their own sake. Social history is not an approach that one can simply slide into from more conventional history; it takes some retooling.

How great a problem this is remains unclear, for social historians have not until recently paid particular attention to dissemination. Their mission has been one of research and conceptualization. Only recently has there been an explicit turn to interest in appropriate teaching styles and in contacts with a wider public, aided by some of the enthusiasm social history findings have generated beyond strictly academic confines. One of the challenges for the future, for academic social historians but also for other interested participants, is to focus on the dissemination possibilities. Many of us would argue that social history offers unusual richness to a wide public audience, given the kinds of subjects and the intimate historical understanding it promotes; but the task is only in its early stages.

Complicating the task are two additional deficiencies in most social history work to date. While some social historians claim the total history approach as their goal, in fact most American practitioners have shunned explicit consideration of the relationship between social history topics and more conventional history subject matter. They have treated social history as a subject area *de facto*. Thus, the social historians' approach to the American Revolution involves calling attention to the roles, and in some cases the political alertness, of lower-class groups whom conventional historians had neglected. It has involved a few venturesome generalizations about a link between changes in family relationships— growing father-son tension—or child-rearing styles and the willingness to participate in revolution.[31] There is to date, however, no "social-historical" interpretation of the American Revolution as a whole that will put all the parts, both novel and conventional, into a single package. Social historians have also been reluctant to link their studies with diplomatic and military history. As a result, these latter fields have declined somewhat, as the flip side of social history's rise, and they have not been re-integrated into a historical view that can encompass them on a new, socio-historical basis. Though perhaps excusable in a new field where practitioners were first excited by their own topical outreach, these omissions constitute conceptual weakness. They also make social history harder to use than it should be. One symptom of that is the continued neglect of most social history topics by mainstream textbooks or their relegation to sections separate from the texts' main flow.

Even worse: social historians sometimes neglect to fit even their own special topics together. To some observers, social history is not so much a field or an approach as a collection of separate subjects, tied together only by their novelty. Thus subgroups, and often journals, exist for topics such as crime, family, childhood, mobility, mental illness, demography, and so on. Social history has not yet splintered from these centrifugal spinoffs, but it is conceivable that it may. Even now the fragmentation complicates the efforts of users of social history to make full sense of what they use. As a symptom, no single text in American social history has yet been attempted.[32]

These two problems are remediable, though this is not to say that they will be remedied. Enough social historians have a sense of the field as a whole to limit the fragmentation; many work in several of the leading subfields, which encourages cross-fertilization. Even demographers, among the most specialized methodologically, routinely now appeal to broader concerns—including family arrangements and individual and collective mentalities—as a means of explaining shifts in birth rates.[33] Some linkages are tentatively developing with more conventional topics. Efforts to relate political behavior to social groups and to deal with the social impact of political policy are cases in point.[34] The further hope must be that, as social historians realize the importance of reaching a wider audience, they will move to complete their conceptual tasks. The interaction between researchers and a broader public should be mutually informative.

The problems are nevertheless real. Social historians have some learning to do, not only about methods of reaching beyond an academic clientele but also about making good some of their broader conceptual claims. At the same time, potential users of social history cannot expect to move into this field without some real reorientation, beyond mastery of new factual material. They need attention to processes, instead of just to events or artifacts. Relatedly, they must see ways that social history links past to present, in contrast to the concentration on dramatic differences between past ways of doing things and their contemporary counterparts that served as a staple of the pots-and-pans approach. It remains valid, of course, to show how different life was when organized in part around the spinning wheel instead of the ready-to-wear shop, but it is also important to show how other aspects of life, like family relationships, flow more subtly from one period to the next. Finally, new users of social history need to open themselves to some reorientation of conventional priorities in history, such that changes in humbler spheres of activity take their place along with superficially more striking landmarks. Who can claim, now, that Romantic art forms or the politics of Reconstruction have proved more important, in shaping subsequent society, than the conversion to an unprecedentedly low birth rate or the related shift in the acceptability of infant death?

Adjustments to a wider usage of social history will thus be neither automatic nor easy for any of the parties involved. It remains only to repeat that it is worth the trouble. It has become unfashionable to profess too much enthusiasm for anything going on in history today. Lament more commonly catches the mood. But social historians must buck this mood; what they are discovering is simply too exciting to allow them to do otherwise. One of the chief gains to be expected from a spread of social history to a wider audience is that some of this enthusiasm will be contagious. This is, at least in individual instances, empirical fact, not just hope or hyperbole. Exposure to social history makes admirers of some who had had no use for history before. For others, attuned already to the historical interest, the same exposure serves as something of a conversion experience: they can never again see the past, or grasp the present, without this new lens. Conversion is indeed a term often used, and it has characteristically energizing results. Some converts, and not just from staid academic ranks, will be drawn into the additionally exciting aspect of social history—that its tasks are uncompleted, that so much remains to be done. Attention to basic processes in the past—the central stuff of social history—leads to a real involvement with process in the present: the process of creating and assimilating new knowledge.

Notes

1. Gertrude Himmelfarb review of *The Past Before Us*, edited by Michael Kammen, in *New York Times Book Review*, August 1979, p. 3; Michael Kammen, editor, *The Past Before Us: Contemporary Historical Writing in the United States* (Ithaca: Cornell University Press, 1980).

2. *Journal of Social History; Comparative Studies in Society and History; Societas: A Review of Social History; Journal of Interdisciplinary History*. Also accessible are two key British journals: *Past and Present* and *Social History*.

3. For an overview of recent scholarship, see Peter N. Stearns, "Toward a Wider Vision: Trends in Social History," in *The Past Before Us*, Kammen, pp. 205–230.

4. Linda Rosenzweig and Peter N. Stearns, editors, *Social History Curriculum for Secondary Schools* (Pittsburgh: Carnegie-Mellon University Press, 1982).

5. Jesse Lemisch, "The American Revolution Seen from the Bottom Up," in *Towards a New Past: Dissenting Essays in American History*, edited by Barton J. Bernstein (New York: Pantheon Books, 1968), pp. 3–45.

6. Joseph Kett, *Rites of Passage: Adolescence in America, 1790 to the Present* (New York: Basic Books, 1979); Lloyd de Mause, editor, *The History of Childhood* (New York: Harper-Row, 1974); W. Andrew Achenbaum, *Old Age in the New Land: The American Experience Since 1790* (Baltimore: Johns Hopkins University Press, 1979).

7. James Henretta, "Social History as Lived and Written," *American Historical Review* 84 (1979): 1293–1333.

8. Edward Shorter, *The Making of the Modern Family* (New York: Basic Books, 1975);

Ellen K. Rothman, "Sex and Self-Control: Middle-Class Courtship in America, 1770–1870," *Journal of Social History* 15 (1982): 409–425.

9. Stephan Thernstrom, *Poverty and Progress: Social Mobility in a Nineteenth-Century City* (Cambridge: Harvard University Press, 1964).

10. Traian Stoianovich, *French Historical Method: The "Annales" Paradigm* (Ithaca: Cornell University Press, 1976); Fernand Braudel, *The Mediterranean and the Mediterranean World in the Age of Phillip II*, 2 vols., rev. 2nd ed. (New York: Harper and Row, Publishers, Inc., 1976).

11. John Demos, *A Little Commonwealth: Family Life in Plymouth Colony* (New York: Oxford University Press, 1971); Philip J. Greven, Jr., *Four Generations: Population, Land, and Family in Colonial Andover, Massachusetts* (Ithaca: Cornell University Press, 1970); Kenneth A. Lockridge, *A New England Town: The First Hundred Years* (New York: W. W. Norton & Company, Inc., 1970); Daniel J. Walkowitz, *Worker City, Company Town: Iron and Cotton Worker Protest in Troy and Cohoes, New York, 1855–1884* (Urbana: University of Illinois Press, 1978); Anthony F. Wallace, *Rockdale: The Growth of an American Village in the Early Industrial Revolution* (New York: W. W. Norton & Company, Inc., 1980).

12. Peter Laslett and Richard Wall, editors, *Household and Family in Past Time* (Cambridge: Cambridge University Press, 1972); Edward Shorter and Charles Tilly, *Strikes in France: 1830–1968* (New York: Cambridge University Press, 1974); Roger Lane, *Violent Death in the City: Suicide, Accident, and Murder in Nineteenth-Century Philadelphia* (Cambridge: Harvard University Press, 1979); Stephan Thernstrom, *The Other Bostonians: Poverty and Progress in the American Metropolis, 1880–1970* (Cambridge: Harvard University Press, 1973); Tamara K. Hareven and Randolph Langenbach, *Amoskeag: Life and Work in an American Factory City* (New York: Pantheon Books, 1978).

13. Carl Degler, *At Odds: Women and the Family in America from the Revolution to the Present* (New York: Oxford University Press, 1980).

14. Lawrence Stone, *The Past and the Present* (Boston: Routledge and Kegan Paul, 1981).

15. Robert Forster and Orest Ranum, editors, *Food and Drink in History* (Baltimore: Johns Hopkins University Press, 1979).

16. Thomas J. Schlereth, *Artifacts and the American Past: Techniques for the Teaching Historian* (Nashville: American Association for State and Local History, 1981).

17. *Annales: Economics, Sociétés, Civilisations*; Stoianovich, *French Historical Method*.

18. Edward P. Thompson, *The Making of the English Working Class* (New York: Pantheon, 1963) .

19. Theodore Zeldin, "Personal History and the History of Emotions," *Journal of Social History* 15 (1982): 339–347.

20. Charles Tilly, "The Old New Social History and the New Old Social History," University of Michigan Center for Research on Social Organization *Working Paper* #218 (Ann Arbor, Michigan, 1980).

21. Carole Shammas, "The Domestic Environment in Early Modern England and America," *Journal of Social History* 14 (1980): 3–24.

22. Lawrence Stone, *The Family, Sex and Marriage: England, 1500–1800* (New York: Harper and Row, Publishers, Inc., 1977).

23. Erik H. Erikson, *Young Man Luther: A Study in Psychoanalysis and History* (New York: W. W. Norton & Company, Inc., 1958); Walter Langer, *The Mind of Adolph Hitler* (New York: Basic Books, 1972).

24. David H. Flaherty, *Privacy in Colonial New England, 1630–1776* (Charlottesville: University Press of Virginia, 1972); Peter N. Stearns, "Adaptation to Industrialization: German Workers as a Test Case," *Central European History* 3 (1970): 303–331.

25. W. Andrew Achenbaum and Peter N. Stearns, "Modernization and the History of Old Age," *The Gerontologist* 18 (1978): 307–313.

26. Roger Lane, "Crime and the Industrial Revolution: British and American Views," *Journal of Social History* 7 (1974): 287–303; Eric Monkkonen, *Police in Urban America, Eighteen Hundred Sixty to Nineteen Twenty* (New York: Cambridge University Press, 1981).

27. Edward Shorter, "Illegitimacy, Sexual Revolution, and Social Change in Modern Europe," *Journal of Interdisciplinary History* 2 (1971): 237–272; Maris A. Vinovskis, "An 'Epidemic' of Adolescent Pregnancy? Some Historical Considerations," *Journal of Family History* 6 (1981): 205–230.

28. Thernstrom, *Poverty and Progress;* Edward Pessen, *Riches, Class, and Power before the Civil War* (Lexington, Mass.: D. C. Heath, 1973); John Bodnar, Roger Simon, Michael P. Weber, editors, *Lives of Their Own: Blacks, Italians, and Poles in Pittsburgh, 1900 to 1960* (Urbana: University of Illinois Press, 1982).

29. Peter Filene, *Him–Her Self: Sex Roles in Modern America* (New York: New American Library, 1976); Joe L. Dubbert, *A Man's Place: Masculinity in Transition* (Englewood Cliffs: Prentice-Hall, Inc., 1979).

30. Michael Marrus, *Rise of Modern Leisure* (St. Louis: Forum Press, 1974).

31. Pauline Maier, *From Resistance to Revolution: Colonial Radicals and the Development of American Opposition to Britain: 1765–1766* (New York: Harper-Row, 1972); Philip Greven, *The Protestant Temperament: Patterns of Child Rearing, Religious Experience, and the Self in Early America* (New York: New American Library, 1979).

32. Gary B. Nash, *Class and Society in Early America* (Englewood Cliffs: Prentice-Hall, Inc., 1970); Nash, *Red, White, and Black: The Peoples of Early America* (Englewood Cliffs: Prentice-Hall, 1974).

33. Maris A. Vinovskis, "Recent Trends in American Historical Demography," *Annual Review of Sociology* 4 (1978): 603–627.

34. Samuel P. Hays, *American Political History as Social Analysis: Essays by Samuel P. Hays* (Knoxville: University of Tennessee Press, 1980).

Suggestions for Additional Reading

The following includes some further discussions of the nature of social history; some obvious classics; several studies, excellent in themselves, which also represent some of the more successful emphases in the new social history; a few more specific studies, as in the history of leisure, suggesting some of the most recent frontiers in the field.

Achenbaum, W. Andrew. *Old Age in the New Land: The American Experience Since 1790.* Baltimore: Johns Hopkins University Press, 1979.

An ambitious synthesis in a new area of social history, with wide chronological sweep and utilization of a variety of sources.

Berkhofer, Robert F. *The White Man's Indian: Images of the American Indian from Columbus to the Present.* New York: Alfred A. Knopf, Inc., 1978.

A fascinating social history of the treatment of Indians, with policy implications.

Cott, Nancy F. *The Bonds of Womanhood: "Woman's Sphere" in New England, 1780–1835.* New Haven: Yale University Press, 1978.

> A perceptive treatment of women's history in a crucial period, using a social-cultural history approach.

Dawley, Alan. *Class and Community: The Industrial Revolution in Lynn.* Cambridge: Harvard University Press, 1976.

> Of several fine works in the genre of local working-class history, probably the most challenging.

Demos, John. *A Little Commonwealth: Family Life in Plymouth Colony.* New York: Oxford University Press, 1971.

> One of two or three studies of colonial New England that still stand as landmarks in the development of American social history.

Genovese, Eugene D. *Roll, Jordan, Roll: The World the Slaves Made.* New York: Random House, 1976.

> Of a host of important social histories of slavery, this stands out for original research and provocative interpretation.

Gordon, Michael. *The American Family in Social-Historical Perspective,* 2nd ed. New York: St. Martin's Press, Inc., 1978.

> A mixed and sometimes turgid collection, but one that does reveal patterns of work in family and demographic history.

Greven, Philip. *The Protestant Temperament: Patterns of Child Rearing, Religious Experience, and the Self in Early America.* New York: New American Library, 1979.

> An exciting effort, as a substantive contribution to the history of child-rearing and as an attempt to link themes from social, intellectual, and political history.

Johnson, Paul E. *A Shopkeepers' Millennium: Society and Revivals in Rochester, New York, 1815 to 1837.* New York: Hill and Wang, 1978.

> One of the few efforts to approach religious experience from the standpoint of social history, and a very good job.

Kammen, Michael, ed. *The Past Before Us: Contemporary Historical Writing in the United States.* Ithaca: Cornell University Press, 1980.

> This survey of current research trends includes many essays which reveal the impact of social history; one essay deals with trends and achievements in the field itself.

Kasson, John F. *Amusing the Million: Coney Island at the Turn of the Century.* New York: Hill and Wang, 1978.

> A fascinating, if specific, introduction to some conceptual themes in the history of leisure.

Katz, Michael. *The Irony of Early School Reform: Educational Innovation in Mid-19th Century Massachusetts*. Cambridge: Harvard University Press, 1968.

> This book illustrates one of the leading approaches of many American social historians, by emphasizing the social control aspects of institutions traditionally interpreted in a more liberal and progressive vein. Katz is a particularly persuasive practitioner in this vein, dealing of course with the social effects of education.

Lane, Roger. *Violent Death in the City: Suicide, Accident, and Murder in Nineteenth-Century Philadelphia*. Cambridge: Harvard University Press, 1979.

> Highly quantitative, and therefore revealing of one of social history's research bases, this study also generates important concepts about changes in patterns of violence in industrial America.

Nash, Gary B. *Red, White, and Black: The Peoples of Early America*. Englewood Cliffs, N. J.: Prentice-Hall, Inc., 1974.

> This is about as close as anyone has come to a general American social history, though it deals only with the early period. It is a superior survey.

Rorabaugh, W. J. *The Alcoholic Republic: An American Tradition*. New York: Oxford University Press, 1979.

> A very readable account of a major aspect of early American leisure, with suggestions as to its subsequent decline. As an example of social history, a neat mix of qualitative and quantitative evidence.

Shammas, Carole. "The Domestic Environment in Early Modern England and America."*Journal of Social History* 14 (1980): 3–24.

> A stunning example of the best kind of social history: imaginative in its use of sources (including evidence on artifacts); linked to important concepts about change in family life and gender roles; providing insight on contemporary behavior while remaining solidly historical.

"Social History Today . . . and Tomorrow?" *Journal of Social History* 10 (1976): 129–255.

> Various essays define the state of social history and indicate problems and patterns for the future.

Stone, Lawrence. *The Past and the Present*. Boston: Routledge and Kegan Paul, 1981.

> A thoughtful description and critique of leading trends in socio-historical research.

Thernstrom, Stephan. *The Other Bostonians: Poverty and Progress in the American Metropolis, 1880–1970*. Cambridge: Harvard University Press, 1973.

> Studies of mobility form one of the leading emphases of American social

historians; and, while various efforts are useful, this book conveys many of the basic issues and methods, by the doyen of this subfield.

Thompson, Edward P. *The Making of the English Working Class.* New York: Pantheon, 1963.

One of the works most cited by American historians and a continuing stimulus to studies of the lower classes.

Lewis W. Hine photographed an Italian mother and her child in 1905 as they waited at Ellis Island, the point of entry for millions of immigrants in the late nineteenth and twentieth centuries.

2

Race, Ethnicity, and Cultural Pluralism in American History

Howard N. Rabinowitz

THE NEW SOCIAL HISTORY has had perhaps its greatest impact on the study of race and ethnicity in American life. With the assistance of innovative approaches and methodological techniques, a new generation of social historians has at times confirmed the assumptions of previous writers, but more often refined or totally revised long accepted interpretations. In this essay, I want to examine the ways that these developments have affected our understanding of the role of race and ethnicity in American life. I will begin by indicating what I think the new social history is, especially what makes it different from the old, and why I think the subject of race and ethnicity has drawn so many of its practitioners. Then I want to examine some models for assimilation in American life before discussing the sources, approaches, and findings of the new social history as they apply to the five most commonly studied topics in the history of race and ethnicity.

There is no single definition of the new social history. Indeed, there is probably no common description of the old social history. For simplicity, however, I would argue that the old social history included a diverse group of topics not strictly political—class structure, family life, but also clothing, recreation, religion, and architecture, which are now considered part of cultural history. Furthermore, as demonstrated in the *History of American Life* series (1927–1948) edited by Arthur Schlesinger, Sr., and Dixon Ryan Fox, the old social history did not approach its topics systematically, either in the use of evidence or in the application of theory.

The new social history is quite different. For one thing, it is the product of an underlying philosophy that calls for the study of "ordinary people," the "common folk," or the "masses." Sometimes social historians talk about studying the "inarticulate," which may refer occasionally to the middle and even upper classes. More often, they concentrate on the working class, in an attempt, as Stephan Thernstrom put it, to study history "from the bottom up."[1] Such an approach seeks to learn about the "people" rather than about their leaders—how working people lived, what they believed, how they interacted with each other and with the rest of society.

Second, the new social history has a new orientation or approach. It is interdisciplinary, with an emphasis on testing a theoretical framework, rather than simply reporting the details of everyday life. In the 1960s, pioneering scholars looked to sociology for their insights and methodology; more recently, there has been a shift of attention to the findings of anthropology and geography.

Finally, as befits a theoretically oriented subdiscipline interested in obscure people, the new social history has developed new research methods based on previously neglected sources. The most important of these sources—manuscript census schedules, wills, tax ledgers, organization records, and city directories—lend themselves especially well to quantitative techniques, which in many early monographs often seemed more important to the authors than the findings themselves. Thus the tools of the old social history, including diaries, letters, and newspapers, often have been neglected, because of their nonquantifiable nature or their inappropriateness for the study of semiliterate people.

The new social historians were naturally attracted to the field of race and ethnicity, where for so long an emphasis, often filiopietistic, on articulate or successful leaders had held sway. In part, the attractiveness of the new approach for historians of race and ethnicity was due to the influence of French and English scholars, but at least as important was the increased visibility of blacks, white ethnics, and other minorities during the 1960s. Thanks to the new sources and methodology, previous generations of ethnic or racial masses could now be examined and treated as subjects of history rather than merely as objects whose lives were determined by the assimilating forces in American life that plunged them into the nation's famous melting pot. As John Briggs expresses it in his examination of Italians in three American communities, "The immigrants were not chameleons totally dependent on their surroundings for their character. They contributed to shaping their future rather than receiving their destinies wholly defined and packaged by others." Likewise, in his study of the Los Angeles Japanese community, John Modell rejects the tendency to view the Japanese in America as victims, accepting instead the new approach to ethnic history that argues, "Neither wholly autonomous nor simply passive recipients of the malign initiatives of majority Americans, minorities have evolved varied attitudes and institutions appropriate to their circumstances." Even slavery could not eliminate such options. According to John Blassingame, "The slave held onto many remnants of his African culture, gained a sense of worth in the quarters, spent most of his time free from surveillance by whites, controlled important aspects of his life, and did some personally meaningful things on his own volition."[2]

Many of the new social historians were primarily interested in seeing whether the forces of modernization and Americanization had indeed stripped immigrants and migrants of their basic values and institutions. This is suggested by the title, if not always the content, of *The Uprooted*, Oscar Handlin's 1951 Pulitzer Prize-winning work on European immigration to the United States. In fact, Handlin's classic has become so much of a target for the new social historians that at times it seems that their findings are almost as much the result of a revolt against *The Uprooted* as a revolt against the discredited idea of America as a melting pot. This is unfortunate. Such parasitic history not only lets someone else establish the questions, but also, because so many of the new generation have misread Handlin's extremely subtle book, it leads to the creation of straw men. Furthermore, Handlin's critics ignore the extent to which he anticipated many of their own arguments, even though choosing to emphasize a different side of the immigrant experience. Finally, it is ironic that Handlin has not received the notice he deserves as the forerunner of the new social history. A student of Arthur Schlesinger's and the mentor of several leading new social historians, including Thernstrom, Handlin stands as a pivotal figure in the writing of social history, not only because of his status as student and teacher, but because his works, beginning in 1941 with *Boston's Immigrants*, have sought to reveal the lives of the very people that interest the new social historians.

Before we examine the ways the new work in the field has revised or sought to revise *The Uprooted* and similar works, it is necessary to look briefly at possible models for the assimilation of racial and ethnic minorities—that is, the process through which foreign or racial outsiders become "Americanized." There are three major theories for the interaction between these groups and the host society. In each case, the view of assimilation contains an "is" and an "ought" dimension: each reflects not only its proponents' description of the assimilation process, but their desires concerning that process, as well.[4]

The most publicized model of assimilation is the traditional melting pot. The view of America as a melting pot is as old as the nation state. A

French visitor, J. Hector St. John de Crèvecoeur, wrote in 1782 of America, "Here individuals of all nations are melted into a new race of men, whose labours and posterity will one day cause great changes in the world." Dismayed by the rise of the Know-Nothing nativist movement during the mid-nineteenth century, Ralph Waldo Emerson subsequently echoed Crèvecoeur's assessment of the nation's uniqueness:

Man is the most composite of all creatures. . . . As in the old burning of the Temple at Corinth, by the melting and intermixture of silver and gold and other metals a new compound more precious than any, called the Corinthian brass was formed, so in this continent,—asylum of all nations—the energy of Irish, Germans, Swedes, Poles and Cossacks, and all the European tribes,—of the Africans, and of the Polynesians,—will construct a new race, a new religion, a new state, a new literature, which will be as vigorous as the new Europe which came out of the smelting pot of the Dark Ages, or that which earlier emerged from the Pelasgic and Etruscan barbarism. *La Nature aime les croisements.*[5]

Nevertheless, as Arthur Mann reminds us, the phrase *melting pot* itself was unknown during most of American history. Webster's, for example, listed it for the first time in its 1934 edition.[6] No one knows who coined it, but it became a popular figure of speech only after Israel Zangwill's play by that title caught the public fancy in the years prior to World War I. Zangwill was a British Jew, whose play was first performed in 1908 and published in book form the following year. The author saw intermarriage as a key to the "immigrant problem," since it led to a little bit of everyone being mixed in the great melting pot. In his opinion, the best American was one of mixed ancestry. Such a view was denounced from different perspectives by many ethnic types and old-stock Americans, but it attracted widespread support, including that of President Theodore Roosevelt, who wrote the author, "I do not know when I have seen a play that stirred me as much."[7]

Another view of the melting pot had already emerged and would be expressed in the immigration laws of the 1920s. According to it, rather than having each group contribute to the melting pot, the immigrants would be Americanized, and their differences would melt away as they became Americans—that is, Anglo-Saxons, though perhaps with funny last names. That was allegedly what had happened to the so-called "old immigrants," who had come from northern and western Europe prior to the late nineteenth century. What emerged therefore was the doctrine of Anglo-Saxon supremacy or Anglo-conformity, which held that more recent newcomers had nothing to add to the values, virtues, institutions, and behavior of old-stock Americans. A response to the great influx of "new immigrants" from southern and eastern Europe between 1880 and 1914, it signaled, like all expressions of xenophobia in American history, a loss of confidence in the country's present and future prospects.

Many still defend that view, most notably in letters-to-the-editor columns and calls in to radio talk shows, but a third model is probably the most popular theory today. This is, of course, *cultural pluralism*, a phrase coined by Horace Kallen, an American Jew who took his degree at Harvard in philosophy. Writing in the teens and early 1920s, most notably in *Culture and Democracy in the United States,*[8] Kallen proposed that every ethnic group live to itself and retain its own language, religion, schools, clubs, history, customs, food, and other aspects of its culture. Because Kallen's ideas changed, over time, and exhibited a troublesome vagueness, they defy easy summary, but his theory was based on a number of assumptions that, as we shall see, did not always hold true. He assumed that immigration would continue; that claims of ancestry were irrepressible (men can change everything, Kallen wrote, except their grandfathers); that the "American creed" guaranteed the equality of all different kinds of men; and that the United States was strong in proportion to its diversity.

Kallen was confident, in the face of much evidence to the contrary, that ethnic pluralism was compatible with national unity. English would remain the official language, and everyone would accept and work within the democratic, capitalistic polity. Sociologist Milton Gordon has since labeled such an intersection of cultures as cultural assimilation or acculturation. Kallen thus substituted for the melting pot the concept of America as an orchestra. Others, while changing the metaphor, have kept its meaning, as in Carl Degler's use of the term *salad bowl* to describe the nature of assimilation.[9] In any case, the constituent elements retain their special character, but blend together to form something greater than the sum of the parts.

Yet the end of large-scale European immigration, the impact of World War II, and other factors seemed by 1950 to have left ethnicity dissolved in the melting pot. Observers stressed the unity of American life; a so-called consensus school flourished among historians, who emphasized the shared values of Americans that cut across class, race, and regional boundaries; and Dwight Eisenhower reigned over America's seemingly "affluent society." Works about *the* American character proliferated, and the new discipline of American Studies enjoyed rapid growth. Within that environment, neither academics nor laymen gave much attention to the presence of cultural diversity produced by racial and ethnic differences. Kallen's views nonetheless finally became fashionable, as a result of the Cold War, the founding of Israel, Third World revolutions, the civil rights movement, and especially the black power-ignited ethnic revival of the 1960s. The determination of individual groups to preserve their cultural heritage led pop and academic sociologists to pick up the cry, pointing to the persistence of ethnic attachment as a sign that something was clearly missing in the core American culture.

As a result, cultural pluralism is today used to describe the accommodation of American society to the diverse ethnic and racial groups in its midst. Indeed, the new social history uses cultural pluralism—that is, intergroup differences based on the persistence of older ethnic ties within the dominant culture—as a take-off point for American ethnic and racial history. Perhaps as important, since it colors so much of this work, the new social historians view such persistence quite favorably and treat it as something that should have happened. In other words, the new social history not only finds evidence of strong ethnic and racial identification, but usually celebrates it, as well, though often expressing dismay at the frequent examples of inequality among groups. And, as in the case of John Modell's sympathetic treatment of the first generation of Japanese Americans in their conflict with the more Americanization-oriented second generation, an author's preference for ethnic persistence does not necessarily depend upon membership in the group being discussed.[10]

So much for background. It is time to look at the extent to which the findings of the new social history have modified our understanding of five broad areas of ethnic and racial history: migration patterns, community formation, mobility, family structure, and politics. The primary point to keep in mind is that this body of work has revealed basic patterns of adjustment that cut across all ethnic and racial groups, while at the same time discovering attitudes, values, and forms of behavior distinctive to certain groups. The new social historians are dealing with shared *and* unique characteristics and trying to account for both the differences and similarities among groups. But whatever the final result, the migrants' personal preferences are central, reflecting a previously unacknowledged control over their own destiny. Even though an author like Richard Griswold del Castillo might acknowledge that "racial discrimination, cultural oppression, and outright violence have been major forces molding the Mexican-American experience," he typically emphasizes that "since the late nineteenth century, Mexican-American history has also been characterized by creative and constructive responses to changing circumstances."[11]

The first two areas—migration and community formation—are closely linked because they involve the extent of "uprootedness" and alienation produced by breaking away from an old, familiar environment and then having to adjust to new surroundings or even, as in the case of immigrants, a new country. In *The Uprooted,* Oscar Handlin argues that "the history of immigration is a history of alienation and its consequences." Though in this book Handlin was writing only of European immigrants, in his other works, including *The Newcomers* and *The American People in the Twentieth Century,* he extended that description to the internal migration of blacks and Hispanics.[12] For Handlin and most other scholars through the early 1960s, what was particularly significant was what was lost as migrants left settled, stable, rural communities in the Old World or the South and were transplanted as individuals to a hostile, strange, urban America. The ties with the past were weakened or even "snipped," as former values and behavior patterns came under attack from Americanizing or modernizing forces. Even if the first generation managed to hold onto the ancestral language, religion, and institutions, it did so in the face of a disorienting and destructive environment. The next generation, by contrast, was quickly assimilated. The struggle between the first and the second generations then made the degree of alienation even more frightening. Virginia Yans-McLaughlin has taken issue with this scenario and characterizes it as being "grounded in a conventional sociological model implying a clear dichotomy, as well as abrupt discontinuities between folk and urban societies."[13] Yans-McLaughlin and others maintain that the act of migration or emigration was not as wrenching as previously thought and that much of the earlier cultural patterns successfully weathered the migration, thus reducing the sense of alienation. Undergirding such assertions is a new interpretation of the migratory process itself.

As early as 1964, in an important and widely discussed article about Southern Italians, Rudolph Vecoli drew attention to the extent of group migration, group settlement in the New World, and "chain migration," which allowed new migrants to join their former neighbors in the same cities or even in the same neighborhoods in America. More recently, Judith Fincher Laird, in a dissertation on a small Mexican community in Nebraska, concludes in a similar vein that "Mexican immigration bore little resemblance to the 'uprooting' experience which Oscar Handlin depicted as characteristic of European immigration. Indeed, continuity rather than alienation, marginality and social disorganization, characterized Mexican immigration."[14]

The work of Josef Barton is especially significant in the development of this altered depiction of the effects of migration. It is also typical of the new emphasis given to the life of the immigrants in the Old World rather than simply focusing on the problems of assimilation in the New. In discussing the migration of Slovaks, Rumanians, and Italians to Cleveland around the turn of the century, Barton shows three stages of migrants—individual pioneers, followed by relatives and friends, and finally even whole villages. Barton also found that the migrants came from all classes and were not driven out of the Old World by destitution or persecution. They represented, instead, the more aggressive and ambitious individuals, who felt threatened by an increasingly unstable economic situation at home and who sought to better their situation in America. In Barton's hands, these migrants look more like the Puritan forefathers fleeing potential economic difficulty in East Anglia than like the starving Irish of the 1840s chronicled by Handlin in *Boston's Immigrants*. And unlike Handlin's late-nineteenth-century migrants in *The Uprooted,* they were highly self-selective. [15]

All recent authors join Barton in seeing individual desires for economic betterment based on the expectation of declining fortunes where they were as more important than religious persecution, hard times, and other crises in determining migration. Some see an even more selective process of chain migration. Using passport records of Italian towns and United States naturalization records, John Briggs stresses the importance of "small family-based migration chains." He reports the greeting given the Italian premier by a local mayor in the province of Potenza "in the name of the eight thousand under my administration, of which three thousand are emigrants in America and five thousand are preparing to join them." Briggs, however, is more impressed with the complexity of the chains than is Barton. He found that the migrants did not concentrate on a handful of destinations in the United States and once in America did not necessarily live only among those they had known back home; but the significant degree of linkage clearly reduced the sense of alienation. Chains were especially important in Mexican migration to southern California during the same period. "After one family situated itself," writes Albert Camarillo, "it would attract relatives and friends from the original home in Mexico: the familial migration network was very common." A Mexican resident who arrived in Santa Barbara in 1916 explained that

One family comes from Durango and establishes itself here. From here it writes there and says come! come! come over, it is good here. It brings others and others. Well, one was here . . . Juan Esparza—he brought twenty-eight families from Durango. [16]

The nature of the migration experience has critical implications for community formation. In the traditional view, the individual immigrant or migrant underwent a painful and isolated adjustment to the new conditions, with only a few voluntary associations unsuccessfully attempting to cushion the shock. But revisionists argue that chain migration and group settlement allowed the transference of pre-migration organizations and values. Even more suggestive of the remaining ties with the past was the surprising amount of reverse migration. That practice has long been known to have been common among the Chinese, but Thomas Kessner estimates that between 1907 and 1911 there was a yearly average of seventy-three repatriates for every one hundred Italian immigrants. Between 1908 and 1912, yearly repatriation for all "new immigrants," excluding Jews, was 42 percent (the Jews had a figure of only 7 percent, which Kessner attributes to greater economic success but which might also simply reflect the unattractive conditions back home).

The return home was often not the final act in the immigrant's saga, however. John Bodnar, in his study of a small community in Pennsylvania, uncovered evidence of significant numbers of Slavs moving back and forth between the United States and Europe. Given the proximity of the homeland, that phenomenon was most marked among Mexican Americans. Mario Garcia argues that most Mexicans who came to El Paso around the turn of the century fully intended to return south. Whether or not immigrants returned home, their primary loyalty often continued to be to the old country. Albert Camarillo found that, from 1910 to 1927, only 0.7 percent of the 849 naturalization petitions at the Santa Barbara Court House had been filed by Mexican immigrants, a pattern of non-naturalization that continued throughout the 1930s. Unfortunately, it is not possible to trace the internal movements of American blacks, but I suspect that the use of oral history will reveal a constant two-way flow between northern cities and the Southern countryside—if not for the original migrants, then at least for their children.[17]

In other words, though some adjustment and change was obviously necessary, the migrants were far from being totally uprooted. The first generation especially joined churches and synagogues, mutual aid societies, and fraternal organizations based on town or district origins in the old country or in the South. Previous scholars, including Handlin, had allowed for such carry-overs, but the new social historians see this behavior as seriously limiting the degree of alienation and sense of loss. Family patterns, about which I will have more to say later, were also transferred, and marriage was carried on within the ethnic group. The process of adjustment was made even easier by ethnically determined residential segregation. Like Barton's white ethnics, Modell's Japanese, and the Mexicans of Camarillo, Garcia, and Griswold del Castillo, blacks also used a high degree of residential segregation to good advantage. As I have argued elsewhere, blacks in the postwar urban South, for example, built in their sections of the cities churches, schools, and fraternal associations that eased the transition to urban life. Some caution is required here, however, as recent work demonstrates that individual groups of white ethnics were not as residentially isolated from each other as it was once believed, and their degree of segregation was certainly less than that experienced by Hispanics, blacks, and Orientals.[18]

Nevertheless, the newcomers quickly established communities that nurtured old forms of behavior, while individuals started to adjust to their new environment. An ethnic group's core values and customs persisted at least until the second generation began the process of assimilation at the primary group level. Rather than simply learn English, adopt American dress, and accept the political and economic system, the "outsiders" now came to interact with members of the dominant society in organizations, forms of recreation, and even in marital relations. Termed *structural assimilation* by Milton Gordon, the extent of this process even today for some groups lags far behind the attainment of cultural assimilation. As John Briggs reminds us, the process of passing old values and identities from generation to generation, often in the absence of outside hostility, remains a major subject for future research.[19]

One historian, James Borchert, draws heavily on anthropological studies and photographs to carry the argument even further, in his discussion of Washington, D.C.'s black alley dwellers. Arguing that "urbanization does not necessarily void the importance of primary groups," he claims that Southern black migrants withstood the modernizing and urbanizing forces of the dominant culture to the extent that successive generations maintained their values in terms of religious behavior, work habits, folklore, and family life. Borchert, however, goes too far in denying the obvious influence of the migratory trauma and new environment. Elizabeth Pleck's finding of a more limited persistence in terms of duration and degree of old habits among Southern migrants to Boston seems more compelling; but Borchert's work serves as a valuable modifer of accepted wisdom concerning black America's move from plantation to ghetto.[20]

The discovery of relatively autonomous communities among post-1865 ethnic and racial groups echoes the findings of social historians, who, during the past decade or so, have studied slave life. Indeed Borchert frequently cites the work of John Blassingame, Herbert Gutman, and Eugene Genovese to document the alleged continuity between the life style of his alley dwellers and that of rural slaves. Much of this work on slavery was a reaction to Stanley Elkins's controversial landmark effort,

Slavery: A Problem in American Institutional & Intellectual Life (1959). Because Elkins emphasizes the disentegrating impact of slavery on the slave's psyche, his book has functioned for the current generation of scholars in black history as the counterpart of Handlin's *The Uprooted.* In both the study of slave and post-1865 minority life, the emphasis is on the ability of minority groups to preserve their cultural values and institutions in the face of a hostile, or at least different, dominant society. The individuals are thus not alienated or isolated, because they have each other and their "community."[21]

Both the new and older books would agree that there was both persistence and change in behavior, but the newer works are more impressed with the extent of the former. In their emphasis on continuity, these studies are part of a broader trend in the writing of American history. Another group of social historians, for example, now argues for the persistence of traditional ways of life long after settlement in colonial America.[22] Thus Borchert argues that "Although urbanization has clearly affected folk migrants, the change is more of degree than of kind. What is most impressive is not the extent of change, but the continuity, the persistence of traditional functions, forms, and outlooks." John Briggs writes of his Italian immigrants' "sense of continuity between past and present." And though more conscious of the examples of acculturation than most other younger scholars and thus demonstrating more affinity with Handlin, Mario Garcia concludes that "first generation immigrants and political refugees, through their re-establishment of spiritual societies common in Mexico as well as the re-enactment of native Mexican religious celebrations, successfully maintained cultural continuity and helped create a sense of community in the barrios." At first glance, it seems that Virginia Yans-McLaughlin's approach might be significantly different. She argues that "The relationship between modernity and tradition . . . is neither dichotomous nor linear but dialectical." In fact, she documents the forces of continuity, even where the clash between the new environment and tradition produced a blend of the old and the new.[23]

The persistence of older values has serious implications for the study of mobility in American history, the third broad topic. Social mobility studies have become practically a cottage industry since the publication, in 1964, of Stephan Thernstrom's *Poverty and Progress,* a study of mobility in Newburyport, Massachusetts, between 1840 and 1880. Indeed, from the mid-1960s to the mid-1970s, social mobility studies were practically *the* new social history. Characterized by increasingly sophisticated theoretical and methodological techniques that now employ computers, these efforts have relied on manuscript census schedules and city directories. All have found little support for the old idea of rags to riches mobility, but neither have they found the static situation more common in Europe. They have documented, instead, limited upward movement throughout the social system, not only for individuals, but between generations—unskilled to semiskilled, upper-blue-collar to lower-white-collar, etc. Such studies also have demonstrated that high rates of geographic mobility have been the rule throughout American history and not the result of the automobile or the emergence of national corporations. Indeed, rates of geographic mobility as well as rates of economic mobility have changed remarkably little over the years.[24]

Not surprisingly, these studies have found differences among various ethnic groups and between natives and immigrants. Thernstrom's *The Other Bostonians* (1973) found a pattern echoed in other accounts for different cities and periods. Yankees did better than immigrants, Jews and Protestants better than Catholics, the sons of the middle class better than those of the poor, Russian Jews and English better than Irish and Italians, but all enjoyed a marked degree of upward mobility. Only for blacks has this not been the case, but at least since 1940, in Boston—and no doubt elsewhere—they too have begun to enjoy the fruits of a fluid social system. Subsequent studies of Mexican Americans have revealed not only a pattern of group immobility similar to that of blacks but also a notable amount of individual downward mobility, explained by the fact that in the Southwest and southern California the Mexicans were the original settlers caught in the midst of a changing society that left only menial jobs for them.[25]

Yet there are serious problems with the works on mobility. Due to the availability of manuscript census schedules and more manageable samples, they are best suited to the nineteenth century and for smaller cities. What is more, the significance of their findings is complicated by a number of factors, including reliance on occupational change as a substitute for other measures of mobility; alteration in job categories, over time; the omission of women; and discrimination against transients, blacks, and the poor. Even more troubling, since it is more subtle, is the prior assumption that mobility is something that all groups sought. In fact, the absence of mobility may be seen by some groups as a "good thing," rather than a sign of failure.[26] Stephan Thernstrom's attempt to deal with problems in the data by claiming that "data that are not perfectly comparable seem to me better than no data at all," is not reassuring.[27] Worse still, while we know the patterns of mobility (many of which have long been suspected from impressionistic evidence), there is much disagreement in accounting for differences among groups. Barton found Italians more upwardly mobile than Slovaks because they placed a higher value on secular education and ambition, but Rumanians did better than both, because education was even more important to them, family size smaller, and their culture more secularly oriented. Kessner found Italians lagging behind Jews, because they were less concerned with education and social mobility, yet John Briggs argues that his Italians were quite interested in these factors, an interest that Briggs claims was brought over from the old country. Thernstrom believes blacks suffered in part because of their lack of skills, but Elizabeth Pleck in her study of Boston blacks identifies white racism as the culprit.[28] The major point, however, is that for whatever reasons, though ethnicity clearly intersects with class, social mobility has a basic ethnic component that must not be ignored.

Ethnicity and race also have a strong though even less well understood impact on the nature of family structure and family life, the fourth area of historical concern. I do not want to devote much space to the family, since Maris Vinovskis and Elizabeth Pleck analyze the contributions of recent research in their essays; but two points must be noted. First, there is a great similarity among groups as far as family structure is concerned. The supposed shift from an extended to a nuclear family, a process at the heart of ideas about the impact of industrialization and modernization, was not a product of migration. In fact, the nuclear family (husband and wife, with or without children) has been the norm in western society since the Middle Ages. Herbert Gutman's work, for example, reveals that even in the alleged matrifocal world of blacks under slavery and freedom, two-parent households were in the majority. There are serious problems with Gutman's work—common sense tells us that slavery must have had a greater impact on the black family than he allows, and his nonlongitudinal "snapshot" research technique and presentist orientation are serious drawbacks—but he provides a needed corrective to previous assumptions about both the nature of American slavery and the status of the black family within it.[29]

The second point worth emphasizing has to do with the effect of the American urban environment on immigrant family life. Here we find some significant evidence of change tending toward homogenization. All recent work on Mexicans, for example, points to the expanded role of women within the family and especially to their greater representation in the labor market in the United States than in Mexico. Nevertheless, authors once again emphasize the degree of continuity between pre- and post-migration life and, especially during the first years after migration, carry-overs from the place of origin clearly led to differences among ethnic, racial, and perhaps class groupings with regard to family values and functions. Despite the increased presence of their wives in the work force, for example, Italian and Mexican men retained their traditional power and authority within the family, even when out of work themselves.[30]

Although more research needs to be done, there seem to be pronounced differences in family size and attitudes, though, as in the case of blacks, class lines produce major variations within groups. Mexicans married young to protect virginity and to promote family growth; Irish and French Canadians married later, so that, though they also were Catholic and established big families, the families are not so large as those among Mexicans. Italians proved more hesitant than Jews to allow their girls and even boys to pursue an education; Barton's Slovaks sought parochial school education for their children, while Italians and Rumanians preferred secular schools; New York's Italian Catholics were more likely than the Irish to send their children to public schools and colleges. Then, too, although the nuclear family is now acknowledged as the dominant form, there are indications that certain ethnic groups, while arranged in nuclear households, had members of the extended family living in separate households nearby, as in the case of French Canadians studied by Tamara Hareven and as with Josef Barton's Slovaks.[31]

We also need to know more about marriage patterns. It seems that members of the first generation most frequently married within the ethnic group. The second generation, however, often married outside the group, indicating significant strides toward structural assimilation. Nevertheless, when deserting the ethnic group, most individuals evidently married within the same religion. Thus, in 1955, in an influential book entitled *Protestant, Catholic and Jew*, the theologian Will Herberg argued for the declining significance in America of ethnicity versus religion. Herbert and others saw a "triple melting pot," in which Italian Catholics married Irish or Polish Catholics, German Protestants married Swedish and English Protestants, and German and East European Jews intermarried.[32] Yet, as in so much else in ethnic history, blacks were left out. Even if the extent of such white ethnic intermarriage by religion is as widespread as claimed, given the resistence to racial intermarriage, it would still make more sense, as David Heer reminds us, to talk of a "double melting pot."[33] But the triple-melting-pot idea held sway until the ethnic revival of the 1960s and 1970s.

One final subject, though technically a part of still another of the proliferating new versions of old subdisciplines, is politics. The new political history (which Samuel Hays considers in another essay in this volume) shares much with the new social history. In an effort to break away from the traditional emphasis on presidential politics, major leaders, and the centrality of such national issues as slavery, the tariff, and the bloody shirt, political historians, especially for the nineteenth century, have attempted to explain much of voting behavior in terms of ethnic and religious loyalties and values. Of course, we have long known that throughout our history the Irish have been Democrats and that Negroes were wedded to the Republicans from emancipation until the New Deal, when they switched to the Democrats. But by using manuscript census data, city directories, precinct registration records, and, in some cases, actual polling books, the new political historians have made far sharper distinctions than ever before and have drawn attention to the importance of such local issues as parochial school attendance, temperance, and sabbatarianism. They have sought to divide the electorate, not along class lines, but rather according to whether or not they were "pietists" or "ritualists," "evangelicals" or "liturgicals." Proponents argue that those whose religious commitment was confined to church-going opposed political parties that took strong moral stands, while the evangelicals or pietists endorsed such efforts.[34] In other words, ethnicity and religious affiliation influenced voting behavior long before the creation of the moral majority, the state of Israel, or Poland's Solidarity Union.

However, the ethnoculturalists, as they are often called, do not command complete control of the field. Nor should they. After all, the history of Southern politics and much of twentieth-century politics does not conform to their model. Then, too, they often ignore the splits within ethnic groups based on class, nativity, and degree of assimilation.[35] The battle between proponents of the importance of cultural as opposed to economic factors or local over national issues in determining voting preference can therefore be expected to continue with ever-escalating sophistication in weaponry.

So much for what has been done by social historians in the treatment of race, ethnicity, and cultural pluralism. I would like to conclude by offering a few suggestions for the possible direction of future work.

First, I think we need more comparative studies. On the one hand, this work should compare the experiences of a single ethnic group in different locations. That might consist of focusing on different cities or even neighborhoods, as is already being done. More ambitiously, however, we need to compare American Italians, for example, with Italians in Argentina or Germany. A common variant would be the comparison of two or more American ethnic groups. The value of the comparative dimension should be obvious. Once we have discerned patterns within a group with respect to family life, migration, social mobility, community formation, or politics, how can we be certain of causative factors without having available control groups? The temptation, for example, to ascribe language problems as the major source of limited mobility for Hispanics is tempered when we study the language problems of Eastern and Southern Europeans at the turn of the century. Similarly, color or race as a factor in limiting black mobility seems less important once the remarkable success of the Chinese and the Japanese Americans is noted. And how can we understand the persistence of old values and patterns of behavior in America without seeing whether or not those characteristics hold for immigrants outside the United States? Daniel Patrick Moynihan, for example, asserts that the Irish development of the boss system in America resulted from their "Irishness," based on conditions in the old country; yet the Irish who went to England and Australia failed to build the same kind of system. Such comparative work will of necessity depend heavily on secondary sources to support primary research on the main target group, but, as in a just-published book on Poles, blacks, and Italians in Pittsburgh by three authors, multi-author monographs can be based on primary research for all groups involved.[36]

This kind of comparative work will naturally depend on continued borrowing from other disciplines, which—as I have noted earlier—is a hallmark of the new social history. Just as we need to lower the barriers that divide disciplines, however, we must begin to end the unnatural division between black history and immigrant history, for in the end we cannot fully understand the history of one minority group without knowing the history of the others. Though probably politically untenable on most campuses today, one positive step in this direction would be the merger of separate ethnic studies programs into a single unit that would put a premium on comparative study.

I also believe that it is time to re-examine our infatuation with the concept of cultural pluralism. After all, things did not work out as Horace Kallen had planned—immigration restriction became national policy, the ancestral language has been transmitted to only a minority of the second and especially the third generation, and increased intermarriage means that, while you cannot change your grandfather, you can change the grandfathers of your posterity. More important, however, Kallen and most defenders of cultural pluralism today overlook the obvious fact that each ethnic group is itself pluralistic. Thus, in his otherwise excellent study, Josef Barton confined his examination of ethnic persistence to those who had already qualified as ethnics through intermarriage and parish or club membership. We learn much about the people who retained their ethnic identity, but, because of the author's filtering process, nothing about those who had in fact already become part of the melting pot. Even when authors such as John Briggs acknowledge the differences within groups, the emphasis remains on shared values, institutions, and behavior. Many authors who describe the splits within a group then proceed to treat the group as a single "community."

Similarly, most new social historians take the discrimination and oppression encountered by their group as a given factor. Only the studies on Mexican Americans tend toward the oppression model once so common in the treatment of blacks and white ethnics, though there are, of course, concessions to what can be termed the new orthodoxy in ethnic history. The revisionists are correct to emphasize the resistance of migrants and immigrants to the forces of Americanization or modernization; but in redressing the balance, they come close to claiming true autonomy for the individuals and ignoring the considerable impact of the new environment in which they had to function. Even among those who claim they are merely arguing for the existence of dialectical rather than dichotomous relationships between culture and environment, once the studies get under way the authors often lose sight of those outside pressures. If not careful, the reader of some works on slavery might get the impression that slavery was at worst a minor annoyance that at times restricted the slave's freedom of movement or limited his earning power. The new social historians have shown that both slave and immigrant life consisted of more than debasing disorganization and oppression; but, though in many respects going beyond Handlin and Elkins, they have not as yet produced a compelling mix of oppression and resistance, defeat and triumph that might enable us to treat *The Uprooted* and *Slavery* merely as period pieces. Perhaps that is not surprising, given the desire to write corrective history, a history that often fails to acknowledge fully the insights of previous authors.

It is only common sense that the forces of modernization and Americanization must have had some impact on at least some of the migrants. Even those who resisted the total remaking of their lives must have made some accommodation to the new ways, while many others must have shed more significant aspects of their cultures. Divisions within the Mexican, Japanese, and black communities studied by Camarillo, Griswold del Castillo, Modell, and Pleck suggest the value of that approach. Yet John Bodnar, Virginia Yans-McLaughlin, and Lawrence Levine are the only ones to use such interaction as an organizing principle, and, as I have noted, the emphasis still remains on continuity.[37] Perhaps, then, it is time to begin to analyze the ethnic map of America by looking at individuals instead of at groups. Possibly, drawing

on the underdeveloped insights of Milton Gordon, Arthur Mann has
provided a useful typology of individual responses to ethnic identity.[38]

The first group Mann calls the "total identifiers," who live out their
lives within the ethnic group. They are the classic cultural pluralists. They
eat with, live with, worship with, and marry their own kind. At present,
total identifiers are a fraction of the population, but their extent at various
times in the past is subject to debate. Perhaps Mexican Americans, for
whom immigration is a continuing process and the homeland so close,
provide the closest current approximation for the kind of cultural identity
so many of the social historians have found in previous generations of
immigrants.

"Partial identifiers" are those who regard ethnic attachment as important, but not all-inclusive. Milton Gordon would see them as having
undergone acculturation, but resisted structural assimilation by keeping
alive contacts at the primary group level, whether with respect to associational, religious, and recreational activities, or with marriage
partners.

"Disaffiliates" grew up in an ethnic or ethno-religious environment,
but have chosen to deviate. They are often found in the world of
academia, the news media, and show business. Most can be termed intellectuals who form a separate group with their own values, rituals, dress,
heroes, fears, and ways of bringing up children. Unlike the partial or total
identifiers, however, the disaffiliates are not tied by a common ancestry.
More of a factor than in earlier years, their number figures to increase with
the expansion of the college-educated population.

"Hybrids" are those of mixed ancestry unable to identify themselves
as a single stock. The product of much intermarriage, they are the children of the melting pot. Perhaps they are like the college professor who
took the columnist Abigail Van Buren to task for saying that a letter-
writer's children were one-quarter Italian. "Abby," wrote Professor
Joseph Ellis, "for nearly fifty years I have tried to get people to see themselves as Americans, not hyphenates. There is no such thing as 'Italian
blood,' one-quarter or otherwise. . . . so let's begin to see people as
people, four quarters' worth all the time."[39]

I think that Mann's model is appropriate, because it removes cultural
pluralism as the norm, deviations from which merit rebuke. Among
many people today, maintaining the values, language, and behavior of
one's ethnic group is as critical as the melting pot was for the founding
fathers or as Anglo-conformity was for the immigration restrictionists.
Thus, Joel Williamson, in an examination of miscegenation and mulattoes

in the United States, expresses concern, though he himself is white, that "the integrity of Negro life is . . . going to be damaged by the large numbers of talented Negroes being recruited into the great white way, where they will strive, consciously and unconsciously, to leave their blackness behind and to gain full membership in the sterile, materialistic club of middle-class America." Similarly, Michael Novak, in celebrating the "unmeltable ethnics," is dismayed by those who surrendered their heritage.[40]

I do not mean to condemn cultural pluralism. In fact, I think that cultural pluralism marks an advance over previous theories of assimilation both as a descriptive and as a prescriptive tool, though I would personally lean in the direction of its expression through the partial-identifier mode. Still, the issue of deviation is most important, especially for blacks, Hispanics, and Indians. It is crucial to remember that you cannot say blacks, Hispanics, or Indians are not like other ethnic groups, since other ethnic groups are not like each other and never were. Like other Americans, therefore, individual Negroes, Hispanics, and Indians have the right to choose whether they want to be total identifiers, partial identifiers, or disaffiliates, or whether they want to contribute to the ranks of hybrids. Neither the 100 percent Americans nor the ethnic purists deserve automatic praise or condemnation.

In the end, a critical matter for debate will be whose responsibility it is to further ethnic identification and what form that identification should take. Is it the job of the family and the ethnic community, or is it the responsibility of the public sector, through its schools, museums, preservation societies, and governments? And when does the desire of one group to perpetuate its way of life infringe on the opportunities sought by other groups for advancement? Historians have begun to pay more systematic attention to the effects and nature of intergroup ethnic conflict—certainly a subject worthy of greater study for both the present and the past.[41]

I think that, in this regard, John Higham's concept of a system of "pluralistic integration" provides some guidelines. Such a system would "uphold the validity of a common culture, to which all individuals have access, while sustaining the efforts of minorities to preserve and enhance their own integrity." The key to such a dual commitment would be the distinction between "nuclei" and "boundaries." Boundaries would be understood to be permeable; ethnic nuclei would be respected as enduring centers of social action. Thus, "Both integration and ethnic cohesion are recognized as worthy goals, which different individuals will accept in different degrees." It is Higham's hope that such a system, which is already partly in place, "implies that invigoration of the nuclei can relieve the defense of ethnic boundaries."[42]

The problem is that it will not always be self-evident where the nucleus ends and the boundaries begin; but, of course, this gets at the whole issue of American nationality or identity and the rights of minorities. It is a problem that we tend to forget confronts all countries. Russia and Canada are only two examples. The problem is particularly great in a nation of immigrants such as ours. After all, as Arthur Mann and John Higham remind us, how much diversity can you encourage without undermining the very foundations of national unity and identity? This is as yet a question that the new social historians in their celebration of diversity have not asked about ethnic and racial past.

Notes

The author wishes to thank Professors Anne Boylan and Arthur Mann for their comments on an earlier version of this essay.

1. Stephan Thernstrom, *Poverty and Progress: Social Mobility in a Nineteenth-Century City* (Cambridge: Harvard University Press, 1964), p. 7.

2. John W. Briggs, *An Italian Passage: Immigrants to Three American Cities, 1890–1930* (New Haven: Yale University Press, 1978), p. xx; John Modell, *The Economics and Politics of Racial Accommodation: The Japanese of Los Angeles, 1900–1942* (Urbana: University of Illinois Press, 1977), p. vii; John W. Blassingame, *The Slave Community: Plantation Life in the Antebellum South* (New York: Oxford Unviersity Press, 1972), p. viii.

3. Oscar Handlin, *The Uprooted: The Epic Story of the Great Migrations That Made the American People*, 2d ed., enlarged (Boston: Little, Brown, 1973); Handlin, *Boston's Immigrants, 1790–1865: A Study in Acculturation* (Cambridge: Harvard University Press, 1941). For criticism of Handlin, see, for example, Virginia Yans-McLaughlin, *Family and Community: Italian Immigrants in Buffalo, 1880–1930* (Ithaca: Cornell University Press, 1977), pp. 18, 26, 57, 62, 181; Briggs, *Italian Passage*, p. 118; Josef J. Barton, *Peasants and Strangers: Italians, Rumanians, and Slovaks in an American City, 1890–1950* (Cambridge: Harvard University Press, 1975), p. 2; Judith Fincher Laird, "Argentine, Kansas: The Evolution of a Mexican-American Community: 1905–1940," (Ph.D dissertation, University of Kansas, 1975), p. 159.

4. The following treatment draws heavily on John Higham, *Send These to Me: Jews and Other Immigrants in Urban America* (New York: Atheneum, 1975), pp. 196–230; Milton M. Gordon, *Assimilation in American Life: The Role of Race, Religion, and National Origins* (New York: Oxford University Press, 1964), chaps. 4–6; Arthur Mann, *The One and the Many: Reflections on the American Identity* (Chicago: University of Chicago Press, 1979), chaps. 5–6.

5. J. Hector St. John de Crevecoeur, *Letters from an American Farmer* (London, 1782; reprint ed., New York: Albert and Charles Boni, 1925), p. 55; Ralph Waldo Emerson, *Journals of Ralph Waldo Emerson*, edited by Edward Waldo Emerson and Waldo Emerson Forbes, 10 vols. (Boston: Houghton Mifflin, 1909–1914), 7:115–116.

6. Mann, *One and the Many*, pp. 97–98.

7. Israel Zangwill, *The Melting Pot* (New York: Macmillan, 1909); Roosevelt quoted in Mann, *One and the Many*, p. 100.

8. Horace M. Kallen, *Culture and Democracy in the United States* (New York: Boni and Liveright, 1924).

9. Gordon, *Assimilation*, pp. 70–71; Carl N. Degler, *Out of Our Past: The Forces That Shaped Modern America* (New York: Harper and Row, 1959), p. 296.

10. Modell, *Economics and Politics of Racial Accommodation, passim,* but especially pp. 84–85.

11. Richard Griswold del Castillo, *The Los Angeles Barrio, 1850–1890: A Social History* (Berkeley: University of California Press, 1979), p. xi.

12. Handlin, *The Uprooted*, p. 4; Handlin, *The Newcomers: Negroes and Puerto Ricans in a Changing Metropolis* (Cambridge: Harvard University Press, 1959); Handlin, *The American People in the Twentieth Century* (Cambridge: Harvard University Press, 1954).

13. Yans-McLaughlin, *Family and Community*, p. 18.

14. Rudolph J. Vecoli, "Contadini in Chicago: A Critique of *The Uprooted*," *Journal of American History* 51 (1964): 404–417; Laird, "Argentine, Kansas," p. 159, as quoted with a muted endorsement in Mario T. Garcia, *Desert Immigrants: The Mexicans of El Paso, 1880–1920* (New Haven: Yale University Press, 1981), p. 197.

15. Barton, *Peasants and Strangers*, especially chaps. 2–3. Barton's immigrants, however, have much in common with those described by Marcus Lee Hansen, whose pioneering work has been ignored by the new social historians. See, for example, Hansen, *The Immigrant in American History* (Cambridge: Harvard University Press, 1940).

16. Briggs, *Italian Passage*, chaps. 1–5, quotation on p. 70; Albert Camarillo, *Chicanos in a Changing Society: From Mexican Pueblos to American Barrios in Santa Barbara and Southern California, 1848–1930* (Cambridge: Harvard University Press, 1979), pp. 144, 279, quotation on p. 146. See also Yans-McLaughlin, *Family and Community*, pp. 58–64; Marc Lee Raphael, *Jews and Judaism in a Midwestern Community: Columbus, Ohio, 1840–1975* (Columbus: Ohio Historical Society, 1979), pp. 16–17; John Bodnar, *Immigration and Industrialization: Ethnicity in an American Mill Town, 1870–1940* (Pittsburgh: Unversity of Pittsburgh Press, 1977), pp. 26–28; Elizabeth Hafkin Pleck, *Black Migration and Poverty: Boston 1865–1900* (New York: Academic Press, 1979), pp. 63–67.

17. Thomas Kessner, *The Golden Door: Italian and Jewish Immigrant Mobility in New York City, 1880–1915* (New York: Oxford University Press, 1977), pp. 28–31; Bodnar, *Immigration and Industrialization*, pp. 28–29, 55, 87–88; Garcia, *Desert Immigrants*, p. 106; Camarillo, *Chicanos*, p. 161. See also Griswold del Castillo, *Los Angeles Barrio*, pp. 119–124. For evidence that proximity to the homeland stimulated similar behavior on the part of at least some French Canadians, see Tamara Hareven, "The Laborers of Manchester, New Hampshire, 1912–1922: The Role of Family and Adjustment to Industrial Life," *Labor History* 16 (1975): 249–265.

18. Barton, *Peasants and Strangers*, pp. 18–22; Modell, *Economics and Politics of Racial Accommodation*, pp. 32–33, 55–75; Camarillo, *Chicanos*, pp. 10–13; Garcia, *Desert Immigrants*, pp. 127–154; Griswold del Castillo, *Los Angeles Barrio*, chap. 5 (the name of the main barrio, Sonora Town, reflects the importance of chain migration); Howard N. Rabinowitz, *Race Relations in the Urban South, 1865–1890* (New York: Oxford University Press, 1978), parts I and II. For the new view of "ghettoization" among white ethnics as compared to blacks, see Sam Bass Warner and Colin B. Burke, "Cultural Change in the Ghetto," *Journal of Contemporary History* 4 (1969): 173–187; Howard P. Chudacoff, *Mobile Americans: Residential and Social Mobility in Omaha, 1880–1920* (New York: Oxford University Press, 1972), pp. 65–68, 75–83; Thomas Lee Philpott, *The Slum and the Ghetto: Neighborhood Deterioration and Middle-Class Reform, Chicago, 1880–1930* (New York: Oxford University Press, 1978), chap. 5;

but see also Kathleen Neils Conzen, *Immigrant Milwaukee: Accommodation and Community in a Frontier City* (Cambridge: Harvard University Press, 1976), pp. 127–136.

19. Gordon, *Assimilation*, pp. 67, 70–71, 80–81, 110–111; Briggs, *Italian Passage*, p. 278.

20. James Borchert, *Alley Life in Washington: Family, Community, Religion, and Folklife in the City, 1850–1970* (Urbana: University of Illinois Press, 1980), *passim*, quotation on p. 240; Pleck, *Black Migration*, p. 3.

21. Blassingame, *Slave Community*; Herbert G. Gutman, *The Black Family in Slavery and Freedom, 1750–1925* (New York: Pantheon, 1976); Eugene D. Genovese, *Roll, Jordan, Roll: The World the Slaves Made* (New York: Pantheon, 1974); Stanley M. Elkins, *Slavery: A Problem in American Institutional and Intellectual Life* (Chicago: University of Chicago Press, 1959).

22. See, for example, Kenneth Lockridge, *A New England Town: The First Hundred Years* (New York: Norton, 1970).

23. Borchert, *Alley Life in Washington*, p. 239; Briggs, *Italian Passage*, p. 272; Garcia, *Desert Immigrants*, p. 213; Yans-McLaughlin, *Family and Community*, p. 22. Two other works that, like Yans-McLaughlin's, emphasize a dialectical relationship between culture and environment, but nevertheless leave the reader more impressed with the high degree of cultural continuity and persistence, are Bodnar, *Immigration and Industrialization*, and Lawrence W. Levine, *Black Culture and Black Consciousness: Afro-American Folk Thought from Slavery to Freedom* (New York: Oxford University Press, 1977).

24. Thernstrom, *Poverty and Progress*. See also Chudacoff, *Mobile Americans*; Kessner, *The Golden Door*; Peter Knights, *The Plain People of Boston, 1830–1860: A Study in City Growth* (New York: Oxford University Press, 1971).

25. Stephan Thernstrom, *The Other Bostonians: Poverty and Progress in the American Metropolis, 1880–1970* (Cambridge: Harvard University Press, 1973); Camarillo, *Chicanos*, pp. 217–225; Griswold del Castillo, *Los Angeles Barrio*, pp. 51–61. See also sources cited in note 24.

26. See, for example, James A. Henretta, "Social History as Lived and Written," *American Historical Review* 84 (1979): 1315–1316; Henretta, "The Study of Social Mobility: Ideological Assumptions and Conceptual Bias," *Labor History* 18 (1977): 165–178; Yans-McLaughlin, *Family and Community*, pp. 34–36.

27. Thernstrom, *Other Bostonians*, p. 330.

28. Barton, *Peasants and Strangers*, chaps. 5–6; Kessner, *Golden Door*, *passim*; Briggs, *Italian Passage*, *passim*; Thernstrom, *Other Bostonians*, pp. 217–218; Pleck, *Black Migration*, chap. 5. For the most successful attempt to minimize the problems inherent in social mobility studies, see Clyde and Sally Griffen, *Natives and Newcomers: The Ordering of Opportunity in Mid-Nineteenth-Century Poughkeepsie* (Cambridge: Harvard University Press, 1978).

29. Gutman, *Black Family*, *passim*.

30. Yans-McLaughlin, *Family and Community*, p. 20 and *passim*; Griswold del Castillo, *Los Angeles Barrio*, chap. 3; Garcia, *Desert Immigrants*, pp. 117–118, 123–124, 201–204. For a somewhat different view, see Camarillo, *Chicanos*, pp. 120, 137.

31. Griswold del Castillo, *Los Angeles Barrio*, chap. 3; Barton, *Peasants and Strangers*, chap. 6; Kessner, *The Golden Door*, chap. 4; Nathan Glazer and Daniel Patrick Moynihan, *Beyond the Melting Pot: The Negroes, Puerto Ricans, Jews, Italians, and Irish of New York City*, 2d ed. (Cambridge: M.I.T. Press, 1970), pp. 201–203. Laurence A. Glasco, "The Life Cycles and Household Structure of American Ethnic Groups: Irish, Germans, and Native-born Whites in Buffalo, New York, 1855," *Journal of Urban History* 1 (1975): 339–364; Tamara Hareven, "Family Time and Industrial Time: Family and Work in a Planned Corporation Town, 1900–1924," 365–389; Myfanwy Morgan and Hilda A. Golden, "Immigrant Families in an Industrial City: A Study of Households in Holyoke, 1880," *Journal of Family History* 4 (1979): 59–68.

32. Will Herberg, *Protestant-Catholic-Jew: An Essay in American Religious Sociology* (Garden City, N.Y.: Doubleday, 1955). See also Ruby Jo Reeves Kennedy, "Single or Triple Melting Pot? Intermarriage Trends in New Haven, 1870–1940," *American Journal of Sociology* 49 (1944): 331–339.

33. David M. Heer, "Intermarriage," in *Harvard Encyclopedia of American Ethnic Groups*, edited by Stephan Thernstrom (Cambridge: Harvard University Press, 1980), p. 521.

34. See, for example, Frederick C. Luebke, *Immigrants and Politics: The Germans of Nebraska, 1880–1900* (Lincoln: University of Nebraska Press, 1969); Paul Kleppner, *The Cross of Culture: A Social Analysis of Midwestern Politics, 1850–1900* (New York: Free Press, 1970); Richard J. Jensen, *The Winning of the Midwest: Social and Political Conflict, 1888–1896* (Chicago: University of Chicago Press, 1971); Ronald P. Formisano, *The Birth of Mass Political Parties: Michigan, 1827–1861* (Princeton: Princeton University Press, 1971); Kleppner, *The Third Electoral System, 1853–1892: Parties, Voters, and Political Cultures* (Chapel Hill: University of North Carolina Press, 1979).

35. For a corrective, see, for example, Arthur Mann, *LaGuardia Comes to Power: 1933* (Philadelphia: Lippincott, 1965).

36. Glazer and Moynihan, *Beyond the Melting Pot*, pp. 223–226; John Bodnar, Roger Simon, and Michael P. Weber, *Lives of Their Own: Blacks, Italians, and Poles in Pittsburgh, 1900–1960* (Urbana: University of Illinois Press, 1982).

37. See, for example, Camarillo, *Chicanos*, pp. 187–191; Griswold del Castillo, *Los Angeles Barrio*, pp. 171–172; Modell, *Economics and Politics of Racial Accommodation, passim*; Pleck, *Black Migration*, pp. 77ff., 118; Bodnar, *Immigration and Industrialization*; Yans-McLaughlin, *Family and Community*; Levine, *Black Culture and Black Consciousness*. For divisions among blacks, see also Rabinowitz, *Race Relations in the Urban South*, especially parts I and II.

38. Mann, *One and the Many*, chap. 8.

39. Letter of Joseph V. Ellis to "Dear Abby," *Albuquerque Journal*, January 26, 1982, p. A-8. Internal evidence suggests that Ellis is a hybrid, though the possibility remains that he might in fact be a disaffiliate.

40. Joel Williamson, *New People: Miscegenation and Mulattoes in the United States* (New York: Free Press, 1980), p. 194; Michael Novak, *The Rise of the Unmeltable Ethnics* (New York: Macmillan, 1972).

41. See, for example, Ronald H. Bayor, *Neighbors in Conflict: The Irish, Germans, Jews and Italians of New York City, 1929–1941* (Baltimore: Johns Hopkins University Press, 1978); Bodnar, Simon, and Weber, *Lives of Their Own*; Bodnar, *Immigration and Industrialization*.

42. Higham, *Send These to Me*, pp. 242–246, quotations on pp. 242, 246.

Suggestions for Additional Reading

General Studies

Dinnerstein, Leonard, Roger L. Nichols, and David M. Reimers. *Natives and Strangers: Ethnic Groups and the Building of America*. 2d ed. New York: Oxford University Press, 1979.

College survey text that incorporates much of the material from the new social history.

Franklin, John Hope. *From Slavery to Freedom: A History of Negro Americans.* 5th
ed. New York: Alfred A. Knopf, 1980.

 The most comprehensive history of blacks in America.

Gordon, Milton. *Assimilation in American Life: The Role of Race, Religion, and
National Origins.* New York: Oxford University Press. 1964.

 Challenging theoretical treatment of the subject that emphasizes the
 importance of cultural pluralism and the variety of responses to assimilation.

Handlin, Oscar. *The Uprooted: The Epic Story of the Great Migrations That Made the
American People.* 2d ed. Boston: Little Brown, 1973.

 Classic "impressionistic" account that has become the target of much of
 the new work in the field. See the excellent new concluding chapter, in
 which the author responds to his critics.

Mann, Arthur. *The One and the Many: Reflections on the American Identity.*
Chicago: University of Chicago Press, 1979.

 Best brief introduction to the study of American ethnicity.

Meier, August, and Elliott Rudwick. *From Plantation to Ghetto.* 3d ed. New York:
Hill and Wang, 1976.

 Best brief interpretive survey of black history.

Thernstrom, Stephan, editor. *Harvard Encyclopedia of American Ethnic Groups.*
Cambridge: Harvard University Press, 1980.

 Indispensable. All you ever wanted to know and more about individual
 groups and key concepts in the study of ethnicity.

White Ethnics (Single Group Studies)

Bodnar, John. *Immigration and Industrialization: Ethnicity in an American Mill
Town, 1870–1940.* Pittsburgh: University of Pittsburgh Press, 1977.

 Uses the Slavs of Steelton, Pennsylvania, as a means of studying the
 interaction of environment and culture.

Briggs, John W. *An Italian Passage: Immigrants to Three American Cities, 1890–1930.*
New Haven: Yale University Press, 1978.

 Uses the experience of Italians in Rochester, Utica, and Kansas City to
 challenge findings of much recent literature concerning alleged Italian
 clannishness, antipathy toward education, fear of social mobility, and
 unselective migration. Immigrant values and attitudes seen as compatible with those in America.

Conzen, Kathleen Neils. *Immigrant Milwaukee, 1836–1860: Accommodation and
Community in a Frontier City.* Cambridge: Harvard University Press,
1976.

Important study of the development of voluntary German identity in the absence of outside hostility and even after economic success.

Goren, Arthur. *New York Jews and the Quest for Community: The Kehillah Experiment, 1908–1922*. New York: Columbia University Press, 1970.

Superb treatment of conflict and co-operation between German and East European Jews.

Handlin, Oscar. *Boston's Immigrants: A Study in Acculturation*. Rev. and enlarged ed. Cambridge, Mass.: Harvard University Press, 1959.

Classic study of the conflict between the Yankees and the Irish (1840–1880) and the resulting group consciousness among both.

Hertzberg, Steven. *Strangers within the Gate City: The Jews of Atlanta, 1845–1915*. Philadelphia: Jewish Publication Society of America, 1978.

Pioneering effort to break out of old methodological and geographical straitjackets.

Nelli, Humbert S. *Italians in Chicago, 1880–1930: A Study in Ethnic Mobility*. New York: Oxford University Press, 1970.

Perceptive and well-written treatment of the forging of Italian identity as a result of immigration and its persistence under the impact of economic and geographic mobility.

Rischin, Moses. *The Promised City: New York Jews, 1870–1914*. Cambridge: Harvard University Press, 1962.

Classic encyclopedic account, especially good on conditions in the immigrant wards.

Yans-McLaughlin, Virginia. *Family and Community: Italian Immigrants in Buffalo, 1880–1930*. Ithaca: Cornell University Press, 1978.

Argues for the persistence of old world patterns of family behavior, though acknowledges existence of a dialectical process.

Blacks, Hispanics, and Orientals

Blassingame, John W. *The Slave Community: Plantation Life in the Antebellum South*. Rev. and enlarged ed. New York: Oxford University Press, 1979.

Despite an exaggerated view of the strength of "community" among slaves, this is now the best brief introduction to the history of American slavery.

Borchert, James. *Alley Life in Washington: Family, Community, Religion, and Folklife in the City, 1850–1970*. Urbana: University of Illinois Press, 1980.

Argues for the persistence of black rural folk values in religion, family life, etc., in the face of modernization and urbanization.

Camarillo, Albert. *Chicanos in a Changing Society: From Mexican Pueblos to Ameri-*

can Barrios in Santa Barbara and Southern California, 1848–1930. Cambridge: Harvard University Press, 1979.

Mainly on Santa Barbara. Emphasizes the persistence of ethnic identity in the face of Anglo hostility and oppression.

Elkins, Stanley M. *Slavery: A Problem in American Institutional and Intellectual Life*. Chicago: University of Chicago Press, 1959.

Controversial book that has been the target of most of the work on slavery published since the early 1960s. Despite undermining most of Elkins's basic contentions, revisionists have not yet dealt successfully with Elkins's basic question: Why didn't more slaves rebel?

Garcia, Mario T. *Desert Immigrants: The Mexicans of El Paso, 1880–1920*. New Haven: Yale University Press, 1981.

Most conceptually oriented of the Mexican studies. Clearest presentation of the mix of continuity and change in Mexican American culture.

Genovese, Eugene D. *Roll, Jordan, Roll: The World the Slaves Made*. New York: Pantheon, 1974.

Typical of recent emphasis in black history on the extent to which blacks were able to control their own lives under slavery. By the country's leading Marxist historian.

Griswold del Castillo, Richard. *The Los Angeles Barrio, 1850–1890: A Social History*. Berkeley: University of California Press, 1980.

Highly quantitative study of employment, family life, and crime patterns.

Gutman, Herbert G. *The Black Family in Slavery and Freedom, 1750–1925*. New York: Pantheon, 1976.

Despite the title, almost the entire book deals with the period prior to 1880, especially before emancipation. Argues for the strength of black families in the face of slavery and other forms of oppression.

Kusmer, Kenneth L. *A Ghetto Takes Shape: Black Cleveland, 1870–1930*. Urbana: University of Illinois Press, 1976.

Best treatment of the development of a Northern ghetto. Comparative approach to the study of urban blacks makes this the best place to get a sense of the literature in the field circa 1975.

Levine, Lawrence W. *Black Culture and Black Consciousness: Afro-American Folk Thought from Slavery to Freedom*. New York: Oxford University Press, 1977.

Through an imaginative use of black folklore material—stories, songs, etc.—shows how a separate black culture emerged during slavery and through interaction with the dominant culture persisted after emancipation.

Modell, John. *The Economics and Politics of Racial Accommodation: The Japanese of Los Angeles, 1900–1942*. Urbana: University of Illinois Press, 1977.

> Greater attention than in most studies to the second generation, which is seen as too intent on accommodating to American expectations.

Pleck, Elizabeth Hafkin. *Black Migration and Poverty: Boston, 1865–1900*. New York: Academic Press, 1979.

> Emphasizes differences among Southern- and Northern-born blacks in Boston in the areas of housing, employment, and family life. Good use of comparative evidence from Northern and Southern cities.

Rabinowitz, Howard N. *Race Relations in the Urban South, 1865–1890*. New York: Oxford University Press, 1978.

> Focuses on Raleigh, Richmond, Montgomery, Nashville, and Atlanta, to examine black urban life and white attitudes, with particular emphasis on the origins and development of segregation.

Multi-Group and Thematic Studies

Barton, Josef J. *Peasants and Strangers: Italians, Rumanians, and Slovaks in an American City, 1890–1950*. Cambridge: Harvard University Press, 1975.

> Methodologically and conceptually rich study that uses three Cleveland ethnic groups to illustrate different attitudes and degrees of assimilation.

Bayor, Ronald H. *Neighbors in Conflict: The Irish, Germans, Jews, and Italians of New York, 1921–1941*. Baltimore: Johns Hopkins University Press, 1978.

> Job competition makes Irish and Jews the bitterest enemies.

Glazer, Nathan, and Daniel Patrick Moynihan. *Beyond the Melting Pot: The Negroes, Puerto Ricans, Jews, Italians, and Irish of New York City*. 2d ed. Cambridge: M.I.T. Press, 1970.

> Controversial, pioneering study of the persistence of ethnicity and the resulting differences among the city's most important groups. New edition contains valuable introduction on the rediscovery of ethnicity during the 1960s.

Kessner, Thomas. *The Golden Door: Italian and Jewish Immigrant Mobility in New York City, 1880–1915*. New York: Oxford University Press, 1977.

> Explains reasons for higher degree of Jewish mobility. Good review of most recent mobility literature, but see Thernstrom for a more thorough discussion of the secondary sources circa 1972.

Thernstrom, Stephan. *The Other Bostonians: Poverty and Progress in the American Metropolis, 1880–1970*. Cambridge: Harvard University Press, 1973.

> Accounts for the relatively high rates of social mobility among Jews, lesser degree of success among Italians and Irish, and relative failure of blacks.

A Milwaukee woman performs a routine domestic task in this photograph taken about 1909 by J. Robert Taylor.

3

Women's History: Gender as a Category of Historical Analysis

Elizabeth H. Pleck

S UBSTANTIAL SCHOLARLY RESEARCH and publication, specialized journals, women's studies curricula, national conferences and organizations, and other professional activities all testify to the increased interest within the last decade in the historical study of women. Perhaps the most significant factor in the emergence of the field was the revival of feminism in the United States in the 1960s. A new self-conscious group came to history with a desire to know its past. That was, at first, a difficult task. Except for an occasional photograph or paragraph devoted to the suffrage movement, women were entirely missing from the typical high school or college textbook. Rarely could a history student name more than a couple of women of achievement in American history. The absence of women from history resulted not simply from an accident of omission, but from the dominant view of what history was. As history evolved over the last one hundred years into a scholarly discipline practiced by professionals, it became preoccupied with the study of the exercise of legal, economic, and political power through the chronicle of wars, diplomacy, great ideas, and the rise of the nation-state. The periods of American history—actually arbitrary demarcations of one length of time from another—followed the major presidencies or wars. Since women so often lacked formal economic and political power, it was easy to exclude mention of them from the study of, say, the Age of Jackson or of Wilson.

Then came the new social history, promising to reshape the study of history and claiming to present those who had been forgotten—the his-

tory of peoples, rather than of nations. The great promise of a democ-
ratized history was never achieved when it came to women, however.
Social history too often turned out to be the history of the common man in
a man-made world. Even in the histories of minorities in the United
States, an important area of inquiry in the last two decades, women were
missing.

The reason for the absence of women in both traditional history and
the new social history was that males had defined themselves as the
subject of history and had ordered historical study to concentrate on male
activities. Historians have tended to value those activities in which males
predominated and to undervalue those in which women predominated,
such as child-rearing and the building of communities. Even more significantly, man has been made the representative of universal human experience. Women, as Simone De Beauvoir argues, have been defined as
the Other, that which was not Man. [1] Never the subject of history, always
the object, women lacked the power to include themselves in history and
to define the terms for their inclusion. Some claim that, because women
are missing from history, most of written history should be considered
"men's history." Actually, much historical writing is concerned not with
people, whether male or female, but with ideas, nation-states, or environments. Nonetheless, when biography is introduced or human experience is discussed, the individual is seen as a male, and the male is seen as
an individual, not as a member of a more powerful and privileged gender.
Perhaps because it is the privilege of an elite to avoid self-conscious inquiry, gender is not seen to define or limit male behavior.

The first effort in women's history has been to compensate for the
invisibility of women from the historical record. Ever since Sarah Hale,
editor of the antebellum *Godey's Lady's Book*, compiled a list of women of
exception, and the suffragist Matilda Gage several decades later pointed
out that a woman, not Eli Whitney, had invented the cotton gin, women
historians have sought to show the contribution of women to their country, to remove and to counter prejudice against women, and to increase
the pride that women feel in the accomplishments of their group.

Clearly, the outstanding contribution of American women from every
religious and racial group has been as community builders, those who
have assessed the needs of their localities for services, raised funds for
institutions, and served as volunteers and paid workers for these institutions. Women have built schools, libraries, kindergartens, homes for
wayward girls, settlement houses, orphanages, societies for the prevention of cruelty to children. Throughout Europe, reformers concerned
about conditions of material and infant health were males; in the United

States, they were mostly females. In England, where the social settlement originated, the prominent settlement house leaders were men, whereas, in the United States, the founders were college-educated women. American men have reformed national politics, the law, and economic life, but women have reshaped their communities and have been prominent advocates of improved welfare for women, children, and animals. American women have also been prominent in abolitionism, the labor and civil rights movements, ecology, radicalism, and the reforms of the Progressive era. Justified as a religious mission and a transfer of female nurturance to community life, this advocacy of community institutions and involvement in reform has served as an antidote to the commercialism of America and the individualistic ethic. Recognition of this involvement of women in reform and community life can lead to new interpretations of American history. The failure of the Jamestown settlement and the success of Plymouth Colony appear due at least in part to the absence of women from the one and to their presence in the other. Similarly, when women Progressives are integrated into the history of that movement, reformers of that era appear to be as concerned with social justice as with economic regulation and social control.

The contribution of women to American history has also been studied through the biographies of individual women. To supplement the *Dictionary of American Biography*, which often omitted the biographies of important American women, Edward T. James, Janet Wilson James, and Paul Boyer edited the three-volume edition of *Notable American Women*, a selection of brief biographical sketches of 1,350 American women who died between 1607 and 1950.[2] A companion volume, edited by Barbara Sicherman and Carol Hurd Green, appeared in 1980, covering 442 women who died between 1951 and 1975.[3] These biographies show the range of female initiative and contribution to American history, especially in the areas of education, reform, and economic life. Biography is at its best when it illustrates not only an exceptional life, but also the relationship of the individual woman to the condition of womankind. Kathryn Kish Sklar's biography of Catherine Beecher traces the ideas and the life of the leading exponent of Victorian womanhood, a highly complex educator and advocate for the advancement of her sex who sought to escape in her own life from the constraints of womanhood she extolled.[4] Jean Strouse's *Alice James*, a biography of the younger sister of William and Henry James, describes the life of an intellectual who made a career out of female invalidism.[5]

The emphasis on famous individuals and on the contributions of women to American history tends to reinforce the idea that the history of women is similar to that of minority groups, whose contributions to American society have been similarly ignored. Akin to a minority group, women have suffered discrimination and denial of economic and political power and have been compelled to establish their own organizations to press for formal political rights. But although women are a distinct grouping within society, they are not a minority. Women are more than half of the American population. Furthermore, women are not segregated from the privileged element of society, but dwell in their midst. Unlike any minority group, they give birth to and rear the privileged group. Indeed, women often hold perspectives more similar to that of the men in their families than to that of women of different social groups. No minority group has included such a diversity of people. Women may indeed share common interests, but they also have opposing ones, as well, because of their diversity. For instance, immigrant, working-class, or minority women have often suffered exclusion from the dominant ideology of gender precisely because such belief systems are built on principles of selectivity.

Moreover, contribution history shows only the manner in which women shaped American history, while the purpose of women's history is to show how American history affected women and affected the definition of womanhood and manhood. The compensatory approach to women's history, no matter how necessary as a remedy for the invisibility of women and their accomplishments, places too much emphasis on those women whose lives departed most from the typical female experience through activism in public life. Women's history, on the other hand, presumes that the ordinary as well as the unusual life experience of women as a group is worthy of historical inquiry.

Calling the field *women's history* is actually something of a misnomer, a convenient shorthand to describe a field whose major concern is actually the evolution of gender, the cultural definition of behavior appropriate for *both* sexes. *Gender*, which varies from one culture to another, is maintained by the forces of socialization, family life, institutions, and ideology. It is a guideline, encouraging behavior considered appropriate and discouraging what is considered inappropriate. *Gender is a social category*, similar to race, class, or age, but it is also an absolutely unique form of social organization. No other social division between two groups, roughly equal in size, exhibits such great disparity in access to resources and formal power. Moreover, women are a social group with powerful and intimate ties with their opposites, based on kinship, shared residence, and common interests in the rearing of children. Thus, while research in women's history focuses largely on the female experience, the conceptual framework is broader—the changing ideas of womanhood and manhood and ways in which actual behavior has met these prescriptions.

Obviously, biology has influenced the definihion of women's experience. Although both sexes are necessary ho produce offspring, only women give birth and are capable of nursing infants. Those women who did not bear children were defined as deviant, while those who did were circumscribed by their definition as mothers. Fatherhood has never served to limit male activity the way motherhood has circumscribed women. In fact, for centuries the ideology of fatherhood has justified hierarchical rule, whether in the family or in the polity. Since reproduction has imposed a greater constraint on women's lives than on men's, the ability to control reproduction marks one of the great freedoms for women. Hence the significance of the fertility decline of the nineteenth century, from an average of eight to four live births per woman. One interpretation of that emphasizes the steady increase in the right of women to refuse their husbands sexual intercourse and to decide how many children they want. That right to abstain was rooted in the ideology of the passionless and pure woman, a Victorian concept long regarded as sexually repressive but actually pivotal in liberating women from the bonds of unwanted pregnancy. But although the history of fertility decline appears as a steady increase in women's control, the history of childbirth (until recently) appears quite the opposite. Until the early twentieth century, nearly every woman who gave birth did so at home, with the aid of female relatives, perhaps her husband, and a midwife. Then childbirth was transformed into a medical illness requiring hospitalization for which a physician (usually a male) was required. Thus, interaction of women and medicine involves the improvement in women's health and life expectancy and the decline in infant mortality, but also the decreasing control of women over the health process.

The study of reproduction and sexuality eventually also leads to examination of marriage and the family, the socially sanctioned forms for sexuality and reproduction. Indeed, the history of gender and the history of the family overlap substantially. Women are not simply half of all the members of the family; they are the creators of it, the nurturers of children—and, in the last two centuries, the major reformers of the family. The two fields appear to be locked into an unhappy marriage, however. On the one hand, women's history has often neglected the technical study of demography in favor of emphasis on the female point of view. On the other, family history has often ignored the variable of gender, resulting in the now familiar problem that male experience in the family as a child, an adolescent, or an elder is considered the universal experience. Both gender and the family can be approached at a general level, each without inquiry into the other, but that approach is taken at the peril of achieving only superficial generalization.

Gender involves much more than just reproduction and sexuality, however. Despite the close and often intimate bonds between the sexes, the social experiences of women differ greatly from that of men. Sociologist Jessie Bernard refers to that divergence in point of view when she describes the "'his' and 'hers' marriage," the different perspectives on marriage held by each partner.[6] The most vivid evocation of the separate world of women has been drawn by Carroll Smith-Rosenberg from the letters and diaries of nineteenth-century middle-class women.[7] Bonds between mothers and daughters were strong, and women expressed unabashed feelings of passion and affection for other women. This female subculture appears to have been grounded in common experience, common rituals of childbirth and nursing of the sick, and common norms, language, and even forms of nonverbal communication.

No aspect of women's experience reflects the restraints of this cultural definition of appropriate behavior more clearly than work. The most unique form of female labor has been women's unpaid work in the home. Children as well as women performed this work, but the responsibility for the division of tasks and their supervision rested with the wife or an older daughter. Indeed, the word *housewife* indicates a form of legal union between a woman and her home. Although Victorian America viewed housework not as work at all, but as a "labor of love," there was always plenty to do, even for the middle-class woman who employed a servant. The situation did not improve even with the growth of technology, first in the nineteenth century, with the installation of indoor plumbing and central heating, and then in the twentieth century, with electricity, refrigeration, vacuum cleaners, and washing machines. Studies of the amount of time that housewives spent performing household chores indicate that, in the period from 1920 to 1965, the amount of time women devoted to housework did not diminish despite such "labor-saving devices." Instead, influenced by advertising and child-rearing experts, women's standards of child care and housekeeping became more meticulous. More recently, it appears that women are devoting less time to housekeeping, perhaps because of the smaller family size of the American family or because of the influence of the women's movement. Yet, despite such recent trends and the increase in the number of men performing housekeeping tasks, housework remains essentially women's work.

Gender has remained just as central when women have worked for pay. The social definition of every woman as an actual or potential housewife and mother has shaped her self-image, sense of self-esteem, decisions about whether or not to accept paid work, and the kind of work she performs. Indeed, women's reproductive capacity has served to justify excluding women from many forms of work and to underscore the view of women as temporary workers. Even female beauty and sexual attractiveness, the traditional asset of many women, has rendered them vulnerable in the workplace. In short, the world of paid work is a sex-segregated one: most women hold jobs in largely female occupations, and most males hold jobs in largely male occupations. Despite the many changes in women's occupational status in the last twenty years, the degree of sex segregation of jobs has remained remarkably constant. As job categories have become filled by members of one or the other sex, it has been assumed that only males or females are fit for them. Once an occupation has been defined as female, it has been invariably associated with lower prestige and pay. Even in the professions, women are crowded into the less prestigious and lower-paid specialties.

The underlying assumption of women's history is that there has been difference, division, and inequality of male to female in history. In every society, women as a group are to some degree and in some way subordinate to men. Every culture segments its social world and its tasks, sometimes even its ideas, into male and female. Labor is often divided in such a way that many of one sex and few of the other are to be found, as in the assignment of women to the care of infants and young children, and of men to warfare. Women's history assumes that these differences are unnatural, not ordained by God or anatomy but instead created by culture and history.

Questioning the naturalness of gender has clear feminist overtones, reflecting the movement's campaign for equality of relations between men and women. Indeed, there is a necessary relationship between feminism and women's history, at least to the extent that feminism assumes that there are questions to be asked. The feminist influence surfaces as well in finding value in what has often been underestimated and overlooked, insisting, for example, that quilting was a major female art form in rural America or that the immigrant mother made an important economic contribution to her family when she took in boarders. But, while the questions in women's history have emerged out of the contemporary issues in the women's movement and from the condition of the sexes today, the tools for studying history remain those of research, evidence, argument, and narration.

For example, the women's movement in this century and the previous one has always tried to measure the progress of women as a group, and some, despairing of ever finding emancipation in the modern world, have sought to find, in the past, evidence of a lost matriarchy. At first, it appeared that it had been found in the colonial period of American history. In the 1920s and 1930s in the United States, women historians such as Elizabeth Dexter, Mary Benson, and Julia Spruill mined a variety of sources, from wills to travelers' accounts, to show the importance of women and the households they presided over in the economic life of the colonies.[8] These historians argued that marriage was, of necessity, a partnership of equals based on mutual recognition of needs. They pointed to the presence of "she-merchants" in a variety of business pursuits, and they insisted that the colonists were not obsessed with gender distinctions. Dexter and her contemporaries believed that women's essential economic contribution to the colonial household and subsistence farm conferred on them status higher than was true in England or in the next century in America. With industrialization, the range of women's economic activities contracted, and women's status declined to that of mere appendages of their husbands. Obviously, these generalizations did not apply to slave women, since the demands of servitude probably actually increased in the nineteenth century, as the institution of slavery became more widespread. However, recent studies have also undermined the interpretation of Dexter and her contemporaries in regard to colonial white women. New research indicates that, in all the colonies, male and female tasks were sharply defined. Very few married women escaped from the constraints imposed by English common law. The belief that women were daughters of Eve who brought sin into the world kept women in their place, or at least increased suspicion toward those who stepped outside of it. (There is some truth in Mary Daly's observation that "when God is male, man becomes a God."[9]) The few documents written by colonial women suggest that they did not regard themselves as worthy and that they were ashamed of their educational and theological inferiority. The only group whose status dramatically declined in the colonial period were Iroquois matrons, those older women of the tribe who lost economic and political power after plow agriculture and the matrifocal long house were abandoned in favor of the single-family farm.

The failure to locate a Golden Age in the colonial past was an important and positive development for the maturity of the field. It showed the importance of considering social diversity in women's history. The whole effort to compress female experience into a single measure of progress or regress was discredited. The interpretation of any period, it was demonstrated, can be only partial without an attempt to measure woman's consciousness, the regard women hold for themselves and their group. Finally, the importance of religion and law in defining woman's place reminded scholars that ideology fixes clear limits on behavior and that transgressors of these limits are severely punished.

Whereas the colonial period can be seen as a time when gender went relatively unnoticed, the nineteenth century appears as a time of heightened rhetoric about gender and attention to the role of the self-made man and the domestically inclined woman. An ideology of separate spheres, which assigned women to the private sphere and men to the public sphere, was enunciated by middle-class women's magazines in the Northeast and by important ideologues of woman's place, such as Catherine Beecher. It arose from and fed into other social changes, such as the removal of productive work from the middle-class home, the "feminization" of the Protestant religion, the growth of female literacy, and increasing attention to the proper care of the child. The ideology of separate spheres differed markedly from previous definitions of womanhood in emphasizing the sexual purity of women as compared to men, female moral superiority, and control over family life. The tone of early research into the effect of this ideology was to present woman as a victim of a conspiracy to entrap her in the home. Closer examination of the writings of nineteenth-century women has shown, however, that women were the major creators of this ideology and that they often used it as a means of gaining autonomy in the home and greater recognition of their worth.

Through the efforts of women reformers, the female domestic sphere was enlarged, first, to include the schoolhouse and, later, other institutions. Women argued that they were uniquely suited to teaching because they were the natural educators of children in the home. Less high-mindedly, women teachers were also willing to accept lower pay than males for these jobs. As a result, teaching became a female-dominated profession by the end of the century. The female public world also grew through the establishment of women's colleges and women's clubs and in the developments of two other female careers in the twentieth century, librarianship and social work.

The ideology of separate spheres had less positive consequences for lower-class women, for it served to accentuate the division of women into the pure and the fallen, the passionless and the passionate. Prostitutes, working women, and female slaves played the Eves to the Victorian lady's Mary. But if the gap between women widened in the Victorian period, the middle-class woman often made efforts to bridge it through reform efforts based on the idea of the common female sensibility that all women shared. Antebellum female moral reform societies hoped to rescue prostitutes, and female abolitionists proclaimed their sisterhood with the woman slave. The sentimental ideal in Victorian literature may have ruined American literary appetites, but the appeal of Harriet Beecher Stowe's *Uncle Tom's Cabin* did more to personalize the evil of slavery than did all the tracts of abolitionist literature combined.

It is more than a mere coincidence that the women's rights movement appeared only about a decade after this unusual insistence on the domestic role of women. Although the movement's emphasis on woman as an individual can be viewed as a rejection of the ideology of separate spheres, the ideology provided a basis for female solidarity, a necessary precondition for the emergence of the movement. Moreover suffragists proved most successful when they shifted from their early emphasis on women's rights as individuals to participate as voters, to claims that the job of the housewife extended to civic reform, since the needs of the family (from clean drinking water to regular garbage collection) were enmeshed with the provision of public services.

A version of the ideology of separate spheres re-emerged in the 1950s and, with less vitality, in the 1970s. With the exception of these two decades, there has been no single ideology of womanhood in this century as clearly articulated as that of the separate spheres. The closest thing to a modern belief system has been the rediscovery of female sexuality, which has been exploited with great success by the movie, cosmetic, fashion, and advertising industries. While the demise of the idea of the separate spheres may have freed women from the stereotype of the home body, it also undercut the basis of female solidarity deriving from woman's identification with the home and her moral superiority. Cast adrift without a point of reference, women defined their identities in every manner except as women.

The major questions in twentieth-century women's history concern the Phoenix-like changes in the women's rights movement. After women were granted the vote, why did the women's movement appear to lose momentum and virtually disappear until the 1960s? Why did the movement re-emerge in the 1960s? Finally, why did the Equal Rights Amendment, first proposed for consideration in 1923, finally fail to be ratified in 1982? There is no simple or single answer to any of these questions, although even a tentative response to any of them must begin by probing the variety of definitions of feminism and how these changed. A more complete answer must consider changes internal to the women's movement and those social forces affecting the movement. Some have examined the ideas, strategies, and leadership of the women's movement and the opposition to feminism. Others have inquired into the character of a period that made for hostility or sympathy for feminism. Social trends in the family, reproduction, female labor force participation, and women's education have been examined to explore their impact on the growth or the decline of the women's movement.

The closer one comes to the present, the more apparent is the need for scholarly study and interpretation of these and other recent changes. The best work in women's history has concerned the history of women in the eighteenth and nineteenth centuries. The history of gender throughout the twentieth century is a project high on the agenda of women's history. Much still needs to be done. The questions of concern in women's history have derived largely from the contemporary women's movement, and that trend will continue; but one might wonder if the field itself will decline because of the recent setbacks for the women's movement. Thus far, there is no cause for concern. Indeed, as the contemporary women's movement has begun to falter, women historians have become more interested in the reasons for the rise and the subsequent decline in feminism and in the ideas and base of support for the opposition to feminism. Moreover, the fundamental changes that gave rise to the women's movement—the growth of women's labor force participation, the increase in the college education of American women, and changes in the American family—continue and still require interpretation.

One indication of the health of the field is the effort to organize materials on women's history. The desire to know more about the lives of women has pressed archivists to catalogue their collections with reference to women and their families. Women's organizations and their leaders have donated their papers to such major women's history archives as the Sophia Smith Collection at Smith College and the Schlesinger Library of Radcliffe College. Oral histories representing a range of female experience—black women community leaders, women active in the suffrage and birth control movements, women pioneers in the West—have proliferated. The task of finding archival records has been made vastly easier through the publication of *Women's History Sources: A Guide to Archives and Manuscript Collections in the United States,* edited by Andrea Hinding, Ames Sheldon Bower, and Clarke Chambers.[10] The guide is a hefty double-volume listing of archival materials on women available in every state.

Also significant have been the efforts of dozens of scholars to disseminate to a wider audience the research of the last decade. Several anthologies reprint some of the major articles in women's history that have appeared in scholarly journals. There are also several textbooks in U.S.

women's history. Many collections of documents on specialized and more general topics have appeared. The American Historical Association offers for sale three pamphlets of special interest. Gerda Lerner's *Teaching Women's History* is an introductory guide to the teaching of the subject that presents a cogent justification of the field, a summary of the major findings of new research, and an extensive bibliography of specialized topics.[11] A report entitled *Recent United States Scholarship on the History of Women*, by Barbara Sicherman, E. William Monter, Joan Wallach Scott, and Kathryn Kish Sklar, surveys recent scholarly literature concerning the history of women, especially in the United States and Western Europe.[12] The AHA also distributes Anne Chapman's *Approaches to Women's History*, a highly innovative high school curriculum in U.S. women's history, conveniently collected in a loose-leaf binder.[13] These three pamphlets contain references to hundreds of books, films, and materials in the field. The "Women in Community Newsletter," published by the Schlesinger Library of Radcliffe College, compiles information about the programs of local community groups that present women's studies research, lectures, and films to public audiences.[14]

Women's history has proven to be one of the most promising and challenging new fields in history. Textbooks and lectures are now integrating this scholarship into American history, and the field of women's history continues to explore new topics of inquiry and to search for new syntheses of change. The achievements in this field in less than a decade have been remarkable. Most of all, women's history has accomplished its most important task: it has redefined the nature of history.

Notes

1. Simone De Beauvoir, *The Second Sex* (New York: Knopf, 1953).

2. Edward T. James, Janet W. James, and Paul S. Boyer, editors, *Notable American Women, 1607–1950: A Biographical Dictionary* (Cambridge: Belknap Press of Harvard University Press, 1971).

3. Barbara Sicherman and Carol Hurd Green, editors, with Ilene Kantrov and Harriette Walker, *Notable American Women, The Modern Period: A Biographical Dictionary* (Cambridge: Belknap Press of Harvard University Press, 1980).

4. Kathryn Kish Sklar, *Catherine Beecher: A Study in American Domesticity* (New Haven: Yale University Press, 1973).

5. Jean Strouse, *Alice James, A Biography* (Boston: Houghton Mifflin, 1980).

6. For Bernard's views, see Jessie Bernard, *The Female World* (New York: Free Press, 1981).

7. Carroll Smith-Rosenberg, "The Female World of Love and Ritual: Relations between Women in Nineteenth-Century America," *Signs: Journal of Women in Culture and Society* I (1975): 1–29.

8. Elizabeth A. Dexter, *Colonial Women of Affairs: A Study of Women in Business and the Professions in America before 1776* (Boston: Houghton Mifflin Company, 1924); Mary Sumner Benson, *Women in Eighteenth-Century America: A Study of Opinion and Social Usage* (New York: Columbia University Press, 1935); and Julia C. Spruill, *Women's Life and Work in the Southern Colonies* (Chapel Hill: University of North Carolina Press, 1938).

9. Mary Daly, *Beyond God the Father: Toward a Philosophy of Women's Liberation* (Boston: Beacon Press, 1973).

10. Andrea Hinding and Ames Sheldon Bower, editors, Clark A. Chambers, consulting editor, *Women's History Sources: A Guide to Archives and Manuscript Collections in the United States* (New York: Bowker, 1979).

11. Gerda Lerner, *Teaching Women's History* (Washington: D.C.: American Historical Association, 1981).

12. Barbara Sicherman, E. William Monter, Joan Wallach Scott, and Kathryn Kish Sklar, *Recent United States Scholarship on the History of Women* (Washington, D.C.: American Historical Association, 1980).

13. Anne Chapman, *Approaches to Women's History* (Washington, D.C.: American Historical Association, 1979).

14. The address of the Schlesinger Library is 3 James Street, Cambridge, Massachusetts 02138.

Suggestions for Additional Reading

Chafe, William H. *The American Woman: Her Changing Social, Economic, and Political Roles, 1920–1970*. New York: Oxford University Press, 1972.

> A survey of twentieth-century U.S. women's history, emphasizing the dramatic changes caused by World War II.

Cott, Nancy F. *The Bonds of Womanhood: "Woman's Sphere" in New England, 1780–1835*. New Haven: Yale University Press, 1977.

> Traces the origins of women's gender group consciousness.

Cott, Nancy F., and Elizabeth H. Pleck, editors. *A Heritage of Her Own: Toward a New Social History of American Women*. New York: Simon and Schuster, 1979.

> A collection of the "classic" articles in the new women's history, emphasizing social and familial experience.

Degler, Carl N. *At Odds: Women and the Family in America from the Revolution to the Present*. New York: Oxford University Press, 1980.

> A bold synthesis of women's history and family history, emphasizing the tensions between the growth of women's identity as individuals and their claims to their husbands and children.

Dublin, Thomas. *Women at Work: The Transformation of Work and Community in Lowell, Massachusetts, 1826–1869*. New York: Columbia University Press, 1979.

How technological change and the growth of the textile industry affected the Lowell mill girls.

DuBois, Ellen Carol. *Feminism and Suffrage: The Emergence of an Independent Women's Movement in America, 1848–1869*. Ithaca: Cornell University Press, 1978.

The growth of the suffrage movement, beginning with its origins in abolitionism.

Flexner, Eleanor. *Century of Struggle: The Woman's Rights Movement in the United States*. Cambridge: Harvard University Press, 1959.

A general survey of the growth of the women's rights movement in labor unions, education, and politics.

James, Edward T., and Janet W. James, editors. *Notable American Women, 1607–1950: A Biographical Dictionary*. 3 vols. Cambridge: Harvard University Press, 1971.

Brief biographical sketches of U.S. women of achievement in diverse fields. An indispensable resource guide to acquire.

Lerner, Gerda, editor. *Black Women in White America: A Documentary History*. New York: Pantheon, 1972.

Short documents emphasizing the social experience and struggle for equality of black women.

Lerner, Gerda, editor.*The Female Experience: An American Documentary*. Indianapolis: Bobbs-Merrill, 1977.

Short, extremely interesting documents that emphasize women's experiences, such as housework, childbirth, family events, etc.

Norton, Mary Beth. *Liberty's Daughters: The Revolutionary Experience of American Women, 1750–1800*. Boston: Little, Brown and Co., 1980.

Describes the unchanging parts of women's experience and also the changes created by the American Revolution.

Pleck, Elizabeth H., and Joseph H. Pleck, editors. *The American Man*. Englewood Cliffs, N.J.: Prentice-Hall, 1980.

Articles and an introduction analyzing the social norms and social experience of American men throughout U.S. history.

Rossi, Alice, editor. *The Feminist Papers: From Adams to deBeauvoir*. New York: Columbia University Press, 1973.

Documents concerning the development of feminist thought.

Ryan, Mary P. *Womanhood in America, from Colonial Times to the Present*. New York: New Viewpoints, 1979.

A social and cultural analysis of stereotypes about feminity.

Sicherman, Barbara, and Carol Hurd Green. *Notable American Women: The Modern Period*. Cambridge: Harvard University Press, 1980.

> Brief biographical sketches of U.S. women of achievement in diverse fields.

Sklar, Kathryn Kish. *Catharine Beecher: A Study in American Domesticity*. New Haven: Yale University Press, 1973.

> The development of the "cult of domesticity," as seen through the life of its leading ideologue.

Chicago's Randolph Street bustled with activity in 1896, when this photograph was taken from the Wabash Elevated Station.

4

The New Urban History: Defining the Field

Kathleen Neils Conzen

THE CONTINUOUS URBANIZATION of its people and the steady growth of its cities in numbers and size has been a constant of American life for much of the country's national history. For a century and a half after 1820, each successive census documented the ever more rapid transformation of a rural people into an urban nation. The first census in 1790 found only about 5 percent of the population in cities and only five cities with populations over 10,000. By the time of the Civil War, almost a fifth of the population was urban; by the turn of the century, almost two-fifths; by 1920, just over half; and by 1970, just under three-quarters. At the time of the Civil War, 93 cities had populations over 10,000; the number rose to 353 within forty years and then increased six and a half times, to 2,301, by 1970. Only two cities had populations of a half million in 1860, but by 1970 the nation had 24 more of that size, each in turn dominating immense urbanized areas inhabited by millions of other urban dwellers.[1]

Behind such statistics lie massive changes in the demographic behavior, life-style choices, and migratory patterns of the American people. The discipline of dense urban living imposed its own special constraints on the social order, affecting the ways in which people earned a living, the rhythm of their daily lives, the nature of their relationships with family members and strangers alike, the ways they governed themselves, the ways they spent their leisure time, the standards of living they enjoyed, the ways they viewed their world. Life cheek-by-jowl with hundreds of thousands of fellow city-dwellers could not help differing in far-reaching ways from the solitary existence of the farmer or the intimate life of the small town.

Thus, when the "new" historians of the 1960s began using innovative methods and theories to uncover the lives of average, "inarticulate" Americans, it was inevitable that they would focus considerable attention on the urban context within which ever greater numbers of ordinary Americans lived. Indeed, the "new urban history" became one of the earliest, most innovative, and most brashly confident of the new histories to emerge from the historiographical ferment of that period. Critics argue, however, that it has also become one of the most sterile fields, infuriatingly elusive in its defining boundaries, methodologically suspect, and conceptually narrow. To its detractors, the "new urban history" has been a blind alley contributing little to our understanding of urban life and serving only to confuse our interpretation of the broader social transformation of which urbanization was a part. The only disagreement has been whether to read the new scholarship out of the field altogether or force on it a stricter urban focus and methodology.[2] If we define this new historiography narrowly and accept a limited interpretation of its findings, the criticism has validity; but if we take a broader view and ask how these new approaches have altered—or should alter—our understanding of the history of American urban life and what kinds of interpretations are converging from the various strands of urban history, whether old, "new," or even "post-new," then it is possible to draw a very different, and perhaps more useful, balance sheet. That is the task of this essay.

For decades, historians have debated about what should and should not be "counted" as urban history. Is urban history somehow the summed history of individual cities? Or is it perhaps the history of the effects of cities or things urban on national history? Or does it somehow involve the history of everything that takes place in the urban setting? Is it the analysis of city-forming decisions? Or should the object of study be some kind of broader social process that results in cities and the interdependencies among and within them? Any and all of these positions have marched under the banner of urban history over the last half century. The debate regarding their respective rights to do so may seem an irrelevant one to the nonspecialist who wanders unsuspecting onto the field of battle, for all of the perspectives have helped to illuminate our understanding of American urban life in one way or another.[3] But we cannot pull this disparate work together and learn how and why our cities became what they are and what the consequences of their evolution have been for urban dwellers and for the nation as a whole, unless we first identify an interpretive perspective that will permit us to distinguish the generic from the particular, isolate causes, and assess consequences.

One way to approach such a perspective is to consider the reasons for city growth in the first instance. A city can be regarded as a relatively large, dense, permanent concentration of heterogeneous persons engaged in nonagricultural pursuits.[4] Note that such a definition involves demographic, physical, functional, and spatial connotations. In actual practice, we also usually require that a city possess a distinctive government of its own; and then, for statistical purposes, we define cities as all such governmental units above a given population-size threshold. But although political status and boundaries are crucial in dictating the actual settlements regarded as urban, far more important conceptually are the functions that cities fulfill, functions that necessitate the defining characteristics of size, density, permanence, heterogeneity, and relative political autonomy. Cities have as their purpose the control and co-ordination of widely dispersed activities across space. For several millennia, mankind has found that clustering in cities encourages more efficient co-ordination and distribution of goods and services and has permitted historically higher degrees of specialization and complementarity than would otherwise have been possible. A city, therefore, is fundamentally *a control point*. Cities grow and multiply when a society reaches a level that both permits and demands increased co-ordination, and life within cities consequently changes as the possible levels of complementarity, specialization, and heterogeneity intensify.

Urbanization, then, is the increase in the proportion of a given population that lives in cities, whether through an increase in the *number* of cities, an increase in their *size*, or both. To the extent that urbanization creates a number of different cities interdependent upon one another and performing different mixes of urban functions for the society of which they are a part, those cities comprise an urban system. Urban functions can be found in settlements of all sizes, often in a hierarchical arrangement whereby cities of successively larger size provide a widening array of services for ever-broadening hinterlands. Americans often call the smallest settlements *towns*, but such settlements are still urban, in a functional sense.

Thus, cities in a society are the common products of a general social process and are systematically linked to one another, so that change in one affects all. They share a common history, which must be taken into account if their own individual histories are to be interpreted or if the consequences of that process for numerous areas of life are to be understood. That translates into a three-fold agenda for urban history.

First, consideration of the shared experience—the process of urbanization itself. Why does a society urbanize? What kinds of population movements are involved? What kind of city system results? What roles do the various cities play in that system?

Second, examination of the ways individual cities respond to this process and how they compare with one another. Why and how does a city grow? How does its physical appearance change? What social structures and institutions do its residents create? What decisions do they take affecting its communal life?

Third, study of more general social, political, and other processes and events that, where they take place in urban settings, are affected in presumably predictable ways by their urban character—social mobility, perhaps, or class conflict, or an election struggle, or caring for the poor. As Louis Wirth argued, in his classic 1938 essay "Urbanism as a Way of Life," the very size, density, and heterogeneous traits that define cities create significant and identifiable constraints and opportunities for human action within their bounds.[5] By extension, this third focus can also become an explicit analysis of the impact of things urban upon national developments, upon national history.

These three foci are conceptually distinct, but interrelated. To use social science jargon, the first involves the process of urbanization as the dependent variable, the thing to be explained. In the second, urbanization becomes an independent variable invoked to help clarify the new dependent variable, the process of forming and transforming a particular city, and the city's transformation becomes a measure of the consequences of urbanization. In the third, both urbanization and a particular city in effect function as variables affecting the way the facets of an urban way of life emerge.[6]

Not all urban history is or has to be written with such a theoretical perspective consciously in mind. If the systemic relationships among the three foci are ignored, however, there are the dangers of causal misinterpretation and irrelevance to any collective body of knowledge about urban life. At least through the 1960s, American urban historians courted these dangers far too frequently, pushing aside calls for greater theoretical coherence through focus on urbanization and its consequences and continuing to rely on the several pragmatic approaches that had come to define the field by then.

Urban history began to crystallize as a field of scholarship only in the 1930s, when the nineteenth-century "boosting" tradition of city history yielded before the first professional city histories, and when historians, reflecting New Deal priorities and perceptions, turned their attention to assessing the significance of the city as opposed to the frontier in American history. Influenced by the old Progressive vision of urban life in constant tension between the forces of corruption and those of reform, historians examined urban governments and other urban institutions, and as the nation entered a new period of consciousness of urban problems after mid-century, the utility value of such urban history mounted. College courses began to proliferate; urban historians took on a kind of collective identity; and, by the late 1960s, the published literature in the field was expanding at a rapid rate. With historians turning to the past for the sources of present ills, virtually every aspect of urban life found its historian, and studies of subjects like public health, transportation, planning, schools, churches, and ethnic and racial communities joined the older studies of city growth, promotion and rivalry, urban culture, and urban influence in the widening canon of urban history.[7]

Along the way, urban theory got short shrift. These were, by and large, city-building studies or studies of phenomena for which the urban setting served more as "site" than as explanation, in the Wirthian sense. Their chronology and interpretive framework remained under the influence of booster and Progressive origins. From the former came the anthropomorphic metaphor of individual city growth explained in terms of stages of infancy, adolescence, maturity, and the like, each stage with its associated problems to be resolved. From the latter came a basically political principal of periodization that posited the turn of the century as the critical watershed separating two major phases of urban history more generally. The implicit framework for analyzing urban phenomena or events often reflected the influence of the early twentieth-century Chicago school of urban sociology, with its emphasis on the intimate links between urban growth, the spatial structure of the city, the mental outlooks of urban dwellers, and the city's moral order and political culture, and its recognition that urbanization generated both processes of social breakdown and personal disorganization and countervailing ordering processes that created new, less personal forms of social and spatial order.[8] But these assumptions were seldom directly addressed. The focus remained largely entrepreneurial or institutional, the form narrative, and the sources, by and large, those of American historians more generally—organizational and governmental records, newspapers, personal papers, and the like.

What such an urban history had yet to come to grips with, despite its richness and variety, were the forces that set this urban phenomenon in motion and the social consequences for urban residents themselves.

These would constitute the agenda of the "new" urban history as it emerged during the late sixties and flowered in the seventies. Stephan Thernstrom and Richard Sennett coined the label to characterize the kinds of work they brought together in a volume of essays on *Nineteenth-Century Cities*, published in 1969. This work, they argued, shared a common interest in exploring the history of ordinary, anonymous people, using quantitative analysis and sociological theory to wrest meaning from the kinds of systematic public records that were the only places that such people left historical footprints. The definition of this new historiography is both specific and curiously limited. Despite the label, there is no mention of either urban settings or urban causation, and Thernstrom himself was shortly to repudiate the label as an inadequate descriptor of work better regarded as social history. Much of the scholarship he had in mind was indeed urban only in the most accidental sense: cities were the most convenient settings in which to observe the social consequences of industrialization, which were the real objects of concern. Nevertheless, the label and even the definition captured something important that was changing our interpretation of American urban history, of which this work, for all its incidental urbanism, was a part: a fundamental reorientation toward social processes and patterns, a new reliance upon systematic sources quantitatively analyzed, and, ultimately, an enhanced willingness to deal with the implications of the broader urbanization framework.[9]

Of all the scholarship in the new urban history, case studies of the populations of individual cities have generated the most excitement and the most criticism. Much of the work has taken its cue from Thernstrom's own path-breaking 1964 study, *Poverty and Progress*, in which he used the methodology of quantitative manuscript census analysis, developed earlier by rural social historians, to explore the reality of social mobility in a small industrial New England city in the nineteenth century. Was it sufficient, he wondered, to explain the relative quiescence of the American working class? Indeed it was, he argued, though the increments were very small and the geographic mobility far more spectacular than the social. In so arguing, he helped set off a search for mobility rates that sent scholars as far afield as Roseburg, Oregon, and Atlanta, Georgia; Omaha, Nebraska, and Poughkeepsie, New York. The same methods could be used to answer other old questions: How successfully were immigrants integrated into American society? Did racial ghettos originate from white prejudice, or from the rural origins of their inhabitants? Did families change in structure and function in the course of industrialization? How destructive was the factory of artisan culture? At last, it seemed, such old historical chestnuts could be cracked open, once and for all, with the lever of solid numbers. No longer would the historian have to rely upon the recollections of an elite memoirist or the jottings of an egoistic diarist or the polemic of a choleric editor. He or she could now trace with exactitude the ways in which individual lives changed, over time.[10]

Tedious hand-counting of the data hampered pioneer research efforts, but the increasing availability of computer time and software programs has made the case study approach more attractive to scholars. Its methodological core is the analysis of sources containing systematic information for lists of urban dwellers. Above all, this means the decennial censuses of the federal government, which, beginning in 1850, collected information on birthplace, age, occupation, residential situation, and the like, for all inhabitants. Available for the years between 1850 and 1880 and for 1900 and 1910 (the 1890 census was almost entirely destroyed by fire, and later censuses are closed to the public), these federal censuses can sometimes be supplemented by state censuses for periods well into the twentieth century. A second basic systematic source is the city directory. By the 1840s, publishers in many cities compiled annual registers, which listed inhabitants alphabetically, with their occupations, frequently their places of employment, and, importantly, the home addresses that are missing from the early censuses. Tax rolls, credit-rating reports, court records, vital records, and organizational membership rosters are examples of other kinds of systematic sources that have proved amenable to similar treatment.[11]

A wide array of information on a given individual can be collected from one or several of these sources and, when converted to machine-readable form, can be aggregated to permit collective statements about the characteristics of particular groups like "the Irish" or "adolescents" or "unskilled laborers" or, indeed, of "unskilled Irish adolescents." Thus, it is possible to lay out and analyze the social structure of a community at a particular point in time. It is also possible to trace a given individual and his offspring through the sources from one time period to the next, in order to analyze social and geographical mobility patterns. The difficulty of tracing females, because of name changes at marriage, has limited most studies to males only. Because numbers quickly become very large as cities grow, the "new" urban historians have cultivated an interest in sampling methods. It is for that reason also that they have tended to confine their studies to single communities. Direct comparison or tracing individuals from one community to another has seemed too laborious a task to merit the effort.

Methodological concerns have been so self-conscious that a reader of journals publishing the "new urban history" might be excused for thinking, at times, that means have overwhelmed ends.[12] At the same time, however, mounting criticism has made it clear that all methodological problems have not been resolved. It is difficult, for example, to estimate what proportion of all urban dwellers found their way into any given source, or how typical were those who did. Even where individuals are present, we cannot always assess the accuracy of any given piece of information. Problems present in one source increase enormously when we try to link sources and assert that the John Doe found in one census is the same John Doe listed in the city directory for that year or in the census ten years later. Tracing those who cannot be linked, and thus presumably died or moved away, is even more difficult. Yet, they usually constituted the majority, and thus the utility of any generalization that cannot take their experience into account becomes questionable.

Even if we assume completeness and reliability of sources and linkages, analytical problems remain. Students of social mobility have to determine what kind of job move constituted significant social mobility in the nineteenth century, but constructing appropriate categories into which to aggregate information on individuals preliminary to such measurement has proved troubling. Should occupations be ranked by the wealth of their practitioners, by the income they produced, by a measure of status somehow derived, or simply by relationship to the means of production? Would a two-class grouping best conform to contemporary perceptions of significant differences, or should it be five classes, or eight? A similar problem has arisen in measuring geographic mobility: what size areal unit captures a significant move? The whole approach necessarily rests on the assumption that the historian can identify the salient social categories in the first instance, and then that his data actually provide appropriate measures for those categories.

Preoccupied with such analytic problems, the "new" urban historians have seldom attempted to achieve comparable statistical sophistication, and rely largely on comparatively straightforward cross-tabulations of data to yield assumptions about relationships. That makes their work relatively accessible to nonspecialists, who nevertheless can easily be put off by the analytical rather than narrative presentation format of much of this work, as well as by the density of inscrutable-looking tables. A more troublesome consequence of such inattention to statistical method has been the failure to employ potentially more powerful explanatory models. Nor has the problem of generalization inherent in the case-study approach been resolved. At best, historians have been able to judge the representativeness of the findings of a particular case study only by comparing such findings with studies of other cities often conducted with quite dissimilar methods and measures. Indeed, the difficulty of adequately exploiting all the sources even for a single city has led to the argument that the best prospects for furthering scholarly knowledge lie in the concentration of major resources on the interdisciplinary, exhaustive study of just one or a few presumably paradigmatic cities. Yet the difficulty remains: how can we know the extent to which findings from a study of one community—often selected only for its proximity to the investigator—bear upon the national issue being explored?[13]

Yet, for all these problems, the findings of such work cannot be ignored. The study of social structure and mobility has documented, first of all, that American cities of all sizes and regions displayed great and increasing disparities of wealth, life-style, and power within their populations, and that such disparities tended to be associated with racial or ethnic origin. In mid-nineteenth-century cities, blacks clearly stood at the bottom of any urban social order, the majority of the Irish did not fare much better, Germans had a strong hold on middling occupations, and the native-born virtually monopolized the upper ranks. Later-arriving immigrant groups similarly tended to move in at the bottom, often with distinctive occupational specializations.[14]

Second, the extreme geographical mobility of these urban populations is evident, though some of the precise mobility rates may be questioned. People changed residences with great frequency, and changed towns with almost equal ease. Sometimes fewer than 40 percent of the householders present in one census year would be there ten years later. By one estimate, more than four times as many families moved into and out of Boston during the 1880s as resided there at the beginning of the decade. A stable core of residents remained, however, made up predominantly of white-collar workers, the native-born, the more mature, and, particularly, property owners. While chances for spectacular social mobility were statistically slight, and most remained within the same general occupational levels, upward mobility definitely outweighed downward mobility for those who persisted, whatever their class. Sons did even better than their fathers, and ethnic differences, while not disappearing, narrowed. More carefully detailed studies have also begun to document the ways in which these patterns were produced by the different levels of opportunity available in various sectors of the economy and branches of industry under the rapidly shifting conditions of industrialization.[15]

Such findings have suggested to some historians the mechanisms by which social order was maintained despite the massive dislocations of industrialization and urbanization. The nineteenth-century city offered sufficient opportunity to some to give them a stake in society. By persisting, they constituted a stable core that supported the institutions and culture of the community in the midst of flux. The unsuccessful, lured by the hope of opportunity ever over the horizon, seldom remained long enough to constitute any kind of organized and enduring challenge. Far from disrupting any sense of community, the economic transformation and its consequent high mobility may have strengthened the commitment of the stable core to cities whose advance also meant the advance of their own fortunes, while at the same time redefining, formalizing, and depersonalizing the channels of community expression. New forms of political participation, voluntary organizations, and religious worship helped integrate newcomers and mediate class relations, while new devices of social control—temperance movements, police, prisons and asylums, schools—dealt with problems created by the rootless and the uncommitted. The very development of class and ethnicity-based residential neighborhoods tended to reduce conflict by creating separate social spheres. In such neighborhoods, however, the more stable workers could also develop a sense of class solidarity, and immigrants could unite to support the kinds of organizations and institutions that would ease the cultural and economic transition of new world life, using traditional family forms, just as middle-class suburbanites developed new ones, to provide order and stability in the face of change.[16]

It is also becoming clear, however, that things did not work out the same way in every city. Towns with booming economies offered greater opportunities and different kinds of problems of social integration than did towns whose economies were stagnant. That was equally true for towns dependent on a heavily capitalized single industry, for example, in comparison with towns performing a wide range of economic functions. The location of a town's major employers could encourage or discourage class or ethnic neighborhoods and thus influence class or ethnic solidarity. A town's particular mix of employment opportunities could support or preclude working-class autonomy. Members of the same immigrant group could do better in one city than in another. One city's elite could be far more unified and powerful than another's.[17]

Too much of the "new urban history" of this type has tended to ignore the influence of the peculiarly urban or of a specific urban setting; yet, the interconnections between the urbanization process and the social proc-

esses and institutional development that occur within urban places remain central. Without explicit attention to the forces stimulating urbanization and shaping a particular city's role within the urban system, we
cannot clarify the evolution of its ecology and society or the decisions of
its community builders. Without an understanding of the constraints and
opportunities created by its structure and its historic culture, we cannot
assess the ways in which it has developed peculiar local variants of national trends. These city studies cannot finesse their lack of urban focus
simply by disclaiming the urban label. The processes studied were urban
in their context and can be understood only by embedding them in urban
history in all of its facets.

To limit our assessment of the achievements and limitations of the
"new urban history" to these case studies of social structure and mobility,
however, is to be over-restrictive. Taking their questions from national
history, these studies have focused attention upon the extent and complexity of social change that accompanied urbanization, and they have,
even if unwittingly, underlined the necessity of examining social change
within the context of the urban system. In so doing, they have made
significant contributions to urban history. Many, of course, have gone
farther. Those case studies concerned with the changing foci of urban
communal life or with the link between social structures and neighborhood formation are clearly and consciously dealing with urban
phenomena, as are those that attempt to show the linkages between social
patterns and local politics.

Other historians have attempted to address even more directly the
relationships between urbanization, particular urban environments, social change, und the institutional life of the city. While their direct concern
may not have been with the social structure itself, their awareness of
social processes, their theoretical orientation, and their willingness to use
quantification, where appropriate, place them squarely within the "new
urban history" thrust. Diverse in its origins, such work can be attributed
to no single motive or impulse. For example, once historians became
aware of the possibilities of quantification, it did not take long to realize
that urban institutions and organizations—city councils, police forces,
poor-relief agencies, schools, law courts—left records that could be
analyzed systematically to say something about policy evolution and
about those who dispensed and received services. Urban institutional
history is thus taking on far greater precision and a larger social dimension than previously. Recent studies of city growth and promotion similarly reflect the influence of the new questions and methods. Moreover,

there are growing areas of intersection between urban history and other of the "new" histories—labor, legal, women's history, to name some examples—contributing to cross-fertilization of approaches and interpretations.[18]

Still others have addressed urbanization theory and urban social processes head-on. Eric Lampard, perhaps the most persistent of those urging the necessity of an urbanization perspective, has also gone the farthest in his own interpretive writing to demonstrate the complex unraveling of the implications of the urbanization process for the urban society and polity and the nation more generally, using the ecological framework of urban sociology, with its emphasis upon the interaction of population trends, environment, technology, and human organization in generating urban change. Similarly, Richard Wade and his students have used the urban theories of the Chicago school of sociology to probe the relationships between city growth, spatial processes, responses to urban problems, and political patterns. Given its strong theoretical orientation, that approach might have been even more hospitable to quantification than it has, in fact, proved to be.[19]

Comparable in its implications is Oscar Handlin's insistence that urban history find its central focus in the reorganization of space within the city, the new modes of maintaining order among its residents, and the new demands it placed upon the human personality as the city's relationship with the world around it changed in response to the rise of the nation-state, capitalism, and new transportation and communication technologies. Handlin, whose 1941 study of *Boston's Immigrants* was perhaps the earliest effort to use manuscript census data to chart urban social patterns, trained at Harvard many of the pioneers of the "new urban history," including not only Thernstrom, but Samuel P. Hays, with his emphasis upon systematic processes of social change and the social analysis of politics, and Sam Bass Warner, Jr. Warner, in a highly influential study, systematically probed building permits and related sources to reconstruct the development of class-segregated suburbs under the impact of new transportation technologies, and then went on to suggest that urban history be analyzed more generally in terms of responses to technological change mediated by often too-unchanging ideology.[20]

In their work and in the students whom they have trained, such scholars have provided urban history with a sense of systematic method and coherent framework, comprehensive enough to provide context for the social structure and mobility studies as well. Some issues, of course, have received more attention than others. Despite several recent efforts to chart social patterns within regional urban systems, historians have remained largely content to let other social scientists work out the details of macro change within urbanization processes and the urban system itself. The processes by which the cities were peopled and the selective attractions of different cities for varying migrant pools remain virtually unexplored. On the other hand, the separation of work from residence and the formation of neighborhoods are being probed in loving detail. Interestingly enough, the influence of new methods and perspectives has been more evident in studies of elite political roles than in studies of the urban mass electorate, despite preoccupation with the mechanics of machine politics and the ready availability from political scientists of appropriate analytical models.[21]

One important consequence of such work has been the re-thinking of periodization within urban history. Is it possible to break up the sweep of American urban history into briefer periods, in order to highlight change and interconnections? Warner's proposed schema was derived from Lewis Mumford's insights regarding the influence of technology upon urban form and from economists' work tracing the shifting orientation of the nation's urban system from trans-Atlantic commerce to interregional trade to specialization for national markets. It posits three stages: the mercantile stage of the colonial period, the commercial-industrializing stage of the mid-nineteenth century, and the mature industrial stage of the twentieth, each with its appropriate urban environment. David Goldfield and Blaine Brownell draw their text periodization even more directly from the spatial form of the city, tracing an evolution from colonial clusters, to the marketplaces of the 1790–1870 period, to the radial centers of 1870–1920, to what they term the post-1920 "vital fringe." Basing his periodization on changing perceptions of scarcity and abundance as they influenced urban governmental functions and political patterns, Zane Miller distinguishes a pre-1825 period of governmental orientation toward the regulation of trade, followed by decades of economic abundance when towns were governed simply as residential communities, then a period dominated by the perception of organic wholeness that lay at the basis of Progressive reforms after 1890, and finally the post-World War II period and the communities of "limited liability" and interest group politics.[22] None of these periodization schemes really copes with the expansion of the system in space as it was being transformed over time, or fully integrates the political with the social, spatial, and economic, but all rest upon a fundamental realization of two basic periods of change at the beginning and the end of the nineteenth century, each reflecting new tasks for cities, new technologies for production, transportation, and communication, and new problems and possibilities posed by new scales of urban living.

Another consequence is the emergence of what might, for want of a better term, be called the "post-new" urban history. The greatest successes of the "new urban history" of whatever stripe have involved the uncovering of patterns of behavior from quantifiable sources. Interpretations of the origins and significance of those patterns have often been less convincing. One problem is that interpretations have often rested upon unexamined assumptions that causes and consequences lie in what can be measured. For example, were the most significant social structures necessarily those formed on the basis of measurable characteristics like occupation or ethnicity, rather than less tractable ones like life-style or education? Another reason interpretations have been unconvincing is that a good part of the variation in patterns has (perhaps consequently) tended to remain statistically "unexplained." Critics early pointed out that the entire logic of mobility research assumed that workers placed high value on mobility; if they did not—and scholars have argued that job security, home ownership, or family values were often the more highly prized—then mobility becomes an irrelevant question.[23]

That has led many to take a closer, often less rigorously quantified, look at the cultures that nurtured these values, gave meaning to social categories, and structured choices. This trend has been particularly evident among historians of nondominant social groups like workers, immigrants, or women. These scholars have traced in the cultural sphere the autonomy and creativity denied the groups in the more public realm. But there is also evidence of growing interest in the cultural values of middle-class urban dwellers, in the meanings they attributed to city living, and in the means by which they sought to order their lives. The material artifacts of the city, particularly its architecture, have proved one way of successfully probing such values. With increasing realization of the extent to which leisure-time and consumption activities, as opposed to the work-place alone, may have come to define significant social patterns, historians are also adding the analysis of popular culture to their tool kit.[24]

On the other hand, we can also see a new willingness to look behind patterns of behavior to the conscious decision-making that structured the urban environment within which behavior took place. The "new urban history" took much of the urban environment as a given factor, assumed the presence of streetcars, sewers, housing, places of employment, and, in re-writing history from the bottom up, often neglected those whose power shaped or constrained the lives of ordinary people. To label recent work probing decisions for mass transit or sewer systems or housing as "post-new" may be to force an unwarranted relationship to the "new urban history," since much of this work simply reflects new refinement of older, policy-oriented concerns for city-building and service provision.[25] Nevertheless, such work, with its heightened awareness of the social inputs and consequences of public policy-making and its meticulous explication of the fiscal, technological, and other constraints on such policy, is fundamental, if the environment within which urban social change took place is to be understood in anything other than a deterministic sense. Simple social-control interpretive models are receding, as historians untangle the complexity of the problems that nineteenth-century urban dwellers had to resolve in order to create a city capable of meeting its basic functional tasks.

How, then, can we draw up a balance sheet of the strengths and limitations of the "new urban history," or more realistically, of American urban history as it has been influenced by these "new," historiographical thrusts? Certainly, much remains to be done. Particularly compelling is the need to come to terms with city-to-city variation. Only when the complex roles of different cities within the evolving urban system are understood, and the relationship of those roles to variations in patterns of behavior within the cities are untangled, will it be possible either to generalize from case studies or to truly capture and explain the unique history of a particular place. In the process, urban historians will also have to pay more attention to the development of local cultures, those historically formed values and norms that help determine goals and set limits on behavior and that can influence not just an ethnic or a class subgroup, but the entrepreneurial enterprise or political behavior of a city's citizens more generally. To interpret such cultures will undoubtedly demand far greater attention to the origins of urban in-migrants and the local cultures they carried with them than has yet been the case. It will also demand expanded attention to urban political behavior beyond current preoccupation with machine and reform phenomena. The necessity for careful exploration of the relative and changing roles of work-place, neighborhood, and leisure-time associations and activities in structuring and giving meaning to the lives of urbanites is evident. So, too, is the equally demanding task of untangling the fiscal and ideological complexities that limited cities as corporate bodies in their attempts to provide for their urban citizens the kind of city services that they desired.[26]

Such a wish list could be expanded indefinitely. Nevertheless, there can be little doubt that the "new" influences on urban history, for all their frequent methodological murkiness, aridity of presentation, and narrowness of focus, have greatly altered and broadened our knowledge of how our cities were fashioned and what life in them has been like. We are now constructing a truly urban history, and in the process, given the centrality of local life to pre-twentieth-century Americans, are also casting a good bit of illumination upon national history. Anyone wishing to interpret the history of life in a particular city, or in cities in general, has available a far wider range of sources, and a far more comprehensive and ultimately also a more personal view of just what that history involved. The daily patterns of living of innumerable individuals, families, and neighborhoods are as central to this "new" urban history as are the decisions of city fathers or the inventions of an Edison or a Ford. The roots of American urban history writing, we noted, lay in the efforts of nineteenth-century urban residents to celebrate and promote the cities they created. Despite its professionalization of method, the "new urban history," paradoxically perhaps, offers even more potential, not only for interpreting local urban history, but also for recapturing the basic historical experience of urban life and understanding, in a very immediate sense, how our cities have come to be what we experience them to be today.

Notes

1. U.S. Department of Commerce, Bureau of the Census, *Historical Statistics of the United States: Colonial Times to 1970* (Washington, D.C.: U.S. Government Printing Office, 1975), pp. 8, 11, 12.

2. Major review essays discussing the "new urban history" include James Henretta, "The Study of Social Mobility: Ideological Assumptions and Conceptual Bias," *Labor History* 18 (1977): 165–178; Bruce M. Stave, "Introduction," in *The Making of Urban History: Historiography Through Oral History*, edited by Bruce M. Stave (Beverly Hills: Sage Publications, 1977), pp. 13–30; John Sharpless and Sam Bass Warner, Jr., "Urban History," *American Behavioral Scientist* 21 (1977): 221–244; Theodore Hershberg, "The New Urban History: Toward an Interdisciplinary History of the City," *Journal of Urban History* 5 (1978): 3–40; Michael H. Frisch, "American Urban History as an Example of Recent Historiography," *History and Theory* 18 (1979): 350–377; and Michael H. Ebner, "Urban History: Retrospect and Prospect," *Journal of American History* 68 (1981): 69–84. Only because they have plowed the ground so well am I able to move this lightly over the field, and the interested reader is encouraged to consult these more detailed explications. This essay also reflects ideas developed in my own "Quantification and the New Urban History," a paper presented at the U.S.-U.S.S.R. Colloquium on Quantitative Methods in History, Tallinn, June 1981.

3. For early examples of this discussion, see William Diamond, "On the Danger of an Urban Interpretation of History," in *Historiography and Urbanization*, edited by Eric F. Goldman (Baltimore: Johns Hopkins University Press, 1941); W. Stull Holt, "Some Consequences of the Urban Movement in American History," *Pacific Historical Review* 22 (1953): 357–371; and particularly Eric E. Lampard, "American Historians and the Study of Urbanization," *American Historical Review* 67 (1961): 49–61, and Roy Lubove, "The Urbanization Process: An Approach to Historical Research," *Journal of the American Institute of Planners* 33 (1967): 33–39.

4. Discussions of the following concepts may be found in Amos Hawley, *Urban Society: An Ecological Approach* (New York: Ronald Pressco, 1971); Charles Tilly, *An Urban World* (Boston: Little, Brown and Co., 1974); Brian J. L. Berry, *The Human Consequences of Urbanization: Divergent Paths in the Urban Experience of the Twentieth Century* (New York: St. Martin's Press, Inc., 1973).

5. Louis Wirth, "Urbanism as a Way of Life," *American Journal of Sociology* 44 (1938): 1–24.

6. This threefold agenda reflects the influence of Lampard, "American Historians," and Hershberg, "New Urban History;" see also Eric E. Lampard, "The Dimensions of Urban History: A Footnote to the 'Urban Crisis'," *Pacific Historical Review* 39 (1970): 261–277.

7. Excellent reviews of these trends include Dwight W. Hoover, "The Diverging Paths of American Urban History," *American Quarterly* 20 (1968): 296–317, and Raymond A. Mohl, "The History of the American City," in *The Reinterpretation of American History and Culture*, edited by William H. Cartwright and Richard L. Watson, Jr. (Washington, D.C.: National Council for the Social Studies, 1973), pp. 165–205.

8. For an introduction to the ideas of the Chicago sociologists, see Robert E. Park, et al., *The City* (Chicago: University of Chicago Press, 1925); for their influence, cf. Richard C. Wade, "An Agenda for Urban History," in *American History: Retrospect and Prospect*, edited by George A. Billias and Gerald N. Grob (New York: Free Press, 1971), pp. 367–398, and Wade, "Urbanization," in *The Comparative Approach to American History*, edited by C. Vann Woodward (New York: Basic Books, 1968), pp. 187–205.

9. Thernstrom and Sennett, editors, *Nineteenth-Century Cities: Essays in the New Urban History* (New Haven: Yale University Press, 1969), pp. vii–viii; Thernstrom, "Reflections on the New Urban History," *Daedalus* 100 (1971): 359–375; Thernstrom, "The New Urban History," in *The Future of History: Essays in the Vanderbilt University Centennial Symposium*, edited by Charles F. Delzell (Nashville: Vanderbilt University Press, 1977), pp. 43–52. Reflecting a broader conception is Leo F. Schnore, "Further Reflections on the 'New' Urban History: A Prefatory Note," in *The New Urban History: Quantitative Explorations by American Historians*, edited by Leo F. Schnore (Princeton: Princeton University Press, 1975), pp. 3–11; see also "Conversation with Samuel P. Hays" in *Making of Urban History*, pp. 315–316.

10. Thernstrom, *Poverty and Progress: Social Mobility in a Nineteenth Century City* (Cambridge: Harvard University Press, 1964). Several of these studies will be noted in following footnotes; since any attempt to list them all would run to several pages, the interested reader should consult a work like *Three Centuries of Social Mobility in America*, edited by Edward Pessen (Lexington, Mass.: D. C. Heath, 1974), or the lists in Stephan Thernstrom, *The Other Bostonians: Poverty and Progress in the American Metropolis, 1880–1970* (Cambridge: Harvard University Press, 1973), or more recently, Robert G. Barrows, "Hurryin' Hoosiers and the American 'Pattern': Geographical Mobility in Indianapolis and Urban North America," *Social Science History* 5 (1981): 197–222.

11. Mark Friedberger and Janice Reiff Webster, "Social Structure and State and Local

History," *Western Historical Quarterly* 9 (1978): 297–314, provides a thorough discussion of these kinds of sources and their use in community history research.

12. A sampling of the most useful of these articles for issues discussed here includes John B. Sharpless and Roy M. Shortridge, "Biased Underenumeration in Census Manuscripts," *Journal of Urban History* 1 (1975): 409–439; Olivier Zunz, William A. Ericson, and Daniel J. Fox, "Sampling for a Study of the Population and Land Use of Detroit in 1880–1885," *Social Science History* 1 (1977): 307–332; Theodore N. Hershberg, Alan N. Burstein, and Robert Dockhorn, "Record Linkage," *Historical Methods Newsletter* 9 (1976): 99–137; Charles Stephenson, "Tracing Those Who Left: Mobility Studies and the Soundex Indexes to the U.S. Census," *Journal of Urban History* 1 (1974): 73–84; Michael B. Katz, "Occupational Classification in History," *Journal of Interdisciplinary History* 3 (1972): 63–88.

13. The final chapter of Thernstrom, *Other Bostonians*, provides an influential attempt to compare the results of various mobility studies. For an argument for the importance of concentrating resources on the interdisciplinary study of a single city, see Theodore Hershberg, editor, *Philadelphia: Work, Space, Family and Group Experience in the Nineteenth Century: Essays Toward an Interdisciplinary History of the City* (New York: Oxford University Press, 1981), pp. 492–495.

14. Cf. Theodore Hershberg, et al., "Occupation and Ethnicity in Five Nineteenth-Century Cities: A Collaborative Inquiry," *Historical Methods Newsletter* 7 (1974): 174–216.

15. Thernstrom, *Other Bostonians*, should be the starting place for anyone interested in the historical study of social mobility. The Boston figure comes from Thernstrom and Peter R. Knights, "Men in Motion: Some Data and Speculations about Urban Population Mobility in Nineteenth-Century America," in *Anonymous Americans: Explorations in Nineteenth-Century Social History*, edited by Tamara K. Hareven (Englewood Cliffs, N.J.: Prentice-Hall, 1971), p. 27. Clyde Griffen and Sally Griffen, *Natives and Newcomers: The Ordering of Opportunity in Mid-Nineteenth-Century Poughkeepsie* (Cambridge: Harvard University Press, 1977), one of the best works of this genre, provides a very detailed discussion of the ways in which various groups were differently affected by the kinds of opportunities available in the various branches of industry.

16. Cf. Michael B. Katz, *The People of Hamilton, Canada West: Family and Class in a Mid-Nineteenth-Century City* (Cambridge: Harvard University Press, 1975); Stuart M. Blumin, *The Urban Threshold: Growth and Change in a Nineteenth-Century American Community* (Chicago: University of Chicago Press, 1976); Don Harrison Doyle, *The Social Order of a Frontier Community: Jacksonville, Illinois, 1825–1870* (Urbana: University of Illinois Press, 1978); Kathleen Neils Conzen, *Immigrant Milwaukee, 1836–1860: Accommodation and Community in a Frontier City* (Cambridge: Harvard University Press, 1976); Virginia Yans-McLaughlin, *Family and Community: Italian Immigrants in Buffalo, 1830–1930* (Ithaca: Cornell University Press, 1977).

17. Cf. Barrows, "Hurryin' Hoosiers;" Michael B. Katz, Michael Doucet, and Mark Stern, "Migration and the Social Order in Erie County, New York: 1855," *Journal of Interdisciplinary History* 8 (1978): 669–701; Michael P. Weber and Anthony E. Boardman, "Economic Growth and Occupational Mobility in Nineteenth-Century Urban America: A Reappraisal," *Journal of Social History* 11 (1977): 52–74; John T. Cumbler, *Working-Class Communities in Industrial America: Work, Leisure, and Struggle in Two Industrial Cities, 1880–1930* (Westport, Conn.: Greenwood Press, 1979); Burton W. Folsom, Jr., *Urban Capitalists: Entrepreneurs and City Growth in Pennsylvania's Lackawanna and Lehigh Valleys, 1800–1920* (Baltimore: Johns Hopkins University Press, 1981).

18. Examples of such work include Jon C. Teaford, *The Municipal Revolution in America: Origins of Modern Urban Government, 1650–1825* (Chicago: University of Chicago Press,

1975); Roger Lane, *Violent Death in the City: Suicide, Accident, and Murder in Nineteenth-Century Philadelphia* (Cambridge: Harvard University Press, 1979); Michael B. Katz, *The Irony of Early School Reform: Educational Innovation in Mid-19th-Century Massachusetts* (Cambridge: Harvard University Press, 1968); Robert Silverman, *Law and Urban Growth: Civil Litigation in the Boston Trial Courts, 1880–1900* (Princeton: Princeton University Press, 1981); for studies of city growth, see, for example, Michael H. Frisch, *Town into City: Springfield, Massachusetts, and the Meaning of Community, 1840–1880* (Cambridge: Harvard University Press, 1972); David R. Goldfield, *Urban Growth in the Age of Sectionalism: Virginia, 1847–1861* (Baton Rouge: Louisiana State University Press, 1977); Gary Lawson Browne, *Baltimore in the Nation, 1789–1861* (Chapel Hill: University of North Carolina Press, 1980).

19. Examples of Lampard's work include "The Urbanizing World," in *The Victorian City: Images and Realities*, edited by H. J. Dyos and Michael Wolff (Boston: Routledge and Kegan Paul, 1973), vol. 1, pp. 3–57, and "The Pursuit of Happiness in the City: Changing Opportunities and Options in America," *Transactions of the Royal Historical Society*, 5th Series, 23 (1973): 175–220; for Wade, see his "Agenda," and "Conversation with Richard C. Wade," in *Making of Urban History*, pp. 159–186.

20. Handlin, "The Modern City as a Field of Historical Study," in *The Historian and the City*, edited by Oscar Handlin and John Burchard (Cambridge: MIT Press, 1963); Handlin, *Boston's Immigrants: A Study in Acculturation* (Cambridge: Harvard University Press, 1941); Warner, *Streetcar Suburbs: The Process of Growth in Boston, 1870–1900* (Cambridge: Harvard University Press, 1962); Warner, "If All the World Were Philadelphia: A Scaffolding for Urban History, 1774–1930," *American Historical Review* 74 (1968): 26–43; Samuel P. Hays, "The Changing Political Structure of the City in Industrial America," *Journal of Urban History* 1 (1974): 6–38. Handlin and Wade were both students at Harvard of Arthur Meier Schlesinger, Sr., whose "The City in American History" [*Mississippi Valley Historical Review* 27 (1940): 43–66] was perhaps the single most important early definition of urban history.

21. Recent attempts to examine social structures within local urban systems include Roberta Balstad Miller's *City and Hinterland: A Case Study of Urban Growth and Regional Development* (Westport, Conn.: Greenwood Press, 1979) and Folsum's *Urban Capitalists*. For a summary of geographers' work on this topic, consult Michael P. Conzen, "The American Urban System in the Nineteenth Century," in *Geography and the Urban Environment: Progress in Research and Applications*, edited by D. T. Herbert and R. J. Johnston (New York: Wiley, 1982), pp. 295–347. Elite studies include Carl V. Harris, *Political Power in Birmingham, 1871–1921* (Knoxville: University of Tennessee Press, 1977), and Eugene J. Watts, *The Social Bases of City Politics: Atlanta, 1864–1903* (Westport, Conn.: Greenwood Press, 1978). For an example of what can be done with electoral analysis, note Martin Shefter, "The Electoral Foundations of the Political Machine: New York City, 1884–1897," in *The History of American Electoral Behavior*, edited by Joel Silbey, et al. (Princeton: Princeton University Press, 1978).

22. Warner, "If All the World"; David R. Goldfield and Blaine A. Brownell, *Urban America: From Downtown to No Town* (Boston: Houghton Mifflin Co., 1979); Zane L. Miller, "Scarcity, Abundance, and American Urban History," *Journal of Urban History* 4 (1978): 131–155.

23. Henretta, "Study of Social Mobility"; Yans-McLaughlin, *Family and Community*; John Bodnar, "Immigration and Modernization: The Case of Slavic Peasants in Industrial America," *Journal of Social History* 10 (1976): 44–71.

24. On interpreting urban architecture, see, for example, Gwendolyn Wright, *Moralism and the Model Home: Domestic Architecture and Cultural Conflict in Chicago, 1873–1913* (Chicago: University of Chicago Press, 1980); on popular culture, Steven A. Riess, *Touching*

Base: Professional Baseball and American Culture in the Progressive Era (Westport, Conn.:
Greenwood Press, 1980), for example, or John F. Kasson, *Amusing the Million: Coney Island
at the Turn of the Century* (New York: Hill and Wang, 1978), or Gunther Barth's synthesizing
City People: The Rise of Modern City Culture in Nineteenth-Century America (New York:
Oxford University Press, 1980).

25. See Charles W. Cheape, *Moving the Masses: Urban Public Transit in New York, Boston,
and Philadelphia, 1880 to 1912* (Cambridge: Harvard University Press, 1980); Martin V. Melosi,
editor, *Pollution and Reform in American Cities, 1870–1930* (Austin: University of Texas Press,
1980); Alan D. Anderson, *The Origin and Resolution of an Urban Crisis: Baltimore, 1890–1930*
(Baltimore: Johns Hopkins University Press, 1977); an earlier work proposing an influential
framework for such analysis is Seymour J. Mandelbaum, *Boss Tweed's New York* (New York:
John Wiley, 1965).

26. Examples of work on city-to-city variation include Richard M. Bernard and Bradley R.
Rice, "Political Environment and the Adoption of Progressive Municipal Reform," *Journal of
Urban History* 1 (1975): 149–174; Sam Bass Warner, Jr., and Sylvia Fleisch, "The Past of
Today's Present: A Social History of America's Metropolises, 1860–1960," *Journal of Urban
History* 3 (1976): 3–117; or J. Rogers Hollingsworth and Ellen Jane Hollingsworth, *Dimensions
in Urban History: Historical and Social Science Perspectives on Middle-Size American Cities*
(Madison: University of Wisconsin Press, 1979). For a persuasive demonstration of the
significance of local political cultures in American cities, see Daniel J. Elazar, *Cities of the
Prairie: The Metropolitan Frontier and American Politics* (New York: Basic Books, 1970).

Suggestions for Additional Reading

Bender, Thomas. *Community and Social Change in America*. New Brunswick: Rutgers University Press, 1978.

> An interpretation of the changing meaning and locus of *community* in the course of American economic transformation.

Blumin, Stuart M. *The Urban Threshold: Growth and Change in a Nineteenth-Century American Community*. Chicago: University of Chicago Press, 1976.

> Concerned for the fate of a sense of community in Kingston, New York, under the impact of urban growth, integrating quantitative measures in readable fashion.

Conzen, Kathleen Neils. *Immigrant Milwaukee, 1836–1860: Accommodation and Community in a Frontier City*. Cambridge, Mass.: Harvard University Press, 1976.

> How immigrants were able to create communities of their own within the framework of opportunity offered on the urban frontier.

Dawley, Alan. *Class and Community: The Industrial Revolution in Lynn*. Cambridge, Mass.: Harvard University Press, 1976.

Traces the changing economic, social, and political fortunes of Lynn shoemakers in the course of industrialization, emphasizing the world view that structured their reactions.

Doyle, Don Harrison. *The Social Order of a Frontier Community: Jacksonville, Illinois, 1825–70*. Urbana: University of Illinois Press, 1978.

Explores the relationships between town founding and growth, social patterns, institutions, and communal order in a small frontier city.

Dykstra, Robert R. *The Cattle Towns*. New York: Knopf, 1968.

Five Kansas cattle towns between 1867 and 1885, and their changing social and political adaptations to the shifting economic base of the cattle trade.

Frisch, Michael H. *Town into City: Springfield, Massachusetts, and the Meaning of Community, 1840–1880*. Cambridge: Harvard University Press, 1972.

Social, cultural, political, and ideological responses to the transformation from New England town to industrial city.

Goldfield, David A., and Blaine A. Brownell. *Urban America: From Downtown to No Town*. Boston: Houghton Mifflin Co., 1979.

Recent interpretive urban history text with emphasis on urbanization as a social process and its consequences for cities and urban dwellers.

Griffen, Clyde, and Sally Griffen. *Natives and Newcomers: The Ordering of Opportunity in Mid-Nineteenth-Century Poughkeepsie*. Cambridge: Harvard University Press, 1977.

Shifts emphasis away from gross measurement of mobility to the factors that influenced different kinds and rates of mobility for different segments of the population and in different economic sectors.

Handlin, Oscar. *Boston's Immigrants: A Study in Acculturation*. Cambridge: Harvard University Press, 1941.

Classic study positing relationship between changing city life and immigrant communities, pioneering in its use of manuscript census data and seductively readable.

Hershberg, Theodore, editor. *Philadelphia: Work, Space, Family and Group Experience in the Nineteenth Century: Essays Toward an Interdisciplinary History of the City*. New York: Oxford University Press, 1981.

Essays reporting the findings and approach of the largest of the multidisciplinary group studies of a single city.

Johnson, Paul E. *A Shopkeeper's Millennium: Society and Revivals in Rochester, New York, 1815 to 1837*. New York: Hill and Wang, 1978.

> Highly readable effort to use quantitative data to chart the changing structure of work and residence and the ways it led to the city's great wave of religious revivalism.

Katz, Michael B. *The People of Hamilton, Canada West: Family and Class in a Mid-Nineteenth-Century City*. Cambridge: Harvard University Press, 1975.

> Sophisticated use of quantitative data to explore changes in family and social structures on the eve of industrialization, drawing a baseline against which to measure the impact of later transformation.

Kusmer, Kenneth L. *A Ghetto Takes Shape: Black Cleveland, 1870–1930*. Urbana: University of Illinois Press, 1976.

> Traces roles of race relations, economic change, and spatial expansion in the formation of a city's black community.

Stave, Bruce M., editor. *The Making of Urban History: Historiography through Oral History*. Beverly Hills: Sage Publications, 1977.

> Interviews with leading "old" and "new" urban historians discussing the context of their work.

Thernstrom, Stephan, and Richard Sennett, editors. *Nineteenth-Century Cities: Essays in the New Urban History*. New Haven: Yale University Press, 1969.

> Essays that, together, constituted the first formal announcement of the "new urban history," emphasizing mobility trends and urban life "from the bottom up."

Thernstrom, Stephan. *The Other Bostonians: Poverty and Progress in the American Metropolis, 1880–1970*. Cambridge: Harvard University Press, 1973.

> Most ambitious, long-term study of geographic and social mobility to date, intergenerational in focus and assessing ethnic and racial differentials, with an important concluding comparative essay.

Thernstrom, Stephan. *Poverty and Progress: Social Mobility in a Nineteenth-Century City*. Cambridge: Harvard University Press, 1964.

> Compellingly presented, classic study of social mobility among unskilled workers in Newburyport, Massachusetts, important in stimulating the mobility concerns of the "new urban history."

Ward, David. *Cities and Immigrants: A Geography of Change in Nineteenth-Century America*. New York: Oxford University Press, 1971.

> Influential brief interpretation of the geographical consequences of the urban-industrial transformation for both the urban system and the spatial structure of the city.

Warner, Sam Bass, Jr. *Streetcar Suburbs: The Process of Growth in Boston, 1870–1900*. Cambridge: Harvard University Press, 1962.

> Classic study of the social and technological factors influencing the developing class segregation of American cities and suburbs.

Andrew Dahl photographed this rural scene in southern Wisconsin between 1873 and 1879.
State Historical Society of Wisconsin

5

Agriculture and Rural Life: The New Rural History

Robert P. Swierenga

I N RECENT YEARS, scholars have sought to apply the concepts, methods, and questions of the new social history to rural life and agriculture. The term that increasingly has come to describe this perspective is the *new rural history*, modeled after the *new urban history*.[1] While urban historians explore the rise and fall of cities, the evolution of their institutions, and the behavior of their inhabitants, rural historians similarly study the demise of rural life and institutions, where the majority of the populace once lived. Similarly, urban historians use quantitative techniques and computer-aided analyses, and so do rural historians. The latter likewise borrow heavily from the social sciences—especially rural sociology, historical geography, demography, agricultural economics, and political science.

The idea of studying rural history in a mode similar to that of urban history appears uncomplicated and hardly path-breaking; yet, to implement it requires a reorientation among historians in their perceptions of rural life and its development. Since the turn of the century, when urban Americans first outnumbered rural dwellers and began to set the cultural tone for society, intellectuals have pictured backwardness, stubborn conservatism—if not reactionism—and a narrow world-view as characteristics of ruralism. H. L. Mencken's expression "hayseed," and Grant Wood's painting of the farm couple in *American Gothic* are the classic images. Cartoonist Al Capp's comic-strip hero Li'l' Abner, the local yokel, and Daisy Mae, his simple, buxom wife, have long reflected the popular perception of rural folk. The stereotyping was mutual, of course. Farmers used the term "slickers" to describe city folk, who, their country cousins said, with a wink, believed milk originated in bottles.

Among academics, similar views prevail. Most professional historians in the twentieth century are urban-oriented. They live and teach in
urban universities and colleges and resonate to urban issues and problems. Stanford scholar Eugen Weber, now a leading rural historian,
frankly admits his past bias: "The history I thought and taught and wrote
about went on chiefly in cities; the countryside and little towns were a
mere appendage of that history, following, echoing, or simply standing by
to watch what was going on, but scarcely relevant on their own account."[2]

Richard Hofstadter, one of the leaders of the consensus school of
American history that gained prominence in the decade after World War
II, denigrated farmers at the expense of urbanites.[3] Liberal reformers, by
tradition, were "urban progressives," whereas rural Americans were
often reactionaries, seeking to restore the lost world of Thomas Jefferson
or, at best, backing into the future.[4] Farmers were wounded yeomen who
espoused anti-Semitism and used conspiracy theories to explain their
suffering in the new international economic order. Rural Americans were
also anti-intellectual book-burners, religious fundamentalists, prudish
Victorians, and teetotaling moralists who foisted their life-style on hap-
less urbanites with the Prohibition Amendment. Hofstadter's totally de-
meaning portrayal of rural Americans is puzzling, given his insightful
statement, oft quoted, that "the United States was born in the country
and moved to the city."[5]

The academic study of the history of rural America is similarly dis-
oriented. Unlike urban history, which, despite its wide diversity, is
viewed as a coherent subject with a rightful place in academia, rural
history remains subsumed under more traditional rubrics—agricultural
and land history, "westward movement" or frontier history, and Southern or Western regional histories. The compilers of the "Recent Articles"
and "Recent Dissertations" listings in the *Journal of American History* and
the *American Historical Review* include a comprehensive "urban" category, but there is no counterpart "rural" section, except for the narrower
topic of "agriculture."

On the one hand, this omission in the schema of categories merely
reflects the fact that rural history has not yet gained prominence as a
subject field among American academics comparable to its status in
Western Europe and Canada;[6] but it may also stem from an implicit assumption on the part of predominantly urban-oriented scholars that rural
history is an anachronism. Rurality as a distinct way of life is declining
rapidly and may well disappear before the year 2000. American scholars
have long conceptualized our national history in the elitist terms of the

"presidential synthesis" or in the story of progress from pioneer log cabins to urban skyscrapers, from dirt paths to vapor trails in the sky. Only coastal cities count. The wide expanse between New York and Los Angeles is merely a "fly-over." To tie one's academic identity to a field of study with such a simplistic image and no future is unthinkable. Even the practitioners themselves prefer terms more in vogue—*social, western, economic, community, local,* and the like—even though such terms have their own presuppositions and givens.

It may be true that rural life will become extinct in the late twentieth century.[7] Technology has eliminated the physical, if not the cultural, boundary line between rural and urban communities, and the rural economy today is totally intertwined with urban industry and commerce. Nevertheless, until at least the late nineteenth century, most Americans lived in rural environs. The story of American history is the tale of the development—and, oftimes, the decline—of rural communities as they have interacted with expanding urban centers. Cities and their "hinterland"[8] have been interdependent: cities have provided services, and rural areas have supplied food products and people, although that trend may be changing, as urbanites desert the cities for small towns and rural areas. At the present time, only one of every thirty-six Americans—2.7 percent of the population—lives on a farm, and there are only six million farmers, nationwide. Nevertheless, nonmetropolitan communities, many of which remain culturally rural, contain one-third of the total United States population and 90 percent of the land area. Thus, rural America has been and continues to be a vital part of the nation's history. Especially is this true for the colonial era and the nineteenth century. In short, social and urban historians cannot explain the national experience without examining rural history as well.

The new social historians increasingly recognize the need to integrate rural and urban history. As Stephan Thernstrom, one of the pioneers, has stated: "I, in fact, prefer that we get them together and just make a new social history."[9] Another urban historian, Kathleen Conzen, author of *Immigrant Milwaukee* (1976), is currently exploring social structural change in a rural Minnesota county in the last century.[10] The late James Malin, the agricultural scholar who, in the 1930s, first developed techniques for studying geographical and social mobility based on the manuscript federal censuses,[11] suggested shortly before his death that the urban historians have been myopic in limiting their studies to the city. "How far is it valid," Malin asked, "to attempt to write integrated rural history or integrated urban history when rural and urban life were not lived in segregated forms? The country town had affinities for its farm patrons as well as for the activities of the metropolitan city." Malin then answered his own sage question by posing a follow-up: "The hazards are great, but what about experimenting with a novel point of view and organizing principle—make the combined rural-urban and mixed conception the central theme of historical study? Familiar facts might then stimulate startling consequences."[12]

Malin was correct to call for an integrated social science approach, in which rural historians explore the nexus between the countryside, market towns, and metropolitan centers. However, the subject of rural history has a rightful place, distinct from urban history. Human behavior in the rural environment has differed over time from that in urban centers; it has had a unique mind-set and value system.[13] As distinct from urban living, rural life-style and activities have involved physical and often social isolation, large family networks with their demands and benefits, family labor relationships, seasonal work patterns, and other features.[14] Historians of rural life must study these distinguishing marks of rurality in order to provide a unified conception of past rural life and social processes. Different forces historically were also at work on the farms and in the cities. While many rural communities failed to cope with the disintegrating forces of modern society and simply disappeared, urban centers grew by leaps and bounds and developed complex differentiated social and economic structures.

The new rural history, like the new urban history, evolved out of the introduction of behavioral methods in the general field of social history in the 1960s. Before describing these, however, we must review antecedents dating back to the turn of the century and the work of Frederick Jackson Turner. Turner's conception of the frontier as a geographical place that developed from virgin land into commercial farms and cities on the prairies has provided the major analytic framework for American historians to the present time. Turner and his students concentrated on the developing agricultural frontier and its equity effects. Did free land ensure political democracy, economic equality, and individual self-reliance, or did avarice and government mismanagement create a society of haves and have nots?

Turner and his successors often disagreed on the meaning of the evidence, in answering these questions. But whatever their conclusions, Turnerians made an innovation in methodology by studying history "from the bottom up," through the case study techniques of the social sciences. Statistical analysis of individual-level data, usually gleaned from manuscript population census and land records, was their hallmark;[15] but their data bases remained severely restricted until the modern advances in data processing in the 1940s and 1950s. Then, for the first time, Turnerians were capable of mastering the extensive files of serial records in county courthouses and the National Archives—population and agricultural census manuscripts, land and tax lists, and civil registers.

Other notable forerunners of the new rural history were Frank Owsley and Merle Curti. Owsley and his research group at Vanderbilt University created massive statewide data files of the Southern "plain folk," the small, non-slave-owning farmers of the pre-Civil War decades, as revealed in census and tax reports. Their detailed studies of the rank and file yeoman farmers—who made up fully 80 percent of the heads of white families—proved, as Turner had concluded in the Midwest, that land ownership was widespread in the South and that "the door of economic opportunity swung open easily" for the plain folk, as it did for the dominant and highly visible planter class. [16] Owsley was an innovator in the application of statistical and social science methods among historians, including nominal record linkage, census-sampling techniques, punch-card processing of data, and electric calculators to compute statistics.

A decade after Owsley's work, Merle Curti and his team of research assistants at the University of Wisconsin embarked on a similar quantitative analysis of the occupational and social structure of a frontier community in Trempealeau County in southwestern Wisconsin. [17] Curti intended "to study microscopically" all gainfully employed persons in a developing rural community in order to test Turner's thesis that the frontier fostered equality of economic opportunity. Like Owsley, Curti chose the manuscript censuses as his primary source and used similar quantitative methods and machine-processing. Curti limited his case study to one county over three decades, but he included more than fifty behavioral variables for its residents. Curti likewise concluded that the thesis of frontier democracy was valid. "Turner's poetical vision of free land and of relatively equal opportunity," Curti concluded, "was for a great many people being realized in Trempealeau County. The story of the making of this community is a story of progress toward democracy." [18] Thus, from the Turnerian tradition and the work of Owsley and Curti came an abiding interest in the process of rural community formation and the socio-economic equality of farmers and rural workers.

Then, in the 1960s, a new type of rural scholar came on the scene, exemplified by Allan Bogue and his students. Bogue was himself a student of Paul W. Gates, the Nestor of American land and agricultural historians, and James C. Malin, a specialist in the adaptation of pioneer settlers in the prairie-grassland environment. Malin's ecological explanation of midwestern rural history in *The Grassland of North America* (1947) and other books provided the first genuine alternative to Turner's geographical determinism. Malin's stress on the social and behavioral aspects of man-land relationships and Gates's emphasis on case studies and on hard evidence of individual actors influenced Bogue greatly.

Bogue's model study, *From Prairie to Cornbelt: Farming on the Illinois and Iowa Prairies in the Nineteenth Century* (1963), is explicitly behavioral. In sharp contrast to the environmental or economic determinism of most agricultural historians, Bogue chose as his main theme the human actors, the farmers, and their creative responses to the challenges of a new environment. "Rather than presenting long general discussions of transportation, agricultural marketing, tenancy, or farmer's movements," Bogue states, in his introduction, "I have tried to emphasize the individual farmer—the man with dirt on his hands and dung on his boots—and the problems and developments that forced him to make decisions about his farm business."[19] The book's chapters carry through this theme: "The People Came," "They Take the Land," "Farms on the Breaking," "How to Farm Sitting Down," "Some are Innovators," "Farmers in the New Settlements," "The Farmer in the 'Old' Community," and so forth. From first to last, Bogue centers his attention on the challenges farmers faced in taking virgin land and, by trial and error, bringing it into full production of corn and hogs.

Bogue's colleague during the writing of the cornbelt book was Samuel P. Hays, who likewise had come to realize the salience of past human behavior in explaining history. The two young scholars influenced and mutually reinforced each other and their graduate students, who usually studied with both. Hays articulated his views in a 1959 paper titled "History as Human Behavior," in which he urged historians to focus on the "human side of the past" rather than on formal institutions and presidential history. "By systematically studying human experience and behavior," Hays asserts, "solid and concrete generalizations [will] emerge regarding past human experience."[20] Whether studying urban or rural communities, Hays's point is that the proper approach is a behavioral one—to learn how people lived, ways in which they related to one another, and how they invested their lives with meaning—all within a broad historical context. Bogue's cornbelt study is clearly cast within this framework, and so is the work of his students.

As a result of the new behavioral approach, there is now more stress on farmers themselves, their family lives and social relations, ethnic and religious backgrounds, community institutions such as churches and clubs, and on comparative cropping and animal husbandry patterns.

Many previously neglected aspects of the rural past are being discovered. One "hidden dimension" in American rural life that Robert Dykstra found, by a careful reading of Kansas cattle-town newspapers, was the perennial conflict *within* local communities between business boosters and cattlemen, on the one side, and local farmers and village laborers on the other.[21] Thus, in addition to rural-urban conflict, there was also cultural conflict within rural communities, even small ones. Farmers in various regions also differed sharply because of economic, social, or geographical conditions. In financial relationships, however, earlier scholars overstressed presumed class conflicts . My books on Iowa frontier land sales and delinquent tax auctions reveal that the intricate credit networks in rural America were far more harmonious than frontier folklore would lead one to believe.[22] Donald Winters reached the same conclusion in his detailed analysis of farm tenants, owner-operators, and landlords in nineteenth-century Iowa.[23] Given certain sets of social and economic conditions, debtors and creditors, renters and landlords, land buyers and land sellers all benefited from their financial dealings and relationships.

The social and demographic history of the countryside is also being illuminated in new and fruitful ways. Robert Taylor studied a large family clan, the Olins, over four generations. He uncovered the family role in the internal migration of this rural group, the Olins, from Vermont to the Midwest in the nineteenth century and the rise of family reunions to preserve the identity of this extended family after their widespread geographical dispersal in the twentieth century.[24] From Taylor's insights, we now understand better the impact of the forces of modernization on a rural family network over the generations. Similarly, Richard Bernard's detailed study of intermarriage in Wisconsin in the period from 1880 to 1920 reveals the ethnic, geographical (urban-rural), and cultural factors in intermarriage and in-marriage patterns. Marital assimilation, Bernard found, was greater in the more rural areas of the state than in the urban center of Milwaukee, largely because the "marriage pool" was smaller in the less-populated and more isolated regions.[25]

American historical geographers have also added to the ethnic and religious dimension of rural history. From the time of settlement to the present, nearly every nationality and church group, in greater or lesser degree, has been represented in the farming population. Rural America, especially the Midwestern frontier, had a remarkable cultural diversity, traces of which still exist today in the countryside.[26] The degree to which these differences in cultural background influenced farming practices has become a major question. Turner and his followers theorized that the frontier experience destroyed the "cultural baggage" of the immigrant pioneers and led to rapid acculturation. The farming practices of immigrant farmers, Turner believed, became indistinguishable from that of their American-born neighbors after a very short period of settlement. Only since the 1960s have scholars systematically tested the long-held theory of rapid assimilation by comparing ethnic cropping patterns, animal husbandry, technological skills, tenure differences, and mobility and persistence rates.

The ethnocultural scholars—as they are called—have discovered many ethnic variations, but have noted also very rapid convergence toward common practices dictated by geographical and environmental conditions in the region studied.[27] One scholar, Robert Ostergren, even went to the unusual effort of tracing a group of Swedish emigrants in Minnesota to their Old Country parish and comparing farming practices before and after migration. The Swedes transplanted their cultural institutions more successfully than they did their farming practices. "When it came to making a living, the immigrants were faced with little choice but to adapt as quickly as possible to the American system. In fact," says Ostergren, "there is little evidence that there ever was much resistance to the dictates of the new environment and the local market economy. The situation was so different from that at home, that one probably did not even seriously contemplate farming in the same manner."[28] However, within a generation, or even sooner, some distinctive traits often reappeared through a process that Terry Jordan calls "cultural rebound."[29] The initial shock of adjustment to a new environment apparently inclined immigrants to ape indigenous American practices; but gradually this initial "artificial" assimilation was reversed, and unique dormant traits reappeared.

The Texas Germans, for example, were an alien group in Texas, confronting an agricultural society that had evolved over two hundred years.[30] Although that uniqueness almost guaranteed the survival of their "European-ness," Jordan found that the German immigrants nevertheless "became Southerners almost from the first." They introduced no new major crops or livestock practices, but rather began cultivating the three Southern staples—corn, cotton, and sweet potatoes. They adopted Southern farmstead architecture and the open-range system, with no barns for wintering stock. They neither dunged their fields nor stall-fed their livestock. If the Germans were imitators from the first, they also clung to Old World cultural traits that made them distinctive for generations among Texas farmers. The Germans were more attracted to the soil and committed to commercial agriculture. They farmed with greater intensity and productivity, were less mobile, and had a higher rate of land-ownership. They diversified more, by actively pursuing market gardening near the major Texas towns, by producing wine and white potatoes (in a sweet potato region), by cultivating small grains, and by using mules instead of horses as draft animals. Many of these surviving characteristics were absent in the earliest years and emerged only later on.

Jordan suggests a four-class typology of the "survival tendencies" of imported agricultural systems by immigrant groups. First of all, there are the old country traits that were never introduced, such as the Texas Germans' failure to dung fields and winter livestock in barns. A second class consists of European traits introduced but not successfully implemented. For Texas Germans, such traits included the use of viticulture, European fruit trees, the farm village plan and communal herding on the West Texan plains, and small-grain production in the East Texas cotton belt. In a third category fall those European traits that survived only the first generation. These included small-scale farm operations, German farmstead structures, and the free-labor system in East Texas. The final class includes long-lived traits. Texas German farmers were distinguishable for generations by their labor-intensive, highly productive, stable, diversified agriculture.

The determining factors in these various outcomes, Jordan believes, were the degree of physical and socioeconomic dissimilarity between the American settlement communities and their European homelands. The mild Texas climate, for example, obviated the need for large barns and winter quartering of livestock. Without barns, manure was lost. The economic milieu likewise encouraged immigrants to adapt farming practices of the region, because those of the native Southerners were proven superior. For that reason, Germans shifted from small farms to the large-scale commercial agriculture common to the region. Moreover, those traits that did survive, either intact or modified, such as intensive farming methods, cheese-making, and cultivating white potatoes, were those that did not interfere with or undermine the economic viability of Texas agriculture. The conclusion is that the more alien the cultural environment, the more defensive and persistent the group. Since the southern United States was not as congenial to European-born farmers as the northern regions, immigrants in the South retained their distinctiveness more than did their compatriots in the North. On the other hand, German wheat farmers in Kansas, Rhine viticulturists in California, and Norwegian dairymen in Wisconsin surrendered their ethnic identity more quickly and blended in with their neighbors from the beginning.

Of course the rapid adjustment of immigrant farmers was due to more than a familiar cultural and climatic environment. Before leaving Europe, immigrants often purchased crude farming manuals and guide books to ease their introduction to America. The also sought direct contacts with American neighbors in order to learn proven farm methods in the area. Many unmarried young men and women "hired out" to Americans as field hands and domestics. If fellow ethnics had previously settled the region, newcomers naturally sought their aid and served "apprentice-ships" under them. Yet, despite rapid acculturation, foreign-born farm-ers always faced a greater adjustment than native-born migrants.

The Texan farmers of German ancestry today still retain some distinc-tive social-cultural traits, but Jordan has concluded that differences in agricultural practices are largely "invisible," if they persist at all. As farm-ers and ranchers, the Germans in Texas are businessmen, first and foremost; they are ethnics only in the farmhouse, in church, and in social clubs.[31] That finding agrees with Bogue's assessment of Midwestern ethnic farmers: cultural differences "were more apparent than real—most obvious in food ways, dress, and lingual traits, and less important when the farmer decided on his combination of major enterprises."[32]

The census research summarized here provides the first solid evi-dence regarding ethnic patterns in agriculture; but these early studies suffer from two limitations that are inherent in the census sources. The first is that all farmers of a given nationality are lumped together, without taking into account local and regional differences in the motherland. The censuses record only the country of birth, of course, and it would be a herculean task to link the census with foreign records at the local level. Yet, in nineteenth-century Europe, farming practices, life-styles, and even language often differed widely between two adjacent provinces in the same country or even between two parishes in the same province. Second, these studies slight the importance of religious group differ-ences, again because the censuses do not report religious or denomina-tional affiliation. Thousands of close-knit, church-centered, ethnic com-munities dotted the landscape of rural America a century ago. These homogeneous clusters of people often had common origins in the old country, and they deliberately sought to create isolated settlements in hopes of preserving their cultural identity and retaining the mother ton-gue for generations to come. Such cohesive sectarian communities dif-fered greatly from settlements composed of a mixture of main-line "church" groups, even if all were Protestant.[33]

Several recent microstudies, all by geographers, take into account the parish backgrounds of American immigrant farmers. These are highly rewarding and suggestive of the direction of future research in agricultural history. John Rice studied farming patterns in a six-township area of frontier Minnesota (Kandiyohi County), which was settled by Swedes, Norwegians, Irish, and Americans from the East.[34] Each of the nationality groups was diverse in origin, except for one group of Swedes, who came from the same parish, Gagnef, in Dalarna Province. Two other Swedish settlements were more diverse, comprising people from many parishes, yet all from the same province. Moreover, each of the three subnational Swedish culture groups was affiliated with the three major church communities in the sample townships. Thus, Rice was able to compare agricultural practices of Swedish cultural groups defined at the national, provincial, and parish levels.

Rice's findings, based on both Swedish and American sources, reveal that farmers from all the nationality groups, except for the Swedes of Gagnef Parish, were similar in their cropping patterns, livestock holdings, persistence rates, and economic status. All the groups concentrated on wheat, but the Gagnef parishioners stand out as unique. They retained their oxen as draft animals into the 1880s, long after the other farmers in the area had switched to horses. The Gagnef community was the most stable by far, and it prospered economically, advancing from the poorest of the Swedish settlements to the wealthiest. Thus, the agricultural experience of the church-centered Gagnef group, transplanted en masse from Dalarna, differed markedly from the neighboring immigrant settlements, including those of Swedes and Norwegians. Religion and its cultural trappings, not nationality per se, determined farming behavior among Minnesota Swedes.

The impact of religion on immigrant farmers was not unique to Minnesota. Russian Germans in Nebraska likewise diverged from the American norm of farming practices in the region.[35] They operated smaller farms, which they owned, debt-free, and they diversified their crop and livestock enterprises to a greater degree than did other ethno-religious groups. Thus, religious values may have been the determining factor among Mennonites in Kansas, as they were for Swedes in Minnesota. A century earlier, in southeastern Pennsylvania, sectarian "plain folk"— Mennonites from the Rhine Valley and Switzerland, Friends (Quakers) from England and Wales, German Baptist "Dunkers," and Moravian Brethren—similarly occupied and used the land differently than did emigrants from mainline European churches—Lutheran, Reformed, Anglican, and Presbyterian. The sect groups valued discipline and cooperation. The Moravians lived communally in agricultural villages, following the European "open-field" system, but the Mennonites and the Quakers lived on family farms. The sects were tightly clustered, geographically; they owned the most valuable farms; and they were the least transient. Although most farmers in Lancaster and Chester counties were involved in general mixed agriculture, with an emphasis on wheat, the Mennonites and the Quakers farmed more intensively, sowed more wheat acreage, and possessed more livestock than did other national and denominational groups.[36] Thus, in a relatively homogeneous agricultural region, the only significant differences in farming behavior derived from religious rather than ethnic origins. The seven Amana villages in Iowa and numerous Spanish-American peasant villages in New Mexico—the latter antedating the Mexican War of Independence from Spain in the 1820s—are additional examples of religiously based communities that to this day use the open-field system of agricultural settlement. In all of these communities, behavioral distinctions in farming can be determined only through microscopic local studies.

This is precisely the nature of the contribution of the new social historians of colonial New England and of the agrarian South of the nineteenth century.[37] These scholars are regional historians, who yet conceive of their work in a holistic way. Through the use of local records, colonial historians have reconstructed the everyday lives of New Englanders in numerous pioneer towns and villages and have described in amazing detail the people's behavior—within the family, the church, the marketplace, and the body politic. These studies have led to a remarkably complete picture of colonial wealth distribution and social mobility; of rates of birth, marriage, and death; of inheritance patterns, officeholding, and church membership.[38] Most use modernization theory as a connecting theme and try to highlight behavioral changes in response to changing community structures. The multiplication of colonial studies even allowed Edward Cook to compose a typology of New England towns based on stages of economic development, differing social structures, and types of political leadership.[39] Given all this attention, it is not surprising that pre-industrial rural communities are now better understood than modern rural communities.

The primary conclusion of the New England studies is that American society before 1820 was familial and communal, not individualistic in the Turnerian frontier sense. Nearly every ethnic and religious group settled together in clustered communities among their own kind. Even families that lived in isolated homesteads rather than in nucleated villages chose to settle near family and friends, because they felt the need to maintain native languages and religious beliefs. While living alone, they accepted the informal communal bonds of language and creed and patronized shops and mills of fellow church members. The commitment to the family and community was so strong in pre-industrial America that many young men who had no immediate prospect of obtaining a farm remained at home as farm laborers or renters rather than migrating west to find land of their own. James Lemon, in his social geographical study of southeastern Pennslyvania, *The Best Poor Man's Country* (1972), found that 45 percent of the adult men studied were landless (two-thirds of them were married, one-third were single). Rather than move west or rebel in anger and frustration at the lack of opportunity, nearly half the people were willing to remain and wait patiently for their patrimony—the family farm, or part of it. In pre-industrial agricultural communities, economic success and security was rare before age forty or forty-five. That was the social reality of life in an age-stratified society where age, wealth, status, and power went together.[40]

James Henretta, a leading colonial economic historian, has offered the best conceptual framework for future research into the mentality of pre-industrial America.[41] The crucial indicator of community values and aspirations, Henretta suggests, was the "behavior of the farm population." Scholars must focus their attention on those activities that dominated the daily lives of the population—that is, "on the productive tasks that provided food, clothing, and shelter." That will show, Henretta maintains, that the family was the primary economic and social unit. Farm work was arranged within the extended family, property was "communal" within the family, but the parent's (usually father's) legal control of the family farm gave him the power to control the terms and the timing of passing the "family land" on to the next generation. Family welfare took precedence over individual rights. Henretta summarizes his thesis in this way:

The agricultural family remained an extended lineal one; each generation lived in a separate household, but the character of production and inheritance linked these conjugal units through a myriad of legal, moral, and customary bonds. Rights and responsibilities stretched across generations. The financial welfare of both parents and children was rooted in the land and in the equipment and labor needed to farm it. Parents therefore influenced their children's choice of marriage partners. Their welfare, or that of their other children, might otherwise be compromised by the premature division of assets which an early marriage entailed. The line was more important than the individual; the patrimony was to be conserved for lineal purposes.[42]

The lineal family was thus the basic unit of entrepreneurial activity and capitalist enterprise in agrarian America.

Following the lead of the colonialists, Southern historians have been in the vanguard since the mid-1970s in developing a holistic model of modern rural history. Vernon Burton, a specialist in South Carolina race relations in the nineteenth century, provided guidelines in a 1976 paper entitled "Southern Community Studies: Methodology and Theory."[43] Burton explains that rural communities should not be studied for antiquarian reasons, or to test traditional hypotheses, such as frontier democracy, or to serve as typical case studies of entire regions; rather, the proper rationale for studying rural communities, according to Burton, is behavioral—to learn "how people lived, how they reacted to and treated others, and what their lives meant to them." The study of *any* local community, he argues, enables scholars to understand "larger human concerns," or, in the words of Samuel P. Hays, to "illuminate broad processes of social change concretely." To achieve that end, Burton argues, the research must be informed by the three elements of sound theory: (1) functionality, or the blending of personal experience and intuition with abstract knowledge; (2) continuity, or the recognition of the interrelationship of human experience in all its complexity; and (3) predictability— that is, understanding past behavior systematically so that one can anticipate future behavior.

To Burton's model must be added a method of differentiating between various communities. Since behavior is in part determined by environment, the selection of a community as a case study is critical. For rural community studies to thrive, it is necessary to develop methods to select for study various types of communities in different regions. We need a systematic typology of communities that takes account of size, spatial organization, degree of urbanization, rate of growth, economic function, etc., such as that Cook provided for New England colonial towns. In that way, each community can be identified and located along various continua. We can then select sample communities for study and begin to develop generalizations about communities as ecological and social systems. Community sampling is the key to the success of these ventures. Nevertheless, the Southern specialists have caught the vision of history "from the bottom up" by concentrating on the "scraps of evidence" left by the inarticulate common people in local community archives and public courthouses.[44] They have capitalized on the computer revolution that makes it possible to use local-level data on thousands of individuals and families to reconstruct past social structures.

Despite the work of the American frontier historians, colonialists, and Southern researchers, it has been European historians, especially the French, who have provided American scholars with a coherent model for rural history. As early as the 1920s, and largely unknown to American scholars, Marc Bloch, a founder of the *Annales* tradition at the Sorbonne in Paris, began pioneering studies in French rural history with the aim of relating the way everyday lives were lived from the Middle Ages until the modern era. Bloch sought to understand the totality of French rural life by roaming over the countryside, speaking with the people, learning their daily routines, and capturing the smell of hogs, hay, and manure. He then sought to explain rural behavior in terms of social science theories borrowed from economics, geography, psychology, sociology, agronomy, cartography, and even folklore.[45]

In the past decade, the *Annales* scholarship has rather suddenly come to the attention of American scholars, and its influence is pronounced. Now available in English translation, the books of Bloch, Fernand Braudel, and Emmanuel LeRoy Ladurie have become mandatory reading.[46] Although there is no counterpart in the American experience to the centuries-long European peasant society—indeed, some argue that the American colonists were "modern" from the outset—the *Annales* concepts have provided a theoretical model that can be adapted to the American story.[47]

Annales historians follow a common theme.[48] They usually describe "the ways things were" in pre-industrial societies, such as the uncouth life-style, the sway of superstition, subsistence farming and a barter economy, geographical isolation and its effects, lawlessness, illiteracy, and poor health. Then they describe the "agencies of change," that is, the institutions that undermined and gradually destroyed the traditional peasant mind-set (*mentalitè*), such as roads and railroads, a market economy, national political campaigns, village schools, seasonal and international labor migration, compulsory military service, and war. Always, the time span is several centuries, so that long-run change can be measured against successive shorter phases of growth and decline. As Ladurie states in *The Peasants of Languedoc* (1966), "I have endeavored in the present book to observe, at various levels, the long-term movements of an economy and of a society—base and super-structure, material life and cultural life, sociological evolution and collective psychology, the whole within the framework of a rural world which remained very largely traditional in nature."[49] Ladurie's masterpiece of "total" history thus combines interdisciplinary theory with original economic and demographic research in order to describe the demise of a traditional peasant society in which the rise in population ran ahead of increases in wealth and food production.

American scholars today are beginning to apply the *Annales* concept of modernization to explain long-lasting social change and periodization, although Marxist and behavioral theories are also employed.[50] Richard

Jensen's notable bicentennial contribution, *Illinois: A Bicentennial History* (1978), offers a practical example of modernization theory as a unifying theme in the state's history. By *modernization,* Jensen means the process of change in basic value systems that led people to behave differently. Illinois residents (and, by implication, all Midwesterners and upland Southerners) displayed three unique ways of thinking about life and styles of behavior: traditional, modern, and post-modern.

Traditionalists are "people who are comfortable with things as they were, who distrust strangers and progress for progress's sake." Authoritarian and male-oriented, they are intensely loyal to self, family, kinfolk, community, race, and often to church congregations. In Illinois, these American counterparts to European peasantry were primarily the Southern-born Scotch-Irish and English Protestants that settled in "Little Egypt," and the Roman Catholic immigrants and blacks that later flooded Northern cities.[51] The "modern" individuals were the "future-oriented, upwardly mobile, reformist Yankees," who arrived in Central Illinois in the 1840s and 1850s and quickly became the dominant group because of their emphasis on efficiency, progress, independence, education, science, technology, and self-discipline. Although predominantly rural farmers, these modernizers represented the most progressive sector in the economy—agriculture. According to Jensen, neither place nor occupation, but, rather, psychological factors and social behavior were determinative. Furthermore, traditionalists, moderns, and, since the 1960s, post-moderns, who reject the Protestant ethic, all continue to co-exist in Illinois. Nevertheless, Southern-born traditionalists were predominant until the Civil War, "the war for modernity," which enabled the Yankee moderns to gain control, a hegemony they have long held but are now losing to the youthful post-moderns.[52] Modernization thus involves a shift from one type of society, usually rural and agricultural, to another, which is usually industrial and (sub)urban.

More recently, Walter Nugent has used the *Annales* concept of systemic change to provide a slightly different periodization of American history. Taking his cue from Braudel's *The Mediterranean and the Mediterranean World in the Age of Philip II* (1949), Nugent distinguishes three periods or "modes" in American history based on mass population data, its movement, distribution, and composition—a long frontier-rural mode from 1720 to 1870, a shorter transition era (the "Great Conjuncture") from 1870 to 1920, and again a longer metropolitan mode since 1920, which Nugent projects into the twenty-first century.

Nugent's frontier-rural period, which resembles Turner's earlier frontier era, interests us.[53] Its characteristics were similar to that of Europe's peasantry—overwhelmingly homogeneous in residence (rural), in occupation (farming), in religion (Protestant), and in ethnicity (Anglo). Eighty percent of Americans remained rural as late as 1860, and most were middle-class, property-owning folk. A high birth rate and large families led to rapid population growth, but territorial expansion kept pace. "Everywhere during the frontier-rural period," Nugent concludes, "the pattern was one of available land attracting settlement, then slow constriction of available land and rising prices for land, high fertility, then land hunger and population pressure from a large and unpropertied second (then third) generation, and finally migration of the young to a new area full of cheap and empty land."[54] The sanguine circumstances led to a very gradual change from subsistence to commercial agriculture, but hand labor with primitive tools, powered by men and horses, remained the norm until the 1860s at least. Only with the spread of the railroad network did the traditional agrarian mode of production and life-style give way to the disorganizing forces of the emerging metropolitan mode.

If, as Nugent asserts, the transformation of traditional rural communities into modern cosmopolitan societies began in the late nineteenth century, the process required several generations to run its course. The isolated, homogeneous, and largely self-sufficient farming communities of the 1900s, with their rituals of local bonding—such as neighborhood threshing rings and barnraisings—gave way slowly to the present-day individualistic, impersonal, and commercialized rural society that is merely a microcosm of urban mass culture.[55]

John Shover in his premier book *First-Majority, Last Minority: The Transformation of Rural Life in America* (1976) insists that the technological revolution in American agriculture after 1945 finally destroyed the rural way of life as it was known for hundreds of years. Using case studies of two counties (Bedford County, Pennsylvania, and Scioto County, Ohio) and two farm families in Michigan and Iowa, Shover describes the social disintegration of the yeoman farmer republic and its replacement in the years after World War II by the agri-industrial empire. He labels this dramatic social change the "Great Disjuncture." With the triumph of agribusiness, the localistic and personalistic frame of reference for portraying country life—symbolized by the "family farm"—became obsolete.[56]

Shover, I fear, is on target. In thirty-five years (1945–1980), rural life has undergone a pervasive and radical change. The history of rural communities, therefore, is the process of adjustment to the destructive forces of modernization and the consequent loss of close and intensive personal relationships. Community has always been a declining phenomenon in rural America. The historian's task is to analyze the changing characteristics of rural communities nationwide and to describe the impact of those changes on the lives of its residents and on society at large.

As this chapter has indicated, the countryside is again a serious subject for historical study. The American behavioralists and the French *Annales* scholars have proven that an interdisciplinary, quantitative, and theoretical approach that analyzes changes in rural society over the centuries can offer a superior means for understanding the evolution of a people. Rural life today may be an anachronism to many. But those who can learn to appreciate the mundane lives of ordinary folk in past societies, when farmers were the first majority, will share in the excitement of the new rural historians as they continue to explore America's agrarian tradition.

Notes

1. Robert P. Swierenga, "The New Rural History: Defining the Parameters," *Great Plains Quarterly* 1 (1981): 211–223; Swierenga, "Towards the 'New Rural History': A Review Essay," *Historical Methods Newsletter* 6 (1973): 111–122; Peter Argersinger, "The People's Past: Teaching American Rural History," *History Teacher* 10 (1977): 403–424; Kathleen Neils Conzen, "Community Studies, Urban History, and American Local History," in *The Past Before Us: Contemporary Historical Writing in the United States*, edited by Michael Kammen (Ithaca: Cornell University Press, 1980), pp. 270–291.

2. Eugen Weber, *Peasants into Frenchmen: The Modernization of Rural France, 1870–1914* (Stanford: Stanford University Press, 1976), p. xi.

3. See, for example, Richard Hofstadter, *Anti-Intellectualism in American History* (New York: Alfred A. Knopf, 1962), pp. 272–282; Richard Hofstadter, *The Age of Reform* (New York: Alfred A. Knopf, 1955), pp. 7–8, 60–93, 121–130.

4. See Daniel Boorstin, *The Lost World of Thomas Jefferson* (New York: Henry Holt, 1948); Marvin Meyers, *The Jacksonian Persuasion, Politics and Belief* (Stanford: Stanford University Press, 1957), pp. vii, 12–15, 140–141, and *passim*.

5. Quoted in Argersinger, "People's Past," p. 406.

6. See, for example, the serial publication, *Canadian Papers in Rural History, 1978–*. In western Europe, the term *agrarian* is more commonly used than *rural*.

7. Cf. Marion Clawson, "The Future of Rural America: A Plan for Population Regrouping," *Current*, no. 148 (1973), pp. 23–28.

8. The term *hinterland*, which is common in economic and urban history, itself reflects an urban bias by implying that cities are the vital centers, dispensing benefits to the "land behind," i.e., the less-developed surrounding area. For works that integrate urban and rural development, see Michael P. Conzen, *Frontier Farming in an Urban Shadow: The Influence of Madison's Proximity on the Agricultural Development of Blooming Grove, Wisconsin* (Madison: State Historical Society of Wisconsin, 1971); Michael P. Conzen, "The Maturing Urban System in the United States, 1840–1910," *Annals of the Association of American Geographers* 67 (1977): 88–108; Roberta Balstad Miller, *City and Hinterland: A Case Study of Urban Growth and Regional Development* (Westport, Conn.: Greenwood Press, 1979).

9. Bruce M. Stave, "A Conversation with Stephan Thernstrom," *Journal of Urban History* 1 (1975): 198.

10. Kathleen Neils Conzen, "Farm and Family: A German Settlement on the Minnesota Frontier" (Paper presented to the American Historical Association, Washington, D.C., December 1976).

11. Robert P. Swierenga, "Quantitative Methods in Rural Land Holding," *Journal of Interdisciplinary History* (in press); Robert Galen Bell, "James C. Malin and the Grassland of North America," *Agricultural History* 46 (1972): 414–424; Allan G. Bogue, "The Heirs of James C. Malin: A Grassland Historiography," *Great Plains Quarterly* 1 (1981): 105–131.

12. Letter, James Malin to the author, October 16, 1973.

13. I define "rural history" as the study of human behavior over time in the rural environment. For a discussion, see Swierenga, "The New Rural History," pp. 212–213.

14. Argersinger, "People's Past," p. 407.

15. Swierenga, "Quantitative Methods in Rural Land Holding and Tenancy Studies."

16. Frank L. Owsley, *Plain Folk of the Old South* (Baton Rouge: Louisiana State University Press, 1949), quotes at pp. 133–135.

17. Merle Curti, *The Making of an American Community: A Case Study of Democracy in a Frontier County* (Stanford: Stanford University Press, 1959).

18. Curti, *American Community*, pp. 3, 15, 227, 448.

19. Allan G. Bogue, *From Prairie to Cornbelt: Farming on the Illinois and Iowa Prairies* (Chicago: University of Chicago Press, 1963), p. 1.

20. Samuel P. Hays, "History as Human Behavior," *Iowa Journal of History* 58 (1960): 193–206, quotes from p. 193.

21. Robert R. Dykstra, "Town-Country Conflict: A Hidden Dimension in American Social History," *Agricultural History* 33 (1964): 195; Dykstra, *The Cattle Towns* (New York: Alfred A. Knopf, 1968).

22. Robert P. Swierenga, *Pioneers and Profits: Land Speculation on the Iowa Frontier* (Ames: Iowa State University Press, 1968); Swierenga, *Acres for Cents: Delinquent Tax Auctions in Frontier Iowa* (Westport, Conn.: Greenwood Press, 1976).

23. Donald L. Winters, *Farmers Without Farms: Agricultural Tenancy in Nineteenth-Century Iowa* (Westport, Conn.: Greenwood Press, 1978).

24. Robert W. Taylor, Jr., "The Olin Tribe: Migration, Mutual Aid, and Solidarity in a Nineteenth-Century Rural American Kin Group" (Ph.D. dissertation, Kent State University, 1979).

25. Richard M. Bernard, *The Melting Pot and the Altar: Marital Assimilation in Early Twentieth-Century Wisconsin* (Minneapolis: University of Minnesota Press, 1980), pp. 119, 124.

26. Robert P. Swierenga, "Ethnicity and American Agriculture," *Ohio History* 89 (1980): 323–344, discusses this subject in detail.

27. Kathleen Neils Conzen, "Historical Approaches to the Study of Rural Ethnic Communities," in *Ethnicity on the Great Plains*, edited by Frederick C. Luebke (Lincoln: University of Nebraska Press, 1980), pp. 1–17; Swierenga, "Ethnicity and American Agriculture," pp. 330–340.

28. Robert C. Ostergren, "A Community Transplanted: The Formative Experience of a Swedish Immigrant Community in the Upper Middle West," *Journal of Historical Geography* 5 (1979): 189–212, quoted at p. 208; Ostergren, "Prairie Bound: Migration Patterns to a Swedish Settlement on the Dakota Frontier," in Luebke, *Ethnicity on the Great Plains*, pp. 73–91; Ostergren, "Land and Family in Rural Immigrant Communities," *Annals of the Association of American Geographers* 71 (1981): 400–411; Ostergren, "Kinship Networks and Migration: A Nineteenth-Century Swedish Example," *Social Science History* 6 (1982): 293–320.

29. Terry G. Jordan, *German Seed in Texas Soil: Immigrant Farmers in Nineteenth-Century Texas* (Austin: University of Texas Press, 1966), p. 192.

30. This paragraph and the four following are summarized from Jordan, *German Seed in Texas Soil*, pp. 194–203. The quotations are on p. 196. See also D. Aidan McQuillan, "Farm Size and Work Ethic: Measuring the Success of Immigrant Farmers on the American Grasslands," *Journal of Historical Geography* 4 (1978): 57–76.

31. Jordan, *German Seed in Texas Soil*, p. 203.

32. Bogue, *Prairie to Cornbelt*, p. 238.

33. See Marianne Wokeck, "Cultural Persistence and Adaptation: The Germans of Lancaster County, Pennsylvania, 1729–76," in *Business and Economic History: Papers Presented at the Twenty-Fourth Annual Meeting of the Business History Conference*, edited by Paul Uselding (Urbana: Bureau of Economic and Business Research, College of Commerce and Business Administration, University of Illinois, 1978).

34. John Rice, "The Role of Culture and Community in Frontier Prairie Farming," *Journal of Historical Geography* 3 (1977): 155–175; Rice, *Patterns of Ethnicity in a Minnesota County, 1880–1905* (Umeºa, Sweden: Department of Geography, University of Umeºa, 1973).

35. Bradley H. Baltensperger, "Agricultural Change Among Nebraska Immigrants, 1880–1900," in Luebke, *Ethnicity on the Great Plains*, pp. 170–189.

36. James T. Lemon, *The Best Poor Man's Country: A Geographical Study of Early Southeastern Pennsylvania* (Baltimore: Johns Hopkins University Press, 1976), pp. 63–64, 81–85, 174.

37. For a detailed survey of the colonial research, see John Murrin's "Review Essay" in *History and Theory* 2 (1972): 226–275. A nineteenth-century counterpart to these colonial studies is Hal Seth Barron's study of Chelsea, Vermont, 1840–1900. See Barron, "The Impact of Rural Depopulation on the Local Economy: Chelsea, Vermont, 1840–1900," *Agricultural History* 54 (1980): 318–335; Barron, "The Tie that Binds: Migration and Persistence in a Settled Rural Community: Chelsea, Vermont, 1840–1900" (Paper presented to the Organization of American Historians, San Francisco, April 1980).

38. Conzen, "Community Studies," p. 277.

39. Edward M. Cook, Jr., *The Fathers of the Towns: Leadership and Community Structure in Eighteenth-Century New England* (Baltimore: Johns Hopkins University Press, 1976).

40. Lemon, *Poor Man's Country*, pp. 43, 83–85, 94–95.

41. James A. Henretta, "Families and Farms: Mentalitè in Pre-Industrial America," *William and Mary Quarterly* 35 (1978): 20.

42. Henretta, "Families and Farms," pp. 25–26.

43. Vernon Burton, "Southern Community Studies: Methodology and Theory" (Paper presented to the American Historical Association, Washington, D.C., December 1976), p. 1. See also Frank J. Huffman, Jr., "Town and Country in the South, 1850–1880: A Comparison of Urban and Rural Social Structures," in Edward Magdol and Jon L. Wakelyn, *The Southern Common People: Studies in Nineteenth-Century Social History* (Westport, Conn.: Greenwood Press, 1980), pp. 239–251.

44. For examples, see the various essays reprinted in Magdol and Wakelyn, *Southern Common People*.

45. Marc Bloch, *French Rural History: An Essay in Its Basic Characteristics* (Berkeley: University of California Press, 1966). This is a translation by Bruce Lyon of Bloch's original 1931 work.

46. Examples of *Annales* scholarship are: Emmanuel Le Roy Ladurie, *The Peasants of Languedoc* (Urbana: University of Illinois Press, 1976); Ladurie, *The Territory of the Historian* (Chicago: University of Chicago Press, 1979); Ladurie, *Montaillou: The Promised Land of Error* (New York: Braziller, 1978); Fernand Braudel, *The Mediterranean and the Mediterranean World in the Age of Philip II*, 2 vols. (New York: Harper and Row, 1976). Analyses and critiques of

the *Annales* are: Troian Stoianovich, *French Historical Method: The Annales Paradigm* (Ithaca: Cornell University Press, 1976); Samuel Kinser, "*Annaliste* Paradigm? The Geohistorical Structuralism of Fernand Braudel," *American Historical Review* 86 (1981): 63–105; Roy L. Willis, "Contributions of the *Annales* School to Agrarian History," *Agricultural History* 52 (1978): 538–548; Robert Forster, "Achievements of the *Annales* School," *Journal of Economic History* 38 (1978): 58–76; James A. Henretta, "Social History as Lived and Written," *American Historical Review* 84 (1979): 1293–1333.

47. Walter Nugent, *Structures of American Social History* (Bloomington: Indiana University Press, 1981), p. 8.

48. This is evident in the works of American scholars writing in the *Annales* tradition: Weber, *Peasants into Frenchmen* and Jerome Blum, *The End of the Old Order in Rural Europe* (Princeton: Princeton University Press, 1978).

49. Ladurie, *Peasants of Languedoc*, p. 289.

50. Nugent, *Structures of American Social History*, pp. 5–6.

51. Richard J. Jensen, *Illinois: A Bicentennial History* (Nashville and New York: American Association for State and Local History and W. W. Norton & Company, Inc., 1978), p. 5.

52. Jensen, *Illinois*, pp. xv, xvii, 75, 178–179.

53. Nugent, *Structures of American Social History*, pp. 54–86.

54. Nugent, *Structures of American Social History*, pp. 72–73.

55. Argersinger, "People's Past," p. 407.

56. John Shover, *First Majority—Last Minority: The Transformation of Rural Life in America* (DeKalb: Northern Illinois University Press, 1976). A more positive prognosis of twentieth-century developments is Gilbert C. Fite, *American Farmers: The New Minority* (Bloomington: Indiana University Press, 1981).

Suggestions for Additional Reading

Argersinger, Peter. "The People's Past: Teaching American Rural History." *History Teacher* 10 (May, 1977): 403–424.

This article provides a framework for teaching rural history with an emphasis on human experience and behavior. Various organizational approaches are evaluated.

Bogue, Allan G. *From Prairie to Cornbelt: Farming on the Illinois and Iowa Prairies.* Chicago: University of Chicago Press, 1963.

A seminal study of Midwestern agricultural development from a behavioral perspective. Bogue is one of the first agricultural historians to investigate the question of cultural differences in crop and livestock mixes among Midwestern ethnic farmers, by analyzing the manuscript population and agricultural censuses.

Conzen, Kathleen Neils. "Historical Approaches to the Study of Rural Ethnic Communities," in *Ethnicity on the Great Plains*, edited by Frederick C. Luebke (Lincoln: University of Nebraska Press, 1980), pp. 1–17.

This seminal essay develops concepts for understanding the process of immigrant cultural adaptation in rural America and the emergence of ethnic identity. Settlement patterns and family relationships are stressed as major determinants.

Conzen, Michael P. *Frontier Farming in an Urban Shadow: The Influence of Madison's Proximity on the Agricultural Development of Blooming Grove, Wisconsin*. Madison: State Historical Society of Wisconsin, 1971.

A historical geographer's analysis of the history and development of a frontier community that was absorbed into a large city.

Curti, Merle E. *The Making of an American Community: A Case Study of Democracy in a Frontier County*. Stanford: Stanford University Press, 1959.

The first manuscript census study to consider socio-economic differences among farmers of the major ethnic groups. More descriptive than analytical, but a truly pioneering work.

Dykstra, Robert R. *The Cattle Towns*. New York: Alfred A. Knopf, 1968.

This award-winning book offers a fresh interpretation of the social history of Kansas cattle-trading centers in the post-Civil War era. The author stresses the social processes and conflicts in local decision-making in frontier communities.

Hays, Samuel P. "History as Human Behavior." *Iowa Journal of History* 58 (1960): 193–206.

A foundational discussion of the significance of behavioral variables in historical analysis.

Henretta, James A. "Families and Farms: Mentalitè in Pre-Industrial America." *William and Mary Quarterly* 35 (1978): 3–32.

This important article explores the relationship between the mental or emotional or ideological aspects of rural people and the structures of their social life, which are revealed through statistical analysis.

Jordan, Terry G. *German Seed in Texas Soil: Immigrant Farmers in Nineteenth-Century Texas*. Austin: University of Texas Press, 1966.

A masterful comparative analysis of cultural distinctiveness among German and non-German farmers in Texas, based on census research and quantitative data.

Lemon, James T. *The Best Poor Man's Country: A Geographical Study of Early Southeastern Pennsylvania*. Baltimore: Johns Hopkins University Press, 1976.

A premier example of the new historical geography that shows the interplay of society and land and its effect on farming practices and social mobility.

Nugent, Walter. *Structures of American Social History*. Bloomington: Indiana University Press, 1981.

A popularized survey of American population changes and their impact on social and economic life. Applies modernization theory in order to explain population patterns that affect the lives of people.

Ostergren, Robert. "Land and Family in Rural Immigrant Communities." *Annals of the Association of American Geographers* 71 (1981): 400–411.

An examination of land-transfer practices in seven Swedish communities in Minnesota. Community differences are related to social and institutional factors and to land-transfer patterns in Sweden.

Owsley, Frank L. *Plain Folk of the Old South*. Baton Rouge: Louisiana State University Press, 1949.

A seminal study, based on the federal population census manuscripts of 1850 and 1860 of numerous Southern states, that portrays the economic life of non-slave-holding farmers.

Shover, John. *First Majority—Last Minority: The Transformation of Rural Life in America*. DeKalb: Northern Illinois University Press, 1976.

This significant book describes the technical revolution in American agriculture in terms of its radical social impact.

Swierenga, Robert P. *Acres for Cents: Delinquent Tax Auctions in Frontier Iowa*. Westport, Conn.: Greenwood Press, 1976.

The only analysis of frontier tax sales and their economic and social significance. Based on local government records.

Swierenga, Robert P. "Ethnicity and American Agriculture." *Ohio History* 89 (1980): 323–344.

A survey of recent primary research on the effect of ethnic and religious-group identity on farming practices and rural life-styles.

Swierenga, Robert P. "The New Rural History: Defining the Parameters." *Great Plains Quarterly* 1 (1981): 211–223.

A theoretical analysis of the new rural history, including a definition and interdisciplinary contributions.

Swierenga, Robert P. *Pioneers and Profits: Land Speculation on the Iowa Frontier*. Ames: Iowa State University Press, 1968.

An economic study of land disposal and speculation in Iowa, emphasizing behavioral aspects and computations of profitability.

Winters, Donald L. *Farmers Without Farms: Agricultural Tenancy in Nineteenth-Century Iowa*. Westport, Conn.: Greenwood Press, 1978.

The only comprehensive analysis of farm tenancy, based on local government records and census reports and employing sound theories of economic development.

William H. Dalrymple, a laborer, and his family posed for this portrait on September 22, 1908 at the Cronis Studio in Salem, Oregon.

Oregon Historical Society, negative number 054G017

6

American Families in the Past

Maris A. Vinovskis

AMERICAN SOCIAL HISTORIANS recently "discovered" the role of the family in our past. Indeed, the history of the family has become one of the most active and challenging areas of research during the past fifteen years. The popularity of this field is illustrated by the fact that, whereas, in the late 1960s, "new" social historians such as John Demos, Philip Greven, and Kenneth Lockridge were often identified narrowly as demographic historians, scholars doing similar studies today are apt to be described more broadly as family historians.[1]

In order to provide some general methodological observations, the first section of this essay will examine changes in the way families in the past have been studied. The achievements and shortcomings of the current research on the American family will then be highlighted by considering four aspects of family life: childbearing, early child development, adolescence, and old age. While neither the general methodological discussion nor the analysis of specific topics can pretend to cover either the richness or complexity of the work on the history of the American family, it is hoped that they will at least convey some of the excitement, attainments, and unresolved problems in this new area of social history.

From Household Size to the Life Course

Though the study of the American family appears to be an entirely new undertaking, a few historians pursued research on this topic many years ago. In the late nineteenth century, Alice Morse Earle explored family life in colonial America, and Arthur Calhoun documented the social history of the family in three volumes published between 1917 and

1919.[2] Most of the early works, however, were largely descriptive and chronicled, rather than analyzed, changes in the American family. The appearance of Edmund Morgan's important book *The Puritan Family*, in 1944, however, heralded the beginning of the field of family history as we know it today—though another two decades were to pass before other scholars joined this effort.[3]

The study of the American family blossomed in the late 1960s and early 1970s with the publication of three major works on colonial America by Demos, Greven, and Lockridge.[4] Using family reconstitution methods borrowed from their French and English counterparts, these studies quickly captured the attention of the profession as a whole. In the process, family history in America became inexorably linked—at least in the minds of the next generation of scholars trained in graduate schools— with quantitative analysis, especially with the use of demographic methods to estimate birth, marriage, and death rates.

The early identification of family history with quantification has had both positive and negative consequences. On the one hand, it has led to the use of demographic techniques that enable historians to reconstruct the lives of ordinary Americans who left their only mark on history in the birth, marriage, or death registers. The use of quantitative indices also has meant that historians now are able to provide a more systematic and rigorous analysis of the American family than those provided by Earle, Calhoun, or even Morgan. On the other hand, the heavy emphasis on quantification has led some individuals—mistakenly—to equate the proper study of the family with the use of numerical data. Yet, some of the best examples of family history are those done without a heavy reliance on numbers.[5] Furthermore, the exaltation of quantification by itself has failed to recognize that the most essential attributes of the social sciences are their conceptual and analytical rigor, rather than just their use of numbers. Thus, the debates between the so-called quantifiers and non-quantifiers in the field of family history frequently are based on a fundamental misunderstanding of the most important characteristics of the "new" social history.

One example of the danger of relying too heavily on numbers without an adequate conceptual basis is the effort to calculate the mean (average) size of households in the past. Reacting against statements by sociologists that most individuals lived in extended families in pre-industrial America and Europe, Peter Laslett and his colleagues set out to demonstrate that few extended families existed in the past. To prove their point, these historians studied mean household size in different cultures and time periods. They found that the mean household size in Western Europe was relatively small and constant—averaging about four persons per household.[6] Mean household size quickly became a convenient way to summarize the characteristics of family life in the past. While this calculation was routinely accepted and practiced by many family historians, a few began to question its conceptual utility.[7] The severest and most damaging criticism came from Lutz Berkner, who called for a more dynamic approach to the study of the family. He argued that, while extended households may constitute only a small proportion of households at any given time, a much larger percentage of them may have been extended at some time during their existence.[8]

As historians moved away from using the mean household size to describe families in the past, they explored other avenues of analysis. One of the most frequent alternatives was to study generations. Greven's analysis of family life in colonial Andover, Massachusetts, traced the lives of the first four generations of settlers in that community. He analyzed the first settlers (first generation), their children (second generation), their grandchildren (third generation), and their great-grandchildren (fourth generation).[9] The use of generations as an analytical construct can be useful if one is studying the transmission of property from the parents to the children or the settlement of a new area; its utility is considerably lessened if one is trying to follow the descendants of these families over many years. In the case of Andover, the lives of the members of the third and fourth generations often overlapped so much chronologically that it is doubtful whether these distinctions had any real meaning for the citizens of that community. Furthermore, this categorization has little analytical clarity, since the same generation contains members from such different age-groups.[10] In trying to follow the same families over such a long time period, perhaps it might be more appropriate to organize the data by birth cohorts (i.e., according to the years in which the individuals are born) or at least to modify Greven's scheme by further subdividing the third and fourth generations on the basis of the ages of their members.[11]

Neither the mean household size nor the concept of generations can provide us with a sense of the dynamics of family life. Sociologists of the family have tried to resolve this problem by defining stages of the family and then organizing them sequentially into a pattern known as the "family cycle." This approach in practice tends to identify variations in family life on the basis of changes in family size caused by the arrival or departure of children. One of the most widely used constructs of the family cycle is the eight-stage model developed by Evelyn Duvall, which starts with "beginning" families (married couple without children) and ends with "aging" families (retirement to death of one or both spouses).[12] The stages in between are triggered by shifts in the size and composition of the household or changes in the social roles of the members within the family. To put the latter factor into operation, Duvall uses changes in the activities of the oldest child. For example, the entry of the oldest child into school marks the beginning of the fourth stage in Duvall's scheme.[13]

The family cycle provides a more dynamic portrayal of the individual family than either the concept of mean household size or generations. On certain questions, especially those related to changes in household composition or the activities of the oldest child, the family-cycle approach can be helpful. Yet, almost by definition, the family cycle is very narrow and constraining, since it cannot incorporate many other important facets of family life in its analysis. For example, information on the work experiences of parents is usually ignored. Furthermore, while the family cycle tries to deal with changes over time, it does not consider the importance of the timing or the sequence of events on the lives of the members of that family.

If the family-cycle model has limited utility today, it is even less applicable historically, when the larger number of children in each household makes any attempt to create stages of the family based on the arrival or departure of children extremely complex and unwieldy. The use of a family-cycle construct also makes less sense in studying the past, when the distinction between members and nonmembers of a household was less rigid than today. For example, the presence of boarders and lodgers as an integral part of the nineteenth-century American household necessitates a reconsideration of the usefulness of present-day family-cycle models such as the one proposed by Duvall.[14]

Historians like Tamara Hareven have recognized the limitations of the existing models of the family cycle for historical analysis and have called for the construction of a new one based on a redefinition of the stages to make them more relevant for recounting the lives of individuals in past societies.[15] Yet, any such effort is likely to be doomed by the conceptual difficulties inherent in trying to encapsulate the complexities of family life as a whole into a manageable set of sequential stages. In fact, despite the continued call for a more appropriate family-cycle model for the past, no one has produced a comprehensive alternative to the Duvall model. Rather than trying to develop an over-all model of the family cycle that can be used for any and all occasions, perhaps historians might more profitably investigate either a particular aspect of family life, such as marriage, or a series of events, such as the transition of children from the home to the school, using a more flexible approach—life-course analysis.[16]

Life-course analysis in some ways signifies a radical departure from earlier efforts to study the family. Rather than trying to categorize and analyze developments in the family as a whole, the life course focuses only on the more limited experiences of the members of that family. Life-course analysis, however, is derived from the earlier efforts to study life histories and pays particular attention to three components of an individual's life—approximate stage of biological development, age-related social roles, and historical position.

At the present time, the life-course approach to the study of family life has a strong following among American family historians—in large part due to the missionary work of Glen Elder, a sociologist who first studied the effects of the Depression of the 1930s upon children growing up during those years.[17] While several scholars have tried to define the life course, no one has really succeeded in succinctly capturing the essence of this approach. One of the best summaries of the life course is provided by Elder:

> The life course refers to pathways through the age-differentiated life-span, to social patterns in the timing, duration, spacing, and order of events; the timing of an event may be as consequential for life experience as whether the event occurs and the degree or type of change. Age differentiation is manifested in expectations and options that impinge on decision processes and the course of events that give shape to life stages, transitions, and turning points. Such differentiation is based in part on the social meanings of age and the biological facts of birth, sexual maturity, and death. These meanings have varied through social history and across cultures at points in time, as documented by evidence on socially recognized age categories, grades, and classes. . . . Over the life course, age differentiation also occurs through the interplay of demographic and economic processes, as in the relation between economic swings and the timing of family events. Sociocultural, demographic, and maternal factors are essential in a theory of life-course variation.[18]

The life-course approach is more a perspective than a formula on how to study the family. It sensitizes one to study particular events or transitions in the lives of family members from a broader perspective, while getting us away from the notion of the existence of any simple, sequential pattern of family stages. Since the life-course approach seeks to place the experiences of individuals within their historical setting, it is well suited for the analysis of family members in the past. Because the life-course approach recognizes the likelihood of changing definitions of social roles, over time, it does not suffer from the presentism evident in most other models of family life.

The life-course approach is the latest, and probably not the last, of our attempts to analyze the family within some analytical framework that is applicable to the past as well as the present. While it appears, over-all, to be a more sensible and useful perspective for studying family life than mean household size, generations, or the family cycle, it too has some glaring shortcomings. Since the life course approach is more of a perspective than an easily stated formula, how to put it into operation is often not clear. Furthermore, the very scope of this approach calls for extensive longitudinal data that are difficult to find in the past. While historians have developed—and should continue to develop—ways of using a life-course perspective based on more limited cross-sectional data, they should also be aware of the methodological limitations that this procedure inevitably places on their findings.[19]

Rather than continuing with a detailed methodological assessment of the study of the American family, let us turn to a more substantive discussion of some of the recent developments in American family history. The four aspects of family life that will be considered are childbearing, early child development, adolescence, and old age. While each of these phases or transitions can be seen from a life-course perspective, this essay will follow them on the basis of the major historiographical debates surrounding them today.

Childbearing

Studies of childbearing in the past did not arise from an interest in the family, but from a need to explain the decline in fertility in the West. As birth rates in the developing countries failed to decline, despite the introduction of modern contraceptive technology in the 1950s and 1960s, demographers and policy-makers began to search for the causes of the earlier decline in fertility in Western Europe, to see what conditions are necessary before a sustained decline in fertility can occur.

Though the study of the decline in fertility in the West was initiated by French and English historians, American scholars, particularly economic historians, joined that effort.[20] The demographic situation in the United States seemed particularly relevant for answering these questions, because the high birth rates in the seventeenth and early eighteenth centuries, similar to those in the developing countries today, began a sustained decline in the late eighteenth and early nineteenth centuries. Though the socio-economic conditions in early America are by no means identical to those in the developing countries, analysis of the interactions of demographic and socio-economic factors in the United States may yield useful insights into the factors necessary for a reduction in fertility.

Three major explanations have been offered to explain the decline in fertility in nineteenth-century America: urbanization and industrialization; the growing scarcity of readily available farmland; and the modernization of nineteenth-century society.[21]

The earliest explanation, still frequently cited, for the decline in fertility in Western Europe and the United States is urban and industrial development. In fact, some sociologists and demographers argue that urbanization and industrialization are necessary preconditions for any fertility decline.[22] Yet, the experience of demographic change in the United States challenges that assertion, because fertility declined in America before the nation was either urban or industrial. Furthermore, it is estimated that more than three-fourths of the decline in fertility during the transition period of 1810 to 1840 occurred in rural areas.[23]

With the failure of the urban-industrial explanation, attention shifted to explaining the reasons for the decline in rural fertility. Led by Yasukichi Yasuba, economic historians argued that the decreasing availability of nearby agricultural land caused farm families to reduce their childbearing. As farmers found it more difficult to find land for their sons, and as they became less dependent upon the labor of their sons to clear their own land, they wanted—and had—fewer children.[24] While this interpretation would seem to call for a comprehensive understanding of nineteenth-century farm life, it was conceptually developed and empirically tested almost entirely with aggregate state or county level data. Though this analysis has since been extended to households, very little effort is made to investigate the life course of members of farm families in order to understand the dynamics of their behavior.[25]

Economic historians continue to adhere to the land-availability explanation for the decline in fertility, but other scholars have seriously questioned both its conceptual and its empirical bases.[26] The model reflects a limited understanding of the behavior of farm families. Though the decreasing availability of nearby farmland made it more expensive for sons to acquire their own farms, it simultaneously raised the value of the father's farm and thereby allowed him, if he chose, to underwrite larger mortgages for his sons. The land availability model also presupposes a high degree of geographic stability among farmers that does not seem to have existed in the nineteenth century. Finally, many of the high correlations found between indices of land availability and fertility at the state or county level were based on methodologically flawed analyses. When these studies were redone, the explanatory strength of the land availability variable was greatly diminished and sometimes altogether eliminated.[27] Future attempts to explain the decline in rural fertility in nineteenth-century America will need to be tied more closely to an analysis of the experiences of farm families with particular attention paid to the process of transmitting property from fathers to sons.

Dissatisfaction with the urbanization-industrialization and the land availability explanations for the decline in fertility encouraged several scholars to consider whether broader changes throughout society, frequently labeled as "modernization," might account for that demographic shift. Their focus on changes within society as a whole, rather than just in the urban-industrial or rural areas, was reinforced by the realization that a parallel decline in birth rates occurred in both the countryside and the towns. [28]

The concept of modernization was widely used in sociology and demography during the 1950s and 1960s, but it was often dismissed because it was so imprecisely defined, mistakenly equated with urbanization and industrialization, or confused with the value-laden notion of progress. [29] More recent uses of the idea of modernization by social scientists, however, avoid most of the earlier shortcomings and demonstrate the utility of this approach for analyzing fertility behavior. [30] Unfortunately, many of the critics of modernization among historians tend to attack the dated work of the 1950s and 1960s without being aware of the recent refinements.

American society in the period from 1750 to 1850 was undergoing major changes that we might label as modernization and that may have encouraged couples to reduce their fertility. There were significant shifts, for example, in the extent and quality of education available to men and women in the antebellum period. The amount of information from newspapers and magazines grew rapidly, as well. America was becoming more commercially oriented, both in its agricultural and its industrial sectors. There was a growing feeling that an individual could and should improve his or her own life—an outgrowth of the reform movements of the early nineteenth century. Finally, the role and status of women in the nineteenth century changed dramatically, at least within their own homes, as middle-class white women attained more power and influence. [31]

Debates over the causes of the decline in fertility in early America continue, but a few tentative generalizations may be hazarded to answer some of the questions posed initially by policy-makers. The decline in fertility in America began well before the nation was either urbanized or industrialized, and therefore these two processes cannot be regarded as a necessary precondition. Second, since the decline in fertility occurred prior to the availability of modern contraceptives, it is necessary to focus on the motivation to reduce fertility, rather than just providing the technology to achieve that goal. Third, the decline in fertility in this country was not preceded or accompanied by a large drop in mortality and therefore does not fit the classic model of the "demographic transition." Fourth, once the decline in fertility began in the United States, areas with the highest levels of fertility experienced the most rapid rates of reduction. That tendency toward a convergence of birth rates after the onset of a fertility decline parallels changes in the developing countries today. Fifth, demographic studies of the United States and Western Europe suggest that fertility decline can occur in a wide variety of socio-economic settings. Finally, research on the past strongly points to the importance of cultural factors influencing the timing and extent of fertility decline. That suggests a possible link between modernization and the reduction of fertility in both the West historically and in the developing countries today.

Most of the historical work on childbearing in America has tried to explain the decline in fertility using aggregate statistics. As simple macro-level explanations such as urbanization-industrialization have proven to be inadequate, we need to re-examine the issue from the perspective of the individual family. Since childbearing is such an important factor influencing family life, historians of the family should begin to study not only the numbers of children born, but their timing and the impact that that may have had upon the lives of the other family members. Despite the extensive and sophisticated literature that we have on the demography of childbearing in the past, we are only beginning to explore this important topic from the perspective of the family.

Early Child Development

Most developmental psychologists assume that young children are the same throughout history. In other words, the basic characteristics of the child are unaltered by the environment. Furthermore, while there may be some variations in the ways children are dealt with across cultures and over time, most psychologists are unaware of these differences or appear to pay little attention to them.

This static image of the young child has been challenged by historians. Philippe Aries initiated the revision, by arguing that children in the Middle Ages were perceived and treated as miniature adults.[32] American historians quickly accepted the findings from Aries and maintained that young children in early America were also seen as miniature adults.[33] This interpretation has been sharply attacked by other historians who have shown, for example, that New England Puritans regarded and treated their young children as distinct from adults. The nature of the young child, as perceived by early Americans, however, was quite different from our image of youngsters today.[34] Colonial Americans assumed that children were capable of learning to read at very early ages. In fact, English educators such as John Locke simply assumed that "when he can talk, 'tis time he should begin to learn to read."[35] The New England Puritans particularly emphasized early education, for religious reasons —so that everyone should be able to read the Bible as soon as possible.[36] That stress on early intellectual development was reinforced by the establishment of infant schools in America in the 1820s. The infant school movement emphasized the importance of sending children under four years old to special schools where they were taught the alphabet and the fundamentals of reading. Though infant schools were initially intended for poor children, middle-class parents quickly began sending their children, as well, when the schools appeared to be highly successful. By the 1830s and 1840s, as many as 50 percent of all three-year-olds were attending public or private schools in many Massachusetts communities.[37] While many of us thought that Headstart was an entirely new undertaking, created in the 1960s to help disadvantaged children, infant schools predated that effort by more than a hundred years.

The image of the young child as intellectually capable of learning to read at such an early age, however, suffered a sudden and unexpected reversal. In the first third of the nineteenth century, there was another segment of the educational movement in Europe and America that stressed the need for the gradual and balanced development of children. These educators felt that children should not be subjected to rapid intellectual development before their minds had physically matured. When Dr. Amariah Brigham announced, in 1833, that early education overstimulated the child's mind and led to insanity, educators and parents reluctantly abandoned teaching young children to read.[38] Thus, during the decades of the 1840s and 1850s, there was a fundamental reorientation in America in the ways that young children were perceived and treated. This change was so successful that when the next effort was made to bring young children into schools called *kindergartens,* their education was cultivated through games, rather than intellectual activities such as reading.[39]

Another fundamental change that occurred in early America was a redefinition of the role of the father in the education and nurturing of his children. Today, most people assume that the mother is the primary and best caretaker of young children. In fact, the movie *Kramer vs. Kramer* startled some Americans by making them realize that among some divorced couples, the father is a more appropriate custodian of the child than the mother. The primacy of the mother's role has been reinforced by historians who point out that, in the nineteenth-century family, the mother was the central figure in the care and education of the young child.[40] Therefore, most of us are quite surprised to learn that, in seventeenth-century New England, the father played a key role in the upbringing of young children.

For Puritans, one of the essential responsibilities for the family was the religious instruction of its children and servants. The task of catechizing was entrusted to the head of the household—almost always the father. It was his duty, with assistance from the mother, to teach the young children and the servants in the household how to read the Bible and to supplement the religous instruction they received in church. To carry out that responsibility, it was necessary for the head of the household to be both literate and religious.[41] In the first two decades of settlement, most fathers were able to discharge their responsibilities, since they were literate and were members of the church. The importance of the father in the home was reinforced further by the suspicion that women like Anne Hutchinson were subverting the Commonwealth when they held religious meetings in the home.[42]

In the second half of the seventeenth century, however, the Puritans encountered an unexpected problem—while women continued joining the church, men did not. That sudden "feminization" of the church placed the ministers and the other leaders of that society in a difficult quandary. On the one hand, they regarded men as trustworthy and literate, but no longer religious enough to catechize the other members of the household. On the other hand, while women were religious, they were regarded as neither literate nor dependable enough to be entrusted with that important task.[43] The Puritans explored many different ways of dealing with that problem. They tried to have ministers visit the homes more frequently to help the parents, and they experimented with requiring school teachers to catechize the children. Yet their efforts were not successful. Instead, the role of women was gradually redefined, and women were given the responsibility for providing religious education to their children. Now it also became necessary for women to be literate in order to teach their children, and that led to an increase in the rate of literacy among New England women from 30 percent , between 1650 and 1670, to 50 percent, between 1787 and 1795.[44] It also encouraged ministers to reconsider the nature of men and women, as they stressed the special propensity of women for religion.[45] By the early decades of the nineteenth century, the role of women as primary caretakers and educators of young children was almost complete. No longer was it expected that the father would predominate or even share in the upbringing and education of young children.

The changing image and treatment of young children in America as well as the shifts in the responsibilities of fathers and mothers for children's care illustrates the sensitivity of even such fundamental aspects of family life to cultural and historical transformations. A relatively static and twentieth-century model of the family cycle, such as the one proposed by Duvall, simply is not able to cope with redefinitions of the characteristics of young children or their interactions with their parents.[46]

Adolescence

Compared to the research on early childhood in the past, the analysis of adolescence or youth is more plentiful and covers a wider variety of topics. In fact, when historians of the family mention children, they usually mean those in their teen-age years. To provide a sense of the richness and complexity of that topic, this section will explore three issues: the concept of adolescence, the transition from school to work, and the recent "epidemic" of adolescent pregnancy.

The idea of adolescence is well established among Americans today. Usually identified with emotional problems created by biological and maturational factors, adolescence is assumed to be nearly universal in our society.[47] Yet anthropologists like Margaret Mead demonstrated many years ago that adolescence as we know it today is not present in many other cultures.[48] Historians are debating whether adolescence existed in the past. Many scholars of the family see adolescence only as a late nineteenth- and early twentieth-century development. According to them, while the concept of youth as a general period of semidependency existed in the period from 1800 to 1875, nothing fully resembling adolescence today had emerged. Yet the transformation of America from an agricultural to an urban-industrial society during those years created sharp discontinuities in the lives of children and created the environment in which adolescence as a stage was to develop.[49] Others have challenged that interpretation by pointing out that, in the early eighteenth century, youths experienced many of the same emotional impulses and tensions that we associate with adolescence today.[50]

At the present time, there is no way to resolve this debate. Part of the disagreement may be caused by the ways in which the participants define the existence or lack of existence of a stage of adolescence. The contending authors also focus on very different time periods, so that they do not directly confront each others' evidence. Finally, the debate is still recent enough that much of the intensive primary work that needs to be completed simply has not yet been undertaken.

Another area that has attracted considerable attention is the study of the transition of youth from the school to the work-place in the nineteenth century. Most of these studies have been done by educational historians, who analyzed the reasons for some children's staying in school while others entered the labor force. Stephan Thernstrom provides an ethnic interpretation of school-leaving in nineteenth-century Newburyport, Massachusetts. He argues that the Irish removed their children from public schools so that the youngsters could earn money to help their families buy their own homes. Compared to other groups, the Irish were much more interested in acquiring their own homes. Thus, Irish parents sacrificed the long-term welfare of their children for their own short-term gains.[51] Michael Katz, on the other hand, rejects that ethnic interpretation and substitutes an economic explanation. Immigrant children were likely to enter the labor force earlier than native-born children, Katz suggests, not because of ethnic or cultural differences in values, but because immigrant families were more dependent upon their children for income just to survive.[52]

As long as historians relied only upon simple cross-tabulations of the relationship between ethnicity and school-leaving or occupation and school-leaving, it was difficult to ascertain the relative importance of these factors. With the introduction of multi-variate techniques, however, it has become possible to separate conceptually and empirically the relative effects of these two variables. Furthermore, improved methods of estimating family consumption needs as well as family income have made it easier to test for the economic pressures on families to send their children to work.[53] A study of school-leaving in eight Essex County, Massachusetts, towns in 1860 and 1880, using multiple classification analysis, found that both ethnicity and occupation of the head of the household affected the likelihood of a child's entering the labor force. Foreign-born children of white-collar and skilled workers, for example, attended school at substantially lower rates than did native-born children of semiskilled and unskilled workers.[54]

While considerable progress has been made in analyzing the ethnic and socio-economic backgrounds of students as they entered the labor force, we still need to examine this transition more closely. For instance, according to the manuscript censuses, most boys who left school acquired a job; many girls, however, apparently left school without obtaining any outside employment. Does that mean that the transition from school to work was different for males and females? Or is the distinction simply an artifact of the way nineteenth-century censuses recorded occupational information for teen-agers?[55] Similarly, did the performance of children in school affect their likelihood of leaving it? Were students who excelled in the classroom less likely to leave than those who did poorly?[56]

The final illustration of historical work on adolescence focuses on the more recent past. The Ninety-fifth Congress enacted the Adolescent Health, Services, and Pregnancy Prevention Act of 1978, to deal with the problem of adolescent childbearing. Both policy-makers and the news media emphasized the "epidemic" nature of adolescent pregnancy and assumed that this problem was a new and growing crisis that necessitated immediate federal action.[57] A more historical perspective, however, would have revealed that this concern was somewhat misdirected. Adolescent pregnancy actually peaked in the United States in 1957.[58] What should have been addressed, but was not, was the dramatic increase in *out-of-wedlock births* among adolescents, which costs taxpayers billions of dollars in welfare payments each year.[59] This problem is not the same as the problem of adolescent pregnancy and requires substantially different legislative action.

That example should alert us to the possibility that contemporary observers of family life can misinterpret events and therefore cannot always be trusted to provide reliable information about family behavior in the past or in the present.[60] Nevertheless, as the passage of the Adolescent Health, Services, and Pregnancy Prevention Act of 1978 and its successor in 1981, the Adolescent Family Life Bill, demonstrate, even misperceptions about family life can be very important in motivating people to undertake courses of action that they might otherwise have rejected. Thus, whenever possible, historians should analyze the intersections between the public and private perceptions of the family and the actual characteristics and experiences of those families, rather than assuming that knowledge of either the attitudinal or the behavioral component is adequate by itself.

Old Age

Contemporary events and concerns often help to determine which issues historians pursue. Investigations of problems of the elderly, for instance, were not undertaken by historians until the 1970s, when interest and funding for research on this topic blossomed. As a result, during the last five years we have explored in detail the role and status of the elderly in the past. Recent studies of the elderly in early America exemplify the difficulties and opportunities whenever one is trying to analyze a hitherto neglected facet of the life course.

Initial studies of the elderly in the colonial period tended to portray them in static terms—usually stressing their high status and the kind and respectful treatment they received.[61] Yet, a closer examination of their lives reveals a more complex and ambiguous existence. While the elderly in early America were revered and venerated if they were physically fit and financially independent, they were treated badly if they were incapacitated and dependent upon their neighbors.[62] Second, the situation of the elderly changed, over time. Whereas the first generation of Puritan ministers, for example, fared well in the New World in their old age, their successors, on the whole, did not do as well. Thus, the idealized image of the elderly in colonial society may be the result of the experiences of the first generation and the expectations and frustrations of those who followed in their footsteps.[63]

The study of elderly ministers in colonial America also raises an important methodological issue in the use of life-course analysis in the past. Ministers in the seventeenth and eighteenth centuries remained in office until they either died or were too incapacitated to preach. The idea of retirement from office at a particular age was unknown.[64] Since many of these ministers survived into their seventies and eighties, how well were they able to function? The answer to that question depends in large measure on what we think most individuals can perform as they age. Rather than turning to the biological or psychological literature on the aging process, most of us probably would guess what it is like to function as an elderly person in our society today. Often, our image of the capabilities of the elderly is based on nothing more than knowing the way our own parents or grandparents behaved as they aged. The life-course approach suggests that we go beyond our implicit assumptions of the ways individuals age and at least consult the existing literature on the aging process for a comprehensive and more informed perspective. But can historians simply use contemporary studies of the elderly to make inferences about them in the past? Investigations of the elderly today, for example, suggest a substantial diminution of physical and mental abilities as most individuals age.[65] Are we to assume, therefore, that that is an invariant pattern that can be applied across all cultures and time periods, so that the capabilities of sixty- or seventy-year-olds in seventeenth-century New England are the same as that of their counterparts today? Or is the functioning of elderly people significantly affected by the social environment in which they live?

Historians need to grapple with such fundamental issues in order to recreate and comprehend the lives of our ancestors. It appears that the level of functioning of the elderly is affected by the expectations that people and institutions have of them. Elderly people who go into nursing homes today tend to deteriorate steadily, both mentally and physically. Part of the explanation is that most nursing homes, which are badly understaffed, reinforce dependent behavior in the elderly, because it takes much more time and effort to encourage patients to make more independent responses. In experimental circumstances, where the elderly in nursing homes are encouraged or even required to take care of themselves as much as possible, there is less physical and mental deterioration.[66] One may speculate, then, that in societies that continue to treat and expect the elderly to be fully functioning and productive members as they age, the physical and mental capacities of the elderly will be higher than in the United States today, where the elderly often face mandatory retirement and the feeling of uselessness. While elderly ministers in colonial America undoubtedly experienced a loss of ability to function over time, the extent of it was probably less than suggested by contemporary studies of the aged in America. While there are no easy ways to resolve this problem, historians should not simply rely on their own personal experiences for assessing the characteristics of aging or accept uncritically the findings from the biological and social sciences that are often based only on an analysis of Americans today.

While there is disagreement over the role and status of the elderly in colonial America, there is even more debate over the approximate time when Americans began to view individuals negatively simply on the basis of their age. David Fischer identifies the growth in negative attitudes and treatment of the elderly with the late eighteenth and early nineteenth centuries.[67] Andrew Achenbaum, on the other hand, sees this shift occurring in the last decades of the nineteenth century.[68] Barbara Rosenkrantz and I date the transition around the mid-nineteenth century.[69] One of the reasons for this continued debate is that historians relying on literary materials can easily disagree amongst themselves, since each one can select a different set of quotations that justify his or her position. Thus, both Achenbaum and Fischer read the nineteenth-century popular magazine, Littell's Living Age, but arrived at very different interpretations of it.[70] What is needed is a more systematic approach to the study of popular literature, which can pinpoint more precisely the time when shifts occurred in the portrayal of the elderly, over time. A recent content analysis of the images of the elderly in Littell's Living Age, from 1845 to 1872, revealed that though the aged were not seen as useful and beneficial as suggested by Achenbaum, neither were they as negatively portrayed during those years as Fischer had argued.[71] Historians of the family should experiment with new and more systematic ways of assessing the manner in which Americans not only treated the elderly, but also the ways in which they perceived them.

* * *

The family in American history is finally receiving the scholarly attention that it deserves. During the next few years, some of the most exciting and challenging work in social history will be done in this area. While serious methodological problems remain to be solved, considerable progress has already been made toward unraveling the intricacies of family life in the past. The future of the family as an important topic of historical research seems assured, but its incorporation within the profession as a whole still remains to be determined. One measure of the larger success of this new field will be the rate at which the issues that it raises and the answers that it provides find their way into the more traditional American history survey courses and textbooks and into the interpretive programs and exhibits of historical agencies and museums.

Notes

I am indebted to the John Simon Guggenheim Memorial Foundation for a fellowship that provided support for the research on which this essay is based.
1. There are several other surveys of the state of family history today. For example, see Carl N. Degler, "Women and the Family," in *The Past Before Us: Contemporary Historical Writing in the United States*, edited by Michael Kammen (Ithaca: Cornell University Press, 1980), pp. 308–326; Maris A. Vinovskis, "From Household Size to the Life Course: Some Observations on Recent Trends in Family History," *American Behavioral Scientist* 21 (1977): 263–287; Tamara K. Hareven, "The History of the Family as an Interdisciplinary Field," *Journal of Interdisciplinary History* 2 (1971): 399–414; Daniel Blake Smith, "The Study of the Family in Early America: Trends, Problems, and Prospects," *William and Mary Quarterly*, 3rd ser., 39 (1982): 3–28.
2. Arthur W. Calhoun, *A Social History of the American Family from Colonial Times to the Present*, 3 vols. (1917–1919; reprint ed., New York: Barnes and Noble, 1960); Alice Morse Earle, *Child Life in Colonial Days* (New York: Macmillan, 1899).
3. Edmund Morgan, *The Puritan Family: Religion and Domestic Relations in Seventeenth-Century New England*, rev. ed. (New York: Harper and Row, 1966).
4. John Demos, *A Little Commonwealth: Family Life in Plymouth Colony* (New York: Oxford University Press, 1970); Philip J. Greven, Jr., *Four Generations: Population, Land, and Family in Colonial Andover, Massachusetts* (Ithaca: Cornell University Press, 1970); Kenneth A. Lockridge, *A New England Town: The First Hundred Years* (New York: W. W. Norton & Company, Inc., 1970).
5. Carl N. Degler, *At Odds: Women and the Family in America from the Revolution to the Present* (New York: Oxford University Press, 1980).
6. Peter Laslett, editor, *Household and Family in Past Time* (Cambridge: Cambridge University Press, 1972).
7. Tamara K. Hareven, "The Family as Process: The Historical Study of the Family Cycle,"

Journal of Social History 7 (1974): 322–329; Michael B. Katz, *The People of Hamilton, Canada West: Family and Class in a Mid-Nineteenth-Century City* (Cambridge: Harvard University Press, 1975); Vinovskis, "Household Size to Life Course."

8. Lutz K. Berkner, "The Use and Misuse of Census Data for the Historical Analysis of Family Structure," *Journal of Interdisciplinary History* 4 (1975): 721–738.

9. Greven, *Four Generations*.

10. Vinovskis, "Household Size to Life Course."

11. Vinovskis, "Household Size to Life Course."

12. Evelyn M. Duvall, *Family Development* (Philadelphia: J. B. Lippincott, 1967).

13. Duvall's scheme has been extended to cover not only changes in the oldest child, but the youngest as well. This led to a twenty-four-stage model of the family cycle, rather than an eight-stage one. Roy Rodgers, *Improvements in the Construction and Analysis of Family Life Cycle Categories* (Kalamazoo: Western Michigan University Press, 1962).

14. John Modell and Tamara K. Hareven, "Urbanization and the Malleable Household: An Examination of Boarding and Lodging in American Families," in *Family and Kin in Urban Communities, 1700–1930*, edited by Tamara K. Hareven (New York: New Viewpoints, 1977), pp. 164–186.

15. Hareven, "Family as Process."

16. Vinovskis, "Household Size to Life Course."

17. Glen Elder, Jr., *Children of the Great Depression: Social Change in Life Experience* (Chicago: University of Chicago Press, 1974).

18. Glen Elder, Jr., "Family History and the Life Course," in *Transitions: The Family and the Life Course in Historical Perspective*, edited by Tamara K. Hareven (New York: Academic Press, 1978), pp. 21–22.

19. An interesting effort to use cross-sectional data to study life course transitions is by John Modell, Frank Furstenberg, Jr., and Theodore Hershberg, "Social Change and Transitions to Adulthood in Historical Perspective," *Journal of Family History* 1 (1976): 7–32. For a critique of this approach, see Vinovskis, "Household Size to Life Course."

20. For reviews of the field of American historical demography, see Kenneth A. Lockridge, "Historical Demography," in *The Future of History*, edited by Charles F. Delzell (Nashville: Vanderbilt University Press, 1977), pp. 53–64; Allan N. Sharlin, "Historical Demography as History and Demography," *American Behavioral Scientist* 21 (1977): 245–262; Maris A. Vinovskis, "Recent Trends in American Historical Demography: Some Methodological and Conceptual Considerations," *Annual Review of Sociology* 4 (1978): 603–627. For a collection of recent work in this field, see Maris A. Vinovskis, editor, *Studies in American Historical Demography* (New York: Academic Press, 1979).

21. There are several other explanations for the decline in fertility. For a more detailed discussion of the alternative theories, see Maris A. Vinovskis, "The Fertility Decline in the West as a Model for Developing Countries Today: The Case of Nineteenth-Century America," in *Fertility Decline in the Less Developed Countries*, edited by Nick Eberstadt (New York: Praeger, 1981), pp. 228–253.

22. J. Potter, "The Growth of Population in America, 1700–1860," in *Population in History: Essays in Historical Demography*, edited by D. V. Glass and D. E. C. Eversley (Chicago: Aldine Publishing Co., 1965), pp. 631–688.

23. Colin Forster and G. S. L. Tucker, *Economic Opportunity and White American Fertility Ratios: 1800–1860* (New Haven: Yale University Press, 1972).

24. Yasukichi Yasuba, *Birth Rates of the White Population in the United States, 1800–1860: An Economic Study*, Johns Hopkins University Studies in History and Political Science 79, no. 2 (Baltimore: Johns Hopkins University Press, 1962).

25. For an analysis of this issue at the household level, see Richard A. Easterlin,

George Alter, and Gretchen A. Condran, "Farms and Farm Families in Old and New Areas: The Northern States in 1860," in *Family and Population in Nineteenth-Century America*, edited by Tamara K. Hareven and Maris A. Vinovskis (Princeton: Princeton University Press, 1978), pp. 22–84.

26. Allan G. Bogue, "Comment on Paper by Easterlin," *Journal of Economic History* 36 (1976): 76–81; Maris A. Vinovskis, *Fertility in Massachusetts from the Revolution to the Civil War* (New York: Academic Press, 1981), pp. 73–88.

27. Maris A. Vinovskis, "Socio-Economic Determinants of Interstate Fertility Differentials in the United States in 1850 and 1860," *Journal of Interdisciplinary History* 6 (1976): 374–396.

28. Vinovskis, *Fertility in Massachusetts*; Robert V. Wells, "Family History and Demographic Transition," *Journal of Social History* 9 (1975): 1–20; Maris A. Vinovskis, *Demographic History and the World Population Crisis* (Worcester, Mass.: Chester Bland-Dwight E. Lee Lectures in History, Clark Press, 1976).

29. For an introduction to this issue, see Richard Bendix, "The Comparative Analysis of Historical Change," in *Social Theory and Economic Change*, edited by Tom Burns and S. B. Saul (London: Tavistock Publications, 1967), pp. 67–86; Neil J. Smelser, *Essays in Sociological Explanation* (Englewood Cliffs, N.J.: Prentice-Hall, 1968), pp. 125–146.

30. Karen A. Miller and Alex Inkeles, "Modernity and Acceptance of Family Limitation in Four Developing Countries," *Journal of Social Issues* 30 (1974): 167–188.

31. For a more detailed discussion of these changes, see Vinovskis, *Fertility in Massachusetts*, pp. 117–144; Richard D. Brown, *Modernization: The Transformation of American Life, 1600–1865* (New York: Norton, 1976).

32. Philippe Aries, *Centuries of Childhood: A Social History of Family Life*, translated by Robert Baldick (New York: Vintage Books, 1962).

33. John Demos, "The American Family in Past Time," *American Scholar* 43 (1974): 428; Michael Zuckerman, *Peaceable Kingdoms: New England Towns in the Eighteenth Century* (New York: Alfred A. Knopf, 1970), p. 73.

34. David E. Stannard, "Death and the Puritan Child," in *Death in America*, edited by David E. Stannard (Philadelphia: University of Pennsylvania Press, 1975), pp. 9–29; Carl F. Kaestle and Maris A. Vinovskis, "From Apron Strings to ABCs: Parents, Children, and Schooling in Nineteenth-Century Massachusetts," in *Turning Points: Historical and Sociological Essays on the Family*, edited by John Demos and Susan Spence Boocock (Chicago: University of Chicago Press, 1978), pp. S39–S80.

35. John Locke, *Some Thoughts Concerning Education*, abridged and edited by F. W. Garforth (Woodbury, N.Y.: Barron, 1964), p. 186.

36. Gerald F. Moran and Maris A. Vinovskis, "The Puritan Family and Religion: A Critical Reappraisal," *William and Mary Quarterly*, 3rd ser., 39 (1982): 29–63.

37. Kaestle and Vinovskis, "Apron Strings to ABCs."

38. Dean May and Maris A. Vinovskis, "A Ray of Millennial Light: Early Education and Social Reform in the Infant School Movement in Massachusetts, 1826–1840," in *Family and Kin in Urban Communities, 1700–1930*, edited by Tamara K. Hareven (New York: New Viewpoints, 1977), pp. 62–99.

39. Kaestle and Vinovskis, "Apron Springs to ABCs."

40. Anne L. Kuhn, *The Mother's Role in Childhood Education* (New Haven: Yale University Press, 1947).

41. Kaestle and Vinovskis, "Apron Strings to ABCs"; Moran and Vinovskis, "Puritan Family and Religion."

42. Lyle Koehler, *A Search for Power: The "Weaker Sex" in Seventeenth-Century New England* (Urbana: University of Illinois Press, 1980).

43. On the feminization of the New England churches, see Gerald F. Moran, " 'Sisters' in Christ: Women and the Church in Seventeenth-Century New England," in *Women in American Religion*, edited by Janet Wilson James (Philadelphia: University of Pennsylvania Press, 1980), pp. 47–65.

44. Kenneth A. Lockridge, *Literacy in Colonial New England: An Inquiry into the Social Context of Literacy in the Early Modern West* (New York: W. W. Norton & Company, Inc., 1974).

45. Laurel Thatcher Ulrich, "Virtuous Women Found: New England Ministerial Literature, 1668–1735," in *Women in American Religion*, edited by Janet Wilson James (Philadelphia: University of Pennsylvania Press, 1980), pp. 67–88.

46. Kuhn, *Mother's Role in Childhood Education*.

47. For an introduction to the issue of adolescence today, see Sigmund E. Dragastin and Glen H. Elder, Jr., editors, *Adolescence in the Life Cycle, Psychological Change and Social Context* (New York: John Wiley, 1975).

48. Margaret Mead, *Coming of Age in Samoa* (New York: Morrow, 1961).

49. John Demos and Virginia Demos, "Adolescence in Historical Perspective," *Journal of Marriage and the Family* 31 (1969): 632–638.

50. N. Ray Hiner, "Adolescence in Eighteenth-Century America," *History of Childhood Quarterly* 3 (1975): 253–280.

51. Stephan Thernstrom, *Poverty and Progress: Social Mobility in a Nineteenth-Century City* (Cambridge: Harvard University Press, 1964).

52. Michael B. Katz and Ian E. Davey, "School Attendance and Early Industrialization in a Canadian City: A Multivariate Analysis," *History of Education Quarterly* 18 (1978): 292.

53. Carl F. Kaestle and Maris A. Vinovskis, "From Fireside to Factory: School Entry and School Leaving in Nineteenth-Century Massachusetts," in *Transitions: The Family and the Life Course in Historical Perspective*, edited by Tamara K. Hareven (New York: Academic Press, 1978), pp. 135–185; Michael B. Katz and Ian E. Davey, "Youth and Early Industrialization in a Canadian City," in *Turning Points: Historical and Sociological Essays on the Family*, edited by John Demos and Susan Spence Boocock (Chicago: University of Chicago Press, 1978), pp. S81–S119.

54. Kaestle and Vinovskis, "Fireside to Factory"; Carl F. Kaestle and Maris A. Vinovskis, *Education and Social Change in Nineteenth-Century Massachusetts* (Cambridge: Cambridge University Press, 1980).

55. Kaestle and Vinovskis, *Education and Social Change*.

56. Very little effort has been made by any educational historians to investigate the activities of children in the classroom. Two scholars who are now looking at this issue are Joel Perlman (Rhode Island schools) and David Angus (Michigan schools).

57. Maris A. Vinovskis, "An 'Epidemic' of Adolescent Pregnancy? Some Historical Considerations," *Journal of Family History* 6 (1981): 205–230.

58. U.S. Congress, House, Select Committee on Population, *Fertility and Contraception in the United States*, 95th Cong., 2d sess., Serial B (1978).

59. For example, Kristin Moore estimated that the federal government disbursed $4.65 billion through Aid to Families with Dependent Children (AFDC) in 1975 to households containing women who bore their first child while teen-agers. (Vinovskis, "Epidemic of Adolescent Pregnancy.")

60. Another example of this type of misperception is on the issue of death in colonial America. Whereas adult New Englanders thought that their life expectancy was very short, in actuality it was quite long—especially in rural areas. (Maris A. Vinovskis, "Angels' Heads and Weeping Willows: Death in Early America," *Proceedings of the American Antiquarian Society* 86 [1976]: 273–302.)

61. David H. Fischer, *Growing Old in America*, expanded edition (New York: Oxford University Press, 1978).

62. John Demos, "Old Age in Early New England," in *Turning Points: Historical and Sociological Essays on the Family*, edited by John Demos and Susan Spence Boocock (Chicago: University of Chicago Press, 1978), pp. S248–S287.

63. Maris A. Vinovskis, " 'Aged Servants of the Lord': Changes in the Status and Treatment of Elderly Ministers in Colonial America," in *Aging from Birth to Death: Socio-Temporal Perspectives*, edited by Matilda Riley and Michael Teitelbaum (forthcoming).

64. Vinovskis, " 'Aged Servants of the Lord.' "

65. On the biological and psychological aspects of aging, see Caleb E. Finch and Leonard Hayflick, editors, *Handbook of the Biology of Aging* (New York: Van Nostrand Reinhold, 1977); James E. Birren and K. Warner Schaie, editors, *Handbook of the Psychology of Aging* (New York: Van Nostrand Reinhold, 1977).

66. E. M. Barton, M. M. Baltes, and M. J. Orzech, "On the Etiology of Dependence in Older Nursing Home Residents During Morning Care: The Role of Staff Behavior," *Journal of Personality and Social Psychology* 38 (1980) 423–431.

67. Fischer, *Growing Old*.

68..W. Andrew Achenbaum, *Old Age in the New Land: The American Experience Since 1790* (Baltimore: Johns Hopkins University Press, 1978).

69. Barbara G. Rosenkrantz and Maris A. Vinovskis, "The Invisible Lunatics: Old Age and Insanity in Mid-Nineteenth-Century Massachusetts," in *Aging and the Elderly: Humanistic Perspectives in Gerontology*, edited by Stuart F. Spicker, et al. (Atlantic Highlands, N.J.: Humanities Press, 1978), pp. 95–125.

70. Fischer, *Growing Old*; Achenbaum, *Old Age*.

71. Jane Range and Maris A. Vinovskis, "Images of Elderly in Popular Literature: A Content Analysis of Littell's *Living Age*, 1845–1882," *Social Science History* 5 (1981): 123–170.

Suggestions for Additional Reading

Achenbaum, W. Andrew. *Old Age in the New Land: The American Experience*. Baltimore: Johns Hopkins University Press, 1978.

> A scholarly and well-written account of our changing attitudes and behavior toward the elderly during the nineteenth and twentieth centuries.

Bane, Mary Jo. *Here to Stay: American Families in the Twentieth Century*. New York: Basic Books, 1976.

> A popular scholarly treatise on changes in the American family during the twentieth century; emphasizes the strengths of the modern family.

Brim, Orville G., Jr., and Jerome Kagan, editors. *Constancy and Change in Human Development*. Cambridge: Harvard University Press, 1980.

> A good collection of essays on the most recent scholarly trends in the study of individual development; emphasizes the importance of changes throughout the entire life course.

Cott, Nancy F. *The Bonds of Womanhood: "Woman's Sphere" in New England, 1780–1835*. New Haven: Yale University Press, 1978.

> One of the best analyses of the transition in the role of women from the colonial period to the nineteenth century

Degler, Carl N. *At Odds: Women and the Family in America from the Revolution to the Present*. New York: Oxford University Press, 1978.

> The best and latest synthesis of recent scholarship on the American family in the nineteenth century.

Demos, John. *A Little Commonwealth: Family Life in Plymouth Colony*. New York: Oxford University Press, 1970.

> Still the best analysis of the colonial family in New England.

Demos, John, and Susan Spence Boocock, editors. *Turning Points: Historical and Sociological Essays on the Family*. Chicago: University of Chicago Press, 1978.

> Useful collection of scholarly essays by historians and other social scientists on the nature of the family in the past.

Dublin, Thomas. *Women at Work: The Transformation of Work and Community in Lowell, Massachusetts, 1826–1860*. New York: Columbia University Press, 1979.

> First-rate discussion of the changes in the role of women in the Lowell textile mills in the antebellum period.

Elder, Glen H., Jr. *Children of the Great Depression: Social Change in Life Experience*. Chicago: University of Chicago Press, 1974.

> A methodologically sophisticated but somewhat difficult-to-read analysis of the impact of the Depression on the lives of young children and families.

Gordon, Michael, editor. *The American Family in Social Historical Perspective*, 2nd ed. New York: St. Martin's Press, 1978.

> The best collection of readings in the history of the American family.

Gordon, Michael. *The American Family: Past, Present, and Future*. New York: Random House, 1978.

> A good textbook on the American family; utilizes and emphasizes recent scholarship on the history of the family.

Gutman, Herbert G. *The Black Family in Slavery and Freedom, 1750–1925*. New York: Pantheon, 1976.

> A very useful analysis of the changes in the black family in the past.

Hareven, Tamara K., editor. *Transitions: The Family and the Life Course in Historical Perspective*. New York: Academic Press, 1978.

Some of the most methodologically sophisticated essays on the study of the nineteenth-century family, using manuscript census data.

Hareven, Tamara K., and Maris A. Vinovskis, editors. *Family and Population in Nineteenth-Century America*. Princeton: Princeton University Press, 1978.

Series of demographic and economic essays on the nineteenth-century family.

Kaestle, Carl F., and Maris A. Vinovskis. *Education and Social Change in Nineteenth-Century Massachusetts*. Cambridge, England: Cambridge University Press, 1980.

An analysis of changes in nineteenth-century education and in the public perception of young children.

Kett, Joseph K. *Rites of Passage: Adolescence in America: 1790 to the Present*. New York: Basic Books, 1977.

A good over-all summary and analysis of changes in youth in the nineteenth and twentieth centuries.

Mohr, James C. *Abortion in America: The Origins and Evolution of National Policy*. New York: Oxford University Press, 1978.

An analysis of changes in American attitudes and practices in regard to abortions in the nineteenth century.

Stannard, David E. *The Puritan Way of Death: A Study of Religion, Culture, and Social Change*. New York: Oxford University Press, 1977.

A highly readable and excellent study of death in colonial America.

Stone, Lawrence. *The Family, Sex and Marriage in England, 1500–1800*. New York: Harper and Row, 1977.

A very scholarly and detailed analysis of the English family that provides a good European background for the study of the American family.

Vinovskis, Maris A., editor.*Studies in American Historical Demography*. New York: Academic Press, 1979.

A collection of twenty-five of the major articles on American historical demography.

A worker at the Wilmington Malleable Iron Company in Delaware paused long enough to have his portrait taken about 1912.

7

Workers and Work in America: The New Labor History

David Brody

THE ATTENTIVE READER, having come thus far into this volume, will already have acquired a fair grasp of the so-called new social history. He or she will know something of its broader contours and will have explored its development in American ethnic history, the family, women, rural life, and the city. The history of workers in America should be seen as one dimension of all those subjects of social history already encountered in this book. When one looks at urban history or at the history of the family or of women, one is in fact also looking in large degree at the history of workers, as well; so the subject matter of this essay will be familiar in some ways, because it has already been dealt with from other avenues. The study of labor history has a distinctive historiography, however, that sets it somewhat apart from other aspects of American social history. In this essay, I would like to start with some accounting of the historical study of workers as it developed in America, and then proceed to trace its recent evolution into a thriving part of the new social history.

The spirit of discovery is strongly felt by scholars seeking to reconstruct the historical experience of ordinary people. They know they are breaking into fresh ground and doing so by means of research methods unknown to earlier generations of historians. That sense of discovery applies to modern labor historians also, and for the same reasons. But labor history is not a new field. It has a long and honorable tradition going back into the late nineteenth century. The scope of that earlier history, however, was very narrowly defined: only the institutions of labor—trade unions, collective bargaining, politics, public policy—were proper subjects of study. In the seminars out of which this book grew, a good deal of debate took place about ways to define the "new" social history. For labor history, what is "new" is always quite clear. It is the determined effort to move beyond the study of institutions to the study of workers themselves. Other fields, such as urban and political history, have gone through a similar struggle, but none has had to battle against so entrenched an institutional perspective as that which dominated American labor history for so many years.

The roots of the subject go back to a great struggle in the late nineteenth century, between two schools of economics. The classical school, dominant in the academies, was highly abstract and deductive. It drew on a set of eternal principles and operated on the assumption of perfectly competitive markets. From this elaborate theoretical framework came highly conservative conclusions. Classical economics argued against any intrusion on the natural operation of the marketplace—against any regulation of business activity, against legislative protection of workers and consumers, and, above all, against trade unions and collective bargaining. In response, there sprang up a rival school, whose intellectual origins derived from the German universities that American graduate students began to attend in growing numbers after the Civil War. The focus was on empirical research, on the study of the economy as it actually operated. From the 1870s onward, bureaus of labor statistics began to gather quantitative evidence, and economic institutions came under closer scrutiny. This "revolt against formalism," as the philosopher Morton G. White has termed it, was in part an intellectual struggle, an attempt to redefine the subject of economics, and in part it was political, an effort to legitimize trade unionism and encourage social and labor legislation. With the formation of the American Economic Association in 1886, this new institutional economics came of age.

Central to its empirical approach was historical study. That was especially stressed by the Germans, who indeed called themselves historical economists. History was one of the crucial ways of breaking out of the abstractions of the classical economics, of creating an empirical base for understanding the way economic systems operated and changed, over time. From the 1880s onward, the historical study of labor began, rooted not in the historical profession that was simultaneously emerging, but in institutional economics. The pioneering scholar was John R. Commons, who settled at the University of Wisconsin. Although Commons did a good deal of contemporary labor economics, his orientation was primarily historical. He began by gathering together the records of workers in America, a task wholly neglected until that time. This enormous undertaking resulted in the publication of the multivolume *A Documentary*

History of Industrial Society. With that as a base, Commons and his students launched the first attempt to write a serious history of American workers. *A History of Labour in the United States,* published in four volumes from 1918 to 1935, remains today the fundamental account, the most comprehensive treatment of the American labor movement in its formative years. [1] Although other centers of research sprung up, most notably at Johns Hopkins, Commons's pre-eminence never wavered, and his numerous students built up what became known as the Wisconsin school of labor history.

Its practitioners were labor economists, and the training they received defined the way they would approach history. They were interested almost exclusively in labor institutions. A huge monographic literature grew up dealing with the histories of individual unions or cataloguing particular structural features of internal union government and variations among collective-bargaining practices. The narrative histories, when they were undertaken, tended to be dismal recitations of events. In part, that was because the labor economists had no literary traditions on which to draw; but in part, too, it was a reflection of the way they defined their subject. Institutions, not people, concerned them, and neither the inherent drama nor the underlying social forces tended to find much place in their accounts. There was also a deep conservatism in the historical work of the labor economists. Their institutional approach had been devised to justify the trade-union movement, and, having accomplished that, they became its defenders. It is perhaps inherent in an institutional approach not to raise larger questions about what is being studied. Many of the economist-historians, too, were practitioners in the field, serving as arbitrators, labor-relations consultants, and government experts. The best of them, like Philip A. Taft, saw the subject very much from the inside. They knew well many labor leaders, and they understood in their bones the way trade unions operated. Such intimacy could produce deeply informed history; it did not lend itself to critical or detached assessment. [2]

The Wisconsin school was singularly fortunate to have, in the person of Selig Perlman, a creative scholar capable of working out the theoretical underpinnings of the Commons approach. Perlman was an exceptional figure in the Commons circle. He had been a youthful Marxist in Europe; he was widely read in European history; he had a speculative cast of mind and, perhaps not incidentally, a quite elegant writing style. In *A Theory of the Labor Movement* (1928), Perlman argued that American workers were "job conscious," that is, that their collective activity sprang from a desire to protect interests on the job and, above all, to defend their job rights in what they saw as a world of restricted opportunity. Job consciousness was by no means unique to America; it was felt no less by European workers. What was exceptional about the American trade-union movement was that it genuinely expressed the job consciousness of its followers. The underlying point had already been addressed by V. I. Lenin, who had argued that, without the leadership of a vanguard of intellectuals, workers were incapable of rising above trade-union consciousness. The distinctive feature of American trade unionism, answered Perlman, was precisely that it was resistant to such penetration. It had not permitted outsiders—intellectuals, radicals, professors—to take over the movement and redirect it toward class struggle and Socialist politics. Although not entirely clear about the sources of this remarkable immunity, Perlman did know that it fostered an "organic" labor movement, one that arose from and truly expressed the will of the working class.[3] Perlman's analysis obviously rested on assumptions about the character of American workers; but that had never been the focus of his research— he had merely reasoned back from his conception of job-conscious unionism and from a sensitive reading of the American conditions acting on labor. While acknowledging that flaw, Perlman's students never moved to correct it. *A Theory of the Labor Movement* was a powerful intellectual defense of the Wisconsin school, but not one calculated to lift its focus beyond the categories of labor institutionalism.

At the time that I was a history graduate student in the 1950s, the Commons tradition was still very much alive and flourishing. Virtually all the work in labor history was being done by labor economists. In 1955, Lloyd Ulman published his brilliant and encyclopedic *The Rise of the National Trade Union;* in 1957 and 1959, Philip Taft published his definitive two-volume history of the American Federation of Labor; and the next year, Walter Galenson brought out his detailed history of the launching of the industrial-union movement, *The CIO Challenge to the AFL.*[4] The Harvard Labor-Management History Series, under the editorship of the eminent labor economist John T. Dunlop, was turning out a steady stream of books. After I finished my thesis in 1958, Dunlop asked me to write a book for the series.[5] In a backhanded way, the invitation said a good deal about the labor history field. It was an experiment, Dunlop told me. He was curious to see what a *historian* might do with the subject he had in mind—a history of trade unionism in the meat industry. That the notion was novel was evident to me due to the trouble my revised thesis was having at the Harvard Press. The labor economists who read my study of steelworkers before the 1930s could not see what contribution I was making to their field. It was, in fact, because of stalemated reviews (I think my manuscript received a record number of readings) that Dunlop became familiar with my work. As a syndic of Harvard Press, he had been called on to decide the issue—which he did, in my favor.

These small events, besides what they revealed of John Dunlop's lively and generous mind, also reflected important changes going on in labor economics and in history. Among younger economists like Gary Becker, the institutional approach was giving way to more theoretical concerns. Human resources had a great vogue in the 1960s, and neoclassical market analysis dominates labor economics today. Although it left behind a rear guard of institutionalists—Taft was churning out books until his death in 1976—that shift opened up the field of labor history. At the same time, the historical profession was changing. History had traditionally been a genteel field, and it had not treated workers as a proper subject of study. When the profession opened up, it did so by recruiting from rural America. It is no accident that the frontier and section, not the city, dominated American historiography for the first third of the twentieth century. The civil rights struggle of the last twenty years has tended to obscure the extent to which American society had been broadly discriminatory in earlier years. Among other things, the elite white-collar occupations had been reserved for white Anglo-Saxon males: not only blacks and women but Catholics and Jews need not apply. A survey of the roster of the American Association of University Professors for that period reveals few women, but more women than people of recent immigrant extraction. As those barriers fell, after World War II, the sons of immigrants and working people entered the historical profession, and some of them began exploring questions related to their own backgrounds, including the history of workers.

No bell struck. The 1950s was an age of political quiescence, of consensus. Not much encouragement could be expected from senior scholars; nor was a labor history topic likely to open any doors in the lean job market of those years. I was perhaps more fortunate than others, in having as my mentor at Harvard Oscar Handlin, the pioneering scholar in immigration history. Even so, I was the only member of my seminar to work on a labor history dissertation, and only two or three of Handlin's long line of students ever did so.[6] Here and there across the country, a scattering of other graduate students were moving in the same direction as well. The members of that first generation—Herbert Gutman, Melvyn Dubofsky, David Montgomery—each had his own intellectual odyssey. My own began with an interest in mass thinking, from a reading of Walter Lippmann, and in wartime repression, from a reading of Katherine Ann Porter's novella *Pale Horse, Pale Rider*. What intrigued me most was the way these issues related to the experience of immigrant workers. Other neophyte labor historians almost certainly shared a similar identification with working-class life. And each one, as he launched his research, was also launching an assault on the institutionalism of the old labor history.

The 1950s constituted a golden age of American historiography. There came of age a remarkable generation of historians—Richard Hofstadter, David Potter, C. Vann Woodward, Oscar Handlin—who emphasized style, analysis that moved on multiple levels, the creative application of the social sciences to the past.[7] All of this stood in shocking contrast to the mechanical research, the one-dimensional analysis, the wooden writing of the existing labor history literature. Young scholars like myself wanted to bring the subtlety and imagination that we saw in Hofstadter's *Age of Reform* or Handlin's *The Uprooted* to the writing of labor history. We wanted to raise the level of the craft. That, almost by definition, meant broadening the focus of labor history. There was a richer history to be explored and more complex questions to be answered than could be found in the story of trade unions. The latter would have to be studied, of course, but as part of the larger history of workers in America. And this conformed, ultimately, to the personal identification that had led us to labor history, in the first place. So, almost as soon as historians entered the field, it was given a thrust in the direction of social history.

Our initial success was, of course, limited. We had to grapple with basic problems of research and conceptualization. For his dissertation study of industrial conflict during the 1870s, Herbert Gutman discovered a rich record in local labor newspapers. David Montgomery uncovered similarly untapped sources for his thesis on labor reform and radical Republicanism, which appeared as his pioneering book *Beyond Equality* (1967).[8] In my case, I originally intended to study the great strike wave of 1919 and its sources in the experience of immigrant workers in wartime America. When that proved too much to handle, I narrowed the topic down to the 1919 steel strike. The material was abundant, for the war period as well as afterward, and my working hypothesis seemed to make sense for the steelworkers. My thesis director, Oscar Handlin, on returning from a sabbatical year in the summer of 1955, approved of what I was doing and suggested that I include a background chapter on the industry and its workers. Handlin's suggestion—casually made, I think—set me off in a new direction. In the end, the "background chapter" turned into two-thirds of the study. What was crucial was the discovery of rich library materials—four volumes of a federal analysis of labor conditions in the steel industry, two statistical volumes on immigrants in the industry in the Dillingham Reports on Immigration, the Pittsburgh Survey, investigations of competition in the steel industry, including stenographic copies of testimony and exhibits in the antitrust suit against United States Steel, and much else from trade journals, company reports, and the labor press. Although I later did research at other libraries, the bulk of what I needed was sitting on the shelves of Widener Library, hitherto unknown to me, and, if known to others, never exploited by them. This material, the fruit of an intense public interest in the steel industry during the Progressive period, enabled me to reconstruct the history of American steelworkers as it had been shaped by technology, management policy, immigration, community, and trade unionism. Into this larger framework I fitted my original interest in the 1919 steel strike.

How large a part accident and discovery played in my writing of *Steelworkers in America: The Nonunion Era* should be all too apparent.[9] But there was nothing accidental about the questions I was asking: *Why did workers come to America? What was their experience inside its mills and factories? How did they accommodate themselves to industrial life? What were the sources of their acquiescence and/or militancy?* These were the kinds of questions inevitably posed by the first generation of historians embarking on the study of labor history. It was in our ability to deal with these questions that we fell short. No one today—certainly no dissertation writer—would settle for my thesis research or cast the subject so broadly. The approved strategy in labor history, as in social history generally, is to cut out a small piece, a local study, and to treat it in depth. Several of Handlin's students, although not in labor history, were actually doing precisely that, just as I was finishing up. Stephan Thernstrom was using the manuscript censuses to measure the upward mobility of common laborers in Newburyport, thereby launching the new field of social mobility studies. Sam Bass Warner was compiling building permits from the basement of the State House in Boston for his pioneering *Streetcar Suburbs*.[10] That I did not follow a similar strategy for the steelworkers could, as with so much else, be ascribed to accident, partly of timing, partly of imagination (watching Warner laboriously reconstruct on an enormous map the housing patterns of Roxbury, West Roxbury, and Dorchester, I thought him crazy). For labor history, in any case, the first forays signified more a sense of promise than of actual achievement in writing the history of workers in America.

In the meantime, labor history was carving its place out within the historical profession. The scholarly superstructure developed swiftly— major archives in Detroit, in Atlanta, at Penn State, and elsewhere, a first-rate journal, and regional associations in many parts of the country. The volume of scholarship grew enormously: the annual bibliography in *Labor History* for 1973 listed sixteen pages of articles, as well as fifty-eight dissertations completed that year. The best books in the field attained a standard of craftsmanship the equal of anything to be found elsewhere in the profession. Sidney Fine's *Sit-Down: The General Motors Strike of 1936–1937* was a model of historical reconstruction based on exhaustive research. Irving Bernstein wrote superb narrative history of American labor during the 1920s and 1930s in his *The Lean Years* and *The Turbulent Years*, as did Melvyn Dubofsky for the Industrial Workers of the World in *We Shall Be All*.[11] Most of the first generation of writing, and much even of the 1970s, dealt with the familiar subjects of labor history—leaders, strikes, organizations, politics. The groundwork was thereby also being laid for future work in the field, however. Far more than would have been the case in the 1950s, labor historians of the next decade were strongly positioned for exploiting fresh possibilities of writing the social history of American workers.

The most important influence came from England. Excepting Frederick Jackson Turner's "The Significance of the Frontier in American History" (1893), probably no single historical work has been so eagerly embraced or has set off so strong a surge of American scholarly activity as E. P. Thompson's *The Making of the English Working Class*.[12] The leading figure in a brilliant constellation of English social historians that included Eric Hobsbawm, George Rudé, and Brian Harrison, Thompson examined dimensions of working-class experience scarcely dreamed of by American students. Class, Thompson argued, "is a *cultural* as much as an economic formation." Following Marx, Thompson found "class experience . . . largely determined by the productive relations into which men are born—or enter involuntarily." But then: "Class-consciousness is the way these experiences are handled in cultural terms: embodied in traditions, value systems, ideas, and institutional forms."[13] Although attentive to the economic forces unleashed by the industrial revolution, Thompson's book was made compelling by his brilliant evocation of an emergent working-class culture. Among the themes that were most striking were Thompson's treatment of the religious roots of industrial morality, the inner meaning of early labor politics and reform, and, most important, the habits and customs of working people as they moved from a preindustrial to an industrial world. Thompson did more than map out a new terrain of working-class life for exploration. By his own loving attention to the concrete and specific, he helped to legitimize the close local study of workers that characterizes so much of the recent research in American labor history. Most of all, the example of his historical imagination—his fertile effort to re-create an earlier world of working people—fired the ambitions of American scholars. They would seek out and bring to life the hidden history of American working-class culture.

The Thompsonian influence found its most comprehensive expression in Herbert Gutman's pioneering essay, "Work, Culture, and Society in Industrializing America."[14] Gutman became the prinicpal American exponent of the Thompsonian approach. An inspiring teacher, Gutman set his many graduate students at the University of Rochester to work on themes suggested by the English social historians. In increasing numbers, dissertations and monographs began to appear—evangelical religion among Lynn shoemakers, the craft traditions of Danbury hatters, leisure in Fall River and Lynn, the New England agrarianism of the Lowell textile girls, the cultural life of Philadelphia workers before the Civil War. The most fully realized of these early forays was Alan Dawley's *Class and Community: The Industrial Revolution in Lynn*.[15] All of this work focused on the industrializing phase of American working-class experience. All of it was local in orientation. All of it was inspired by English examples, and, almost always, the influence was explicitly and gratefully acknowledged.

Very quickly, however, the English models were modified to accommodate to what was specific to the American experience. The ethnic factor, especially, had to be taken into account, for, historically, immigrants had made up the bulk of America's industrial labor force. To a large degree, labor historians realized, the cultural dimensions of American working-class experience took ethnic forms. In his study of iron molders of Troy, New York, for example, Daniel Walkowitz treated them first as workers, then considered their Irish associational activities, and finally revealed that the web of ethnic relationships with police and politicians made the molders a powerful presence in Troy in the years after the Civil War.[16] Ethnic identity was a shaping force for labor solidarity, evident in such various ways as the strike militancy of Slavic miners, the labor boycott as an Irish device in New York City, and the role of ethnic groups in the local labor politics of the Knights of Labor. Other studies stressed ethnocultural tensions as an obstacle to class developments, as, for example, in the Kensington riots of 1844 or in the conflicts between Irish and Cornish hard-rock miners and between French-Canadian and American textile workers. In *The Indispensable Enemy*, Alexander Saxton identified the hatred of the Chinese as a defining experience in California working-class life in the nineteenth century.[17]

The ethnic approach, as it was pushed further, opened up new doors for understanding the work experience in America. In an illuminating study of the Amoskeag mills of Manchester, New Hampshire, for example, Tamara Hareven revealed how important the family system was in the recruitment and work patterns of the French Canadian cotton workers.[18] The movement of immigrants into American industry, we now see, was not random, but—rather—flowed through well-defined networks based on family and village ties. Deeper complexities emerge from a recent study of Italians, Poles, and blacks in Pittsburgh during the first third of the twentieth century. Although the three groups arrived with identically low skill levels, they experienced very different work careers in Pittsburgh. The Italians gravitated to casual and outdoor labor, avoided the factories, and moved up into entrepreneurial occupations. The Poles concentrated in the factories and remained there, with little upward mobility, for generation after generation. The blacks likewise did factory work, but never achieved the stable patterns of the Poles. These differences were attributable partly to ethnic preferences, especially the different preferences of the Italians and the Poles, but partly also to the relationship between family structures and job opportunities. Once inside an industrial plant, Polish workers secured substantial control over recruitment; almost invariably, sons entered the factories through family and personal connections. That, in turn, strengthened the tight family structures of the Polish working-class communities. Sons handed their pay over to their families, lived at home until they married, settled in the same neighborhoods afterward, and rarely moved far up the occupational ladder. The sons of black workers, on the other hand, could not rely on their fathers for jobs. The result was a quite different family pattern among working-class blacks: young people left at an early age, and the predominant unit was the isolated nuclear family of parents and children.[19] The ethnic orientation has thus permitted the exploration of intricacies of working-class experience that would have been wholly inaccessible to earlier generations of labor historians.

The scholars studying ethnicity and work, unlike those interested in ethnicity and working-class culture, would probably not classify themselves as labor historians. This points to a second force, beyond that deriving from England, that has strongly advanced the historical study of workers in America, namely the growth of the new social history in all its guises. The hallmark throughout has been an unremitting focus on the "plain people"—to use Peter Knights' phrase—and these are in the main working people.[20] The compartmentalizing of fields—the chapter headings in this volume provide an adequate index—necessarily are eroding, as historians press forward in their studies of the "plain people." The social historian may start out thinking he is studying city life, politics, or immigrants, and, depending on where his research carries him, may discover himself on the terrain of other disciplines. In the preceding paragraph on work and ethnicity, the attentive reader should have noticed that the key linkage occurs through family structure. (Tamara Hareven, an editor of the *Journal of Family History*, would doubtless identify herself as neither an ethnic nor as a labor historian, but as a family historian.) Questions of social mobility also figure strongly in the discussion. And, indeed, the topic has been treated by scholars primarily interested in social mobility, as in Thomas Kessner's *The Golden Door: Italian and Jewish Immigrant Mobility in New York City*.[21] Such fruitful intermingling of interests enlivens the new social history generally and enormously expands the pool of information available for any given field. As compared to twenty years ago, today's labor historian can draw on a vastly larger literature exploring the history of the American worker.

He is able also to borrow from what is innovative in the new social history. Quantitative methodology, never of much interest to the Commons school, has become an important tool in labor history. A number of old questions have thereby yielded fresh answers. By measuring the occupational composition of its membership, for example, Alan Dawley has shown that the organization of the Knights of St. Crispin was not an artisan revolt against the modernization of the shoe industry. The social origins and career lines of trade-union leaders have been traced in Warren Van Tine's *The Making of the Labor Bureaucrat, 1870–1920*.[22] As more complex questions are tackled, more sophisticated use is sure to be made of computers and statistical analysis. This, in turn, depends on another kind of borrowing from the new social history, namely from the innovative themes it is addressing. Labor historians now commonly deal with questions of social mobility, neighborhoods, family patterns, and living standards in their studies of working-class communities.

So far, we have treated the new labor history as essentially the beneficiary of influences coming from elsewhere; but there have been forces at work very specific to the study of labor history. One was ideological. Labor history, Eric Hobsbawm has remarked, "is by tradition a highly political subject."[23] It had not been so in the United States, at least not in Hobsbawm's sense. Not Marxists, but the followers of Commons and Perlman dominated, and they wrote a labor history celebratory of pure-and-simple unionism. There was an American radical school, exemplified especially in the prolific writings of Philip Foner, but it was vastly less consequential than its European counterparts. Only in the 1960s did a strong radical wave sweep the American field; but, when it did so, it took forms very much encouraging of a social history orientation.

In part, that was the doing of E. P. Thompson and other English social historians, who wrote out of a Marxist tradition; American enthusiasts who seized on their brilliant findings tended to absorb their class framework, as well. More crucial, probably, were two developments indigenous to the American radical scene. One was the corporate-liberal interpretation advanced by James Weinstein in his *The Corporate Ideal in the Liberal State*. Far from challenging the power of American business, Weinstein argued, liberal reform was really a strategy by the corporate sector to shore up the status quo. Among Weinstein's key themes was the easy co-optation of the labor movement: unions were a ready partner of big business in the battle against socialism and the incipient radicalism of American workers.[24] By so denigrating American trade unionism, the corporate-liberal argument weakened the legitimacy of traditional labor history and encouraged scholars to focus their attention more directly on the experience of the workers themselves. The positive impulse in that direction—and powerful it was—came from the New Left. From the late 1960s onward, partly as a result of the surge of labor militancy in the United States and in Europe, partly as a result of the waning energy of the student movement, the New Left shifted its ground and took up the cause of the worker. Rallying cries for "history from the bottom up" and for a "history of the inarticulate" were soon strongly felt within labor history. The initial tendency was to seek out the true history of American radicalism in the "self activity" of the workers. Much attention was given to mass militancy, as, for example, in Jeremy Brecher's *Strike!* The most influential of New Left labor historians, Staughton Lynd, extolled the insurgent movements of the 1930s and located their failure in the institutional rigidity of the Communist Party. The oral-history collection *Rank and File*, edited by Lynd and his wife, Alice, remains a powerful statement of the notion of the worker as indispensable actor of American labor history.[25] The ideological sources of this writing, however, were quickly spent, and its balder formulations soon left behind; but the rank-and-file orientation survives. Among the younger generation of labor historians are many who passed through the radical movements of the 1960s; they retain from that experience a continuing determination not to be distracted from the hard task of writing labor history with workers at its center.

Nothing is more fascinating to the student of history than the way a new perception on the past opens up. In the early 1970s, such an event was happening in American labor history. Both social history and the English school had taught labor historians to see workers as members of communities, as bearers of religious beliefs, ethnic identities, political affiliations. Their specific identities as workers, especially as craft members, were likewise primarily related to their ways of life. Now a different focus emerged: what was the experience of workers on the job? While it is not altogether clear what prompted that question in the early 1970s, it certainly had roots in New Left traditions and in the rampant shop-floor unrest that was seen, for example, in the Lordstown strike of 1972. In the mysterious ways in which historical thinking moves, in any case, a number of writers at roughly the same moment began to study workers within the work place. They were, moreover, preoccupied with one theme—the ongoing struggle between workers and managers over control of the labor process.

Scholars have come to shop-floor history from two directions. One group, very much influenced by Harry Braverman's *Labor and Monopoly Capital: The Degradation of Work in the Twentieth Century*, has concerned itself with the managerial assault on the autonomy of workers. Taking as his text Frederick W. Taylor's *Principles of Scientific Management*, Braverman stressed above all the unceasing compulsion American management has felt to rationalize production. This imperative, Braverman argued, was inherent in the capitalist system, and the invariable consequence was the alienation of the worker from his work. Attracted by its implications for corporate capitalism, a group of radical economists have been drawn into the historical study of this problem. Their findings have been ably synthesized in Richard Edwards's *Contested Terrain: The Transformation of the Workplace in the Twentieth Century*. Labor-segmentation theory, a related argument developed by some of the same scholars, focuses on the way corporate employers secure the compliance of labor. Their workers become a permanent work force, fitted into a rationalized job structure and adequately rewarded, but also held in check by an ever-present reserve army of casual workers made up of women and minorities. Historians, while not on the cutting edge of this kind of analysis, have done important work in establishing the managerial context. Most notable on labor policy is Daniel Nelson's *Managers and Workers: Origins of the New Factory System*, and, on the larger managerial structure, Alfred D. Chandler's *Visible Hand: The Managerial Revolution in American Business*.[26]

The other side of the story—the response of workers—has been very much the province of labor historians. They have been especially influenced by the work of David Montgomery. Montgomery has written provocatively on the autonomy of craft workers in the nineteenth-century factory and a workers' ethic of manliness underlying that independence, and on the evolution of the trade-union agreement as a device for formalizing and enforcing traditional work rules. He has identified the first two decades of the twentieth century as the critical period in the struggle over workers' control. The strike waves of those years constituted labor's response, largely futile, to management's aggressive deployment of machinery and managerial techniques in American factories.[27] Like Gutman, Montgomery has been a prolific graduate teacher—the University of Pittsburgh became a major center in labor history during his tenure there—and his students have begun to explore on many fronts the themes of workers' control.

Another research strategy, rich in its potential, thus has opened up, pursuing the worker—not out into the community, but into the factory and at his workbench. What is especially important is the access that shop-floor history gives to the modern period of labor history. With a few notable exceptions, studies of working-class culture have been confined to the nineteenth century. The study of shop-floor activity will not be thus limited. The struggle of workers to retain control over the job and of managers to subordinate them to a rationalized system of production is a continuing story that does not end at any given stage of industrialization. Thus shop-floor history holds special significance for labor historians of the modern period, for it permits them to get at the experience of working people even in the age of mature collective bargaining.

Readers of this and other essays recounting the new social history may well be thinking, "All very interesting, but what meaning is being added to our sense of the American past?" No question strikes more directly at the heart of the historian's task. If his or her work is not absorbed into the way society understands its history, then those labors ultimately become futile. On this central question, the verdict is not yet in. At the level of historical *experience*, the new scholarship is certainly contributing richly. Whether our larger *understanding* is also advancing—whether social history will provide a new framework and chronology for perceiving the American past—remains much more problematic.

In 1979, Daniel J. Walkowitz published his *Worker City, Company Town: Iron and Cotton-Worker Protest in Troy and Cohoes, New York, 1855–1884.*[28] The book, exceptional for its comparative focus, is otherwise a model example of the new labor history. It is deeply researched; it rests on a substantial quantitative base; it offers a complex analysis thoroughly grounded in interdisciplinary scholarship. It is a sober, densely argued monograph meant for a scholarly audience, and, as such, very favorably received. But Walkowitz's project found also an altogether different kind of expression. Employing the same body of information, Walkowitz wrote and produced a historical drama, "Molders of Troy," which was broadcast nationwide on public television after the appearance of his book. While the characters in the play are fictitious, they convey the same historical truth that is contained in Walkowitz's monograph. What should be taken from this episode is not (or at least not primarily) the idiosyncrasy of the frustrated film-maker disguised as historian; what should be observed, rather, are certain imperatives in the new labor history. First, Walkowitz's research revealed to him, not bloodless institutions or abstractions, but a real world of nineteenth-century workers, and, in their losing defense of that world against the onslaught of modernizing employers, genuine historical drama. Second, Walkowitz felt the need to disseminate this history in a form more accessible than his monograph. To some degree, of course, the second point derives from the first: the material lends itself to dramatic treatment. There is also, however, the conviction that this lost history should be made a part of the American past.

The dissemination of social history scholarship may well move out of the traditional literary channels by which history has found its public in the past. The story of the plain people of America has begun to be told with genuine historical insight in a remarkable flow of films—*Rosie the Riveter, With Babies and Banners, Hero of America, Northern Lights, Hester Street* come readily to mind. There is the fact also that social history creates a symbiotic relationship between scholar and audience. For one thing, the local focus of social history gives its findings a concrete and immediate meaning for local residents. For another, the local residents are an essential source of information: oral history is not only a research tool, but also a means of drawing the informant into the process. Finally, many groups studied by social historians—women, minorities, workers —are impelled by their own contemporary crises to seek out their past, as evidenced, for example, in the enormous success of the film *Roots*. All these elements can be seen in the Baltimore Neighborhood Heritage Project, in which actors recreate before local audiences the history of their neighborhoods, based on the residents' own accounts and on sophisticated research in urban records. The intersection of lay and scholarly interests takes many forms—the meetings of labor history and ethnic societies, the exhibits mounted at local museums, the many oral-history projects under way.

When a social historian asks pensioned immigrant workers or long-time residents of a city neighborhood about their past, those questioned are likely to respond that they have no history worth telling, that *history* is about heroes, cowboys and Indians, Washington and Lincoln, maybe Rockefeller. The social historian vehemently denies that, and, in so doing, is impelled, as Walkowitz was, to show plain Americans that they *do* have a history. He does so, not simply out of altruism, but also to serve his own scholarly interests. In order to inform the social historian, neighborhood residents and immigrant workers must know they have a history. It is this symbiotic relationship, felt more or less by all social historians, that is the surest guarantee that the historical experience of ordinary

Americans—the findings of the new scholarship—will be assimilated into the nation's past.

But what larger meaning will be invested in such a people's history? No clear synthesis has yet emerged. The new labor historian, for one, finds himself in a very different intellectual setting from the scholars of the Wisconsin school. By its nature, institutional history provided for its adherents a clear framework—none was clearer than the American trade union, with its well-defined structure and rules. On a larger scale, Selig Perlman's *Theory of the Labor Movement* performed the same function. As historians pushed out beyond trade union history, they necessarily left the safe haven of Perlman's explicit framework. The thrust of the current scholarship goes strongly against the construction of a new one. Research has focused itself on the intensive local study of workers. We have, moreover, developed an acute sense of the complexity and variety of American working-class experience, in which all lines of inquiry— family, ethnicity, mobility, technology, custom—converge to form an intricate network of connections. At its best, the new labor history has been highly imaginative at establishing linkages between various aspects of working-class experience and at conveying the totality of that experience at a given time and place; but such an approach, necessarily inward-looking, militates against systematic thinking about a new synthesis for American labor history.

For a while, *The Making of the English Working Class* seemed a sufficient guide. The enormous enthusiasm for Thompson's great book derived not only from our discovery of the richness of labor history, but equally from the expectation that, once we had acquired a comparable body of information, we would then go on to write our own *Making of the American Working Class.* Thompson's class formulation may serve admirably in the English setting. Thus, Gareth Stedman Jones, pushing his research into late nineteenth century, has written confidently of "the basic consistency of outlook reflected in the new working-class culture which spread over England after 1870." And further: "The distinctiveness of a working-class way of life was enormously accentuated. Its separateness and impermeability were now reflected in a dense and inward-looking culture." Like Gareth Stedman Jones, we have been busily gathering the evidence of American working-class culture; but labor historians cannot share Jones's confidence of discovering for American workers a "basic consistency of outlook" and a "distinctive . . . way of life."[29]

Thompson's class analysis turned on the interaction between a settled population of English working people, especially cloth-making and metal-working artisans, and a new industrial order that was demonstrably antagonistic to working people's customs and values. Early America, advanced as England in most other ways, lacked such a pre-industrial laboring population. While colonial artisans have been intensively studied in recent years, such research has neither assumed nor discovered that the roots of an American working class are to be found in the laboring people of pre-industrial America. Unlike England, moreover, the recruits to American industrialism were sharply divided along ethnic, racial, and religious lines. And the defining issue—labor's struggle for political rights—was largely absent from the United States: the ballot came to American workers early and without much conflict. For all we have learned from Thompson and his English colleagues, American labor historians cannot expect to develop a new synthesis along the lines of *The Making of the English Working Class*. If not through the idea of a unified working-class culture, then where is the alternative approach for American labor history? No answer is yet at hand.

In this quandary, labor history is at one with the entire field of social history. The problem of synthesis served, indeed, as the theme of Bernard Bailyn's presidential address before the American Historical Association in 1981. The vitality of the new scholarship is evident at every hand—in the volume of research under way, in the accumulating monographic literature, in the prominence given social history within the historical profession. This momentum can be sustained, however, only if it leads to a synthesis that will provide guidance for future scholarship and, more important, help to reshape the existing perception of American social development. The truncated state of the field—rich in its findings, unclear as to larger meaning—places synthesis high on the agenda of American labor historians and of social historians generally.

Notes

At various points in this essay, the author refers to material that he has discussed in another essay, "The Old Labor History and the New: In Search of an American Working Class," *Labor History* 20 (1979): 111–126.

1. John R. Commons, et al., editors, *A Documentary History of Industrial Society*, 10 vols. (Cleveland: A. H. Clark Company, 1910–11); Commons, et al., *A History of Labour in the United States*, 4 vols. (New York: Macmillan Company, 1918–1935).

2. For further treatment of this point, see my "Phillip Taft: Labor Scholar," *Labor History* 19 (1978): 9–22.

3. Selig Perlman, *A Theory of the Labor Movement* (New York: Macmillan Company, 1928).

4. Lloyd Ulman, *The Rise of the National Trade Union: The Development and Significance of Its Structure, Governing Institutions, and Economic Policies* (Cambridge: Harvard University Press, 1955); Philip Taft, *The A.F. of L. in the Time of Gompers* (New York: Harper, 1957) and

The A.F. of L. from the Death of Gompers to the Merger (New York: Harper, 1959); Walter Galenson, *The CIO Challenge to the AFL: A History of the American Labor Movement, 1935–1941* (Cambridge: Harvard University Press, 1960).

5. Brody, *The Butcher Workmen: A Study of Unionization* (Cambridge: Harvard University Press, 1964).

6. Handlin's students are listed in Richard L. Bushman, et al., editors, *Uprooted Americans: Essays to Honor Oscar Handlin* (Boston: Little, Brown and Co., 1979), p. 366.

7. Richard Hofstadter, *The Age of Reform: From Bryan to F.D.R.* (New York: Knopf, 1955); David M. Potter, *People of Plenty: Economic Abundance and the American Character* (Chicago: University of Chicago Press, 1954); C. Vann Woodward, *Origins of the New South, 1877–1913* (Baton Rouge: Louisiana State University Press, 1951); Oscar Handlin, *The Uprooted: The Epic Story of the Great Migrations that Made the American People* (Boston: Little, Brown, 1951).

8. For Montgomery's assessment of the way themes first opened in his book have since been picked up and elaborated, see "An Afterword on Bibliography," in the reprinted edition of *Beyond Equality* (Urbana: University of Illinois Press, 1981), pp. 507–515. The current emphasis on community history can likewise be traced back to Gutman's early work. See especially "The Worker's Search for Power," in *The Gilded Age: A Reappraisal*, edited by H. Wayne Morgan (Syracuse: Syracuse University Press, 1963), pp. 38–68; and "Class, Status, and Community Power in Nineteenth-Century American Industrial Cities—Paterson, New Jersey: A Case Study," in *The Age of Industrialism in America: Essays in Social Structure and Cultural Values*, edited by Frederic Cople Jaher (New York: Free Press, 1968), pp. 263–287.

9. Brody, *Steelworkers in America: The Nonunion Era* (Cambridge: Harvard University Press, 1960).

10. Stephan Thernstrom, *Poverty and Progress: Social Mobility in a Nineteenth-Century City* (Cambridge: Harvard University Press, 1964); Sam Bass Warner, Jr., *Streetcar Suburbs: The Process of Growth in Boston, 1870–1900* (Cambridge: Harvard University Press, 1962).

11. Sidney Fine, *Sit-Down: The General Motors Strike of 1936–1937* (Ann Arbor: University of Michigan Press, 1969); Irving Bernstein, *The Lean Years: A History of the American Worker, 1920–1933* (Boston: Houghton Mifflin, 1960) and *The Turbulent Years: A History of the American Worker, 1933–1941* (Boston: Houghton Mifflin, 1970); Melvin Dubofsky, *We Shall Be All: A History of the Industrial Workers of the World* (Chicago: Quadrangle Books, 1969).

12. Frederick Jackson Turner, "The Significance of the Frontier in American History," *Annual Report of the American Historical Association for 1893* (Washington: Government Printing Office, 1894), pp. 199–227; Edward P. Thompson, *The Making of the English Working Class* (New York: Pantheon, 1963).

13. Quoted in Brody, "Old Labor History and New," p. 123.

14. Herbert Gutman, "Work, Culture, and Society in Industrializing America," *American Historical Review* 78 (1973): 531–587.

15. Alan Dawley, *Class and Community: The Industrial Revolution in Lynn* (Cambridge: Harvard University Press, 1976). Other examples include Paul Faler, "Cultural Aspects of the Industrial Revolution: Lynn, Massachusetts, Shoemakers and Industrial Morality, 1826–1860," *Labor History* 15 (1974): 367–394; John T. Cumbler, *Working-Class Community in Industrial America: Work, Leisure, and Struggle in Two Industrial Cities, 1880–1930* (Westport: Greenwood Press, 1979); Thomas Dublin, *Women at Work: The Transformation of Work and Community in Lowell, Massachusetts, 1826–1860* (New York: Columbia University Press, 1970).

16. Daniel Walkowitz, "Statistics and the Writing of Working Class Culture . . . Iron Workers in Troy," *Labor History* 15 (1974): 416–460.

17. Alexander Saxton, *The Indispensable Enemy: Labor and the Anti-Chinese Movement in California* (Berkeley: University of California Press, 1971).

18. Tamara K. Hareven and Randolph Langenbach, *Amoskeag: Life and Work in an American Factory City* (New York: Pantheon, 1978).

19. John Bodnar, Roger Simon, and Michael P. Weber, *Lives of Their Own: Blacks, Italians, and Poles in Pittsburgh, 1900 to 1960* (Urbana: University of Illinois Press, 1982).

20. See Peter R. Knights, *The Plain People of Boston, 1830–1860: A Study in City Growth* (New York: Oxford University Press, 1971).

21. Thomas Kessner, *The Golden Door: Italian and Jewish Immigrant Mobility in New York City, 1880–1915* (New York: Oxford University Press, 1977).

22. Dawley, *Class and Community*; Warren R. Van Tine, *The Making of the Labor Bureaucrat: Union Leadership in the United States, 1870–1920* (Amherst: University of Massachusetts Press, 1973).

23. Eric Hobsbawm, "Labor History and Ideology," *Journal of Social History* 7 (1974): 371.

24. James Weinstein, *The Corporate Ideal in the Liberal State, 1900–1918* (Boston: Beacon Press, 1968).

25. Jeremy Brecher, *Strike!* (San Francisco: Straight Arrow Books, 1972); Alice and Staughton Lynd, editors, *Rank and File: Personal Histories by Working-Class Organizers* (Boston: Beacon Press, 1973).

26. Harry Braverman, *Labor and Monopoly Capital: The Degradation of Work in the Twentieth Century* (New York: Monthly Review Press, 1974); Frederick W. Taylor, *The Principles of Scientific Management* (New York: Harper and Brothers, 1911); Richard C. Edwards, *Contested Terrain: The Transformation of the Workplace in the Twentieth Century* (New York: Basic Books, 1979); Daniel Nelson, *Managers and Workers: Origins of the New Factory System in the United States, 1880–1920* (Madison: University of Wisconsin Press, 1975); Alfred D. Chandler, *The Visible Hand: The Managerial Revolution in American Business* (Cambridge: Belknap Press, 1977).

27. David Montgomery, *Workers' Control in America* (New York: Cambridge University Press, 1979),

28. Daniel Walkowitz, *Worker City, Company Town: Iron and Cotton Worker Protest in Troy and Cohoes, New York, 1855–1884* (Urbana: University of Illinois Press, 1978).

29. Quoted in Brody, "Old Labor History and New," p. 123.

Suggestions for Additional Reading

Bernstein, Irving. *The Lean Years: A History of the American Worker, 1920–1933*. Boston: Houghton Mifflin, 1960.

Bernstein, Irving. *The Turbulent Years: A History of the American Worker, 1933–1941*. Boston: Houghton Mifflin, 1970.

Comprehensive narrative treatment of this period.

Braverman, Harry. *Labor and Monopoly Capital: The Degradation of Work in the Twentieth Century*. New York: Monthly Review Press, 1974.

Seminal work on the economic forces leading to the rationalization of work processes in the American economy.

Brody, David. *Workers in Industrial America: Essays on the Twentieth-Century Struggle*. New York: Oxford University Press, 1980.

> Historiographical and thematic essays in modern American labor history.

Dawley, Alan. *Class and Community: The Industrial Revolution in Lynn*. Cambridge: Harvard University Press, 1976.

> Community study of shoemakers, much influenced by E. P. Thompson, showing the impact of the industrial revolution and workers' response.

Dublin, Thomas. *Women at Work: The Transformation of Work and Community in Lowell, Massachusetts, 1826–1860*. New York: Columbia University Press, 1979.

> Study of Lowell mill girls, imaginatively using mill records and census data to show the response of a first generation of American industrial workers to the factory system.

Dubofsky, Melvyn. *We Shall Be All: A History of the Industrial Workers of the World*. Chicago: Quadrangle Books, 1969.

> The most recent and fullest treatment of the Wobblies.

Friedlander, Peter. *The Emergence of a UAW Local, 1936–1939: A Study in Class and Culture*. Pittsburgh: University of Pittsburgh Press, 1975.

> An interesting application of new approaches to the factory environment, relying heavily on oral history.

Gutman, Herbert. *Work, Culture and Society in Industrializing America: Essays in America's Working Class and Social History*. New York: Knopf, 1976.

> Important collection of essays by one of the leading practitioners of the new labor history. The title essay is especially important.

Laslett, John H. M. *Labor and the Left: A Study of Socialist and Radical Influences in the American Labor Movement, 1881–1924*. New York: Basic Books, 1970.

> The best and most comprehensive study of the role of Socialists in the American labor movement.

Meier, August, and Elliott Rudwick. *Black Detroit and the Rise of the UAW*. New York: Oxford University Press, 1979.

> Shows the interaction of the black community with the industry and the union during the unionizing period.

Montgomery, David. *Workers' Control in America*. New York: Cambridge University Press, 1979.

> Important collection of essays by a major labor historian who has pioneered in the study of shop-floor relationships and their impact on collective labor action.

Nelson, Daniel. *Managers and Workers: Origins of the New Factory System in the United States, 1880–1920*. Madison: University of Wisconsin Press, 1975.

A study of Taylorism, how it arose out of the conditions of large-scale production and what its consequences were.

Perlman, Selig. *A Theory of the Labor Movement*. New York: Macmillan Company, 1928.

The most influential statement about the "exceptionalism" of the American labor movement.

Taft, Philip. *The A.F. of L. in the Time of Gompers*. New York: Harper, 1957.

Taft, Philip. *The A.F. of L. from the Death of Gompers to the Merger*. New York: Harper, 1959.

The standard account and an excellent example of institutional labor history.

Tentler, Leslie Woodcock. *Wage-Earning Women: Industrial Work and Family Life in the United States, 1900–1930*. New York: Oxford University Press, 1979.

Good example of the interaction of women's and labor history, with an interesting thesis on the causes of female subordination.

Walkowitz, Daniel. *Worker City, Company Town: Iron and Cotton Worker Protest in Troy and Cohoes, New York, 1855–1884*. Urbana: University of Illinois Press, 1978.

Highly detailed, thoroughly researched comparative study of the sources of protest in two industrial towns.

Yans-McLaughlin, Virginia. *Family and Community: Italian Immigrants in Buffalo, 1880–1930*. Ithaca: Cornell University Press, 1977.

Blends ethnic, women's, and community history to reveal the lives of immigrant workers.

In 1947, Joe Rudis, a photographer from the *Nashville Tennessean* newspaper, recorded last-minute campaign efforts outside a voting precinct on North First Street in Nashville.

Nashville Tennessean

8

Politics and Social History: Toward a New Synthesis

Samuel P. Hays

FOR MORE THAN two decades, now, social history has played an increasingly significant role among American historians. It continues to do so. Some concern has arisen, however, about its larger meaning. What is the relevance of the research and writing already completed? What new syntheses does it imply? These concerns of meaning and significance appear now in only limited degree, but here I wish to focus on them more directly. I will do so through a consideration of the relationship between social history and political history. When one asks about the significance of research on the family, women, blacks, ethnic groups, or the community, one inevitably turns to ideas about the larger social and political order. Hence I wish to explore the implications for political history of these new ventures in social history and to suggest some reverse implications, as well. In so doing, I hope to provide some directions of thought for placing the new social history in a more satisfactory historical context.

At the outset, it is well to note that much of what is now called the "new social history" grew out of political history. In the 1950s, several years before such historians as Stephan Thernstrom[1] or Sam Bass Warner[2] completed their studies of vertical mobility and suburbanization, and a decade before interest focused on ethnic history, women's history, and black history, a number of historians began to take a new tack in political history by examining voting behavior. These historians had become quite unhappy about what was called "presidential history"—that is, the practice of dividing political history into four-year presidential terms. The first critique of the "presidential synthesis," written by

Thomas Cochran, appeared in 1948.[3] Cochran argued that it does not make sense to divide political history into four-year presidential-term units, when, in fact, social and economic change has a more continuous and evolutionary character. Political attitudes and values and their social roots must be understood in more developmental terms, with history divided into stages embedded in the processes of change, themselves, rather than in the formal structure of the political system. One way of exploring this is through the study of popular voting patterns and their roots in social and economic circumstance. One of the first to take that approach was Lee Benson, who published, in 1961, a monograph analyzing the popular voting base of Jacksonian politics in New York, emphasizing especially ethnic and cultural factors.[4] Benson's path-breaking study sparked increased attention to this dimension of political behavior, and many historians soon found themselves immersed in the social data that would make studies of political history more meaningful.

My own involvement in social history came about through an interest in the local community as a voting unit. In 1957, students in my graduate seminar at the State University of Iowa each took one county and sought to reconstruct its voting patterns and its varied local community life. They observed significant differences in the voting patterns of rural townships, often located in the same county, and in urban wards within the same city. Carroll County, Iowa, was the most interesting example, because its regular pattern of square townships revealed a marked distinction between heavily Democratic precincts in the northwestern part of the county and equally heavily Republican ones in the southeast. The variation was striking. The more readily available explanation for the difference was ethnicity and religion. The townships did not seem to be significantly different with respect to occupation or property values, but they were quite different in ethno-cultural composition. The voters in northwest Carroll County were Germans, Lutherans and Catholics, and those in the southeast were Yankees, Methodists and Presbyterians.[5]

That method of analysis led directly to the community. We observed communities that were distinctive in their ethnic and religious characteristics and in the settlement patterns that had developed around such personal and community ties. One township in northwest Carroll County proved to be particularly interesting. In 1906, the township, formerly 60 percent Democratic, was divided into two precincts, one voting about 85 percent Democratic and the other about 30 percent. The latter precinct comprised a sizeable number of German Presbyterians, who voted quite differently from the German Lutherans dominant in the other precinct.

Similar analysis of German areas throughout Iowa indicated that German Methodists and German Presbyterians were considerably more Republican than were German Lutherans and German Catholics. Such patterns as those made the community the primary focus of concern in voting studies.

In the early 1960s, growing interest in the analysis of popular voting led to the development of the first large computerized collection of data for general research at the Inter-University Consortium for Political Research at the University of Michigan. Through a national network of historians, a considerable amount of county-level election data was located and recovered, then forwarded to Ann Arbor and computerized. It covered political races since 1824 for the offices of president and governor and for congressional and senatorial seats, and involved slightly more than 95 percent of the theoretically extant data. Yet, county-wide data had limitations, because it tended to obscure community patterns smaller than the county. Minor civil division data, such as township and ward voting returns, seemed to capture community patterns far more effectively. Clearly, county-level data made it impossible to analyze voting patterns in urban counties, which included many quite diverse communities. As a result, the Ann Arbor data became useful primarily to those who wished to determine, on a county level, patterns in voting from year to year or between races for offices such as president or governor. But in relating voting to underlying demography, county-level data had far less analytical potential than did data from smaller units.

During a seminar held at Ann Arbor in 1964, some historians experimented with computerizing township election data. The project entailed keypunching Wisconsin precinct data for the 1890s, which was available in the printed sources. It was a massive job, because there were as many precincts in Wisconsin as there are counties in the entire nation. There were many technical problems in both keypunching and programming, which, within the time and funds available, were not surmounted. Yet, some of us still felt that the best results could come from township and ward voting analysis, because this was the only way to bring the research to the real world of daily life. We therefore encouraged students to work at the township-ward level, doing their own calculations, rather than using the Ann Arbor county data. This, I think, reflected an important dividing line between those historians who wanted to use the voting data as a way of examining community values and those whose interests were limited to establishing data correlations. My own interests tended to go in the former direction; it was at this point that I began to concentrate more on exploring ethnicity and religion as social phenomena than on voting analysis.

The interest in popular voting has given rise to a goodly body of historical writing. Much of the literature focuses on the Midwest, the locale for studies by Paul Kleppner,[6] Richard Jensen,[7] and Frederick Luebke.[8] The volumes by Kleppner and Jensen cover a number of states, especially those of the Old Northwest Territory, while Luebke's study is of Nebraska. The ethnic differences displayed in the Midwest were very sharp. Belgian Catholic coal miners might well be Democratic, while Welsh Presbyterian miners were Republican. Most of these analyses found that cultural differences lay beneath partisan political differences. The central cultural issues were prohibition, sabbatarianism, and language, and these issues formed the basis, although not exclusively so, for the predominant pattern of voting from the early 1850s, when a new pattern of partisan loyalties arose, until the depression of the 1890s, when another pattern emerged. These years, from 1853 to 1893, have come to be called the "Third Party System."[9]

The Kleppner analysis was especially striking. Kleppner emphasized that cultural values involved in party differences could be thought of in terms of two different religious orientations, pietism and ritualism. Pietism grew out of Methodist Arminianism, which stressed that one's religious destiny could be influenced by one's own actions and was not subject to predestined fate. The emphasis lay on personal transformation and commitment to extending the gospel to others. This differed markedly from older religious styles, which tended to stress faithful observance of historical customs and their transmission from one generation to the next. Ritualists included both Lutherans and Catholics. The evangelical thrust of Methodism tended to lead to vigorous action to change the world, such as prohibition, while the more liturgical and ritualistic thrust tended to emphasize protection of the freedom to practice one's customary faith. These cultural differences tended to be associated, in turn, with the Republican party on the one hand and the Democratic party on the other. They reflected deep-seated values in the individual, the family, the kinship network, and the community.[10]

Further analysis refined these patterns. Different proportions of ethnic groups within a community, for example, led to variations in voting. If German Lutherans and German Catholics confronted each other daily, religious differences often seemed more important than their common interest in opposing prohibition or restrictions on Sabbath activities. If the prohibition issue became sharply salient, on the other hand, these two groups of Germans might come together in their voting. Kleppner noted the way in which the Republican party veered back and forth between conflicting strategies. Attempts to dislodge the Lutherans from the Democratic party by emphasizing Lutheran-Catholic differences in religion were undermined by efforts to respond to prohibitionists, which tended to force German Lutherans back into the Democratic party. For party strategists, that gave rise to continual shifts in tactics.

From election to election—and even for different races in the same election—there was considerable voting consistency, reflecting a habitual type of behavior that indicated that persistent attitudes in party choice were rooted in strong ethno-cultural commitments. No self-respecting Norwegian, wrote a Norwegian diarist from northern Iowa, would think of going to church on Sunday and voting for Grover Cleveland on Tuesday. Because of these close connections between ethno-cultural attitudes and party loyalties, the years from 1853 to 1893 constitute the "classic period" of American political parties, when party identification and loyalty reached a peak in American history. One can also associate the decline in party identification, which began in the late nineteenth century, with the erosion of ethno-cultural loyalties from older to younger generations.[11]

In the late 1960s, several tendencies evolved out of these beginnings in social analysis. One group began to speak of the "new political history" and to concentrate on the statistical problems of voting analyses in order to perfect quantitative techniques. From an initial interest in two variables, such as voting and ethnicity, that group became interested in multivariant analysis. They took up legislative voting, relating roll-call votes to personal characteristics of legislators or their constituencies. These activities tended to direct research away from the focus on the community and into the statistical analysis of formal political activities somewhat isolated from the social context.

Others, however, found that the analysis of voting patterns led them more directly into ethnic and cultural history. They were interested in the seeming power of these elements of human behavior and began to explore such elements in their own right. That tack was toward more purely social history and was greatly augmented by those new ventures which arose from the political climate of the 1960s, such as ethnic studies, black history, women's history, family studies, and working-class history. The general tone of this "new social history" was much like that which surrounded the search for voting patterns—a dissatisfaction with traditional categories of political history that seemed to be divorced from underlying social and economic affairs. Some spoke of the history of the "inarticulate," and others of history "from the bottom up." All shared the conviction that the wellsprings of human belief, values, and action were rooted deeply in the social order.

By the late 1960s, increasing numbers of doctoral dissertations focused on ethnic communities or adopted a community context for examining specialized topics in social history, such as the history of labor or that of women. Of particular significance was the use of a comparative method, which was potentially more powerful analytically than earlier approaches. One could compare Polish and Italian communities in a given city, or several Polish communities in the same or different cities. Others compared the subcultures of a single ethnic group. Nora Faires, for example, analyzed German subcultures in nineteenth-century Pittsburgh, using census data and records from seven German churches listing births, christenings, marriages, and deaths. The varying value styles reflected in these churches were then ranged on a continuum. Qualitative evidence was used to flesh out the quantitative data. That led to the identification, for example, of one Lutheran church that was most distinctive: of the seven studied, it was the most cosmopolitan and eclectic in its religious outlook, the only one with a stained-glass window depicting Abraham Lincoln, the one most involved in such evangelical tendencies and issues as prohibition and opposition to slavery, the only German church to permit Louis Kossuth to speak in it during his mid-nineteenth-century tour of America, and the one church on the rolls of which one could identify refugees from the 1848 German revolution. Other German churches seemed to be far too traditionalistic to harbor these influences. [12]

Community analyses took many forms. Those of colonial New England did not grow out of ethno-cultural analyses, but rather reflected the general spirit of the "new social history." Labor history began to stress the analysis of working-class communities, and the history of women was organized often in a similar fashion. Jay Kleinberg examined working-class women in Pittsburgh, not as factory workers but in terms of their work in the household. [13] Kleinberg's study emphasized changes in household technology—from heating and cooking with wood to using the gas stove, from laundering with the washboard to using the wringer-machine—and class variations in acquisition and use of such innovations, all within the context of the community. Religion as a field has received less attention than others. While most agree on the desirability of shifting from the old denominational and theological history to a focus on patterns of religious values, that realization has led to little such analysis. That may well be due, in part, to the limited amount of historical data on religious affiliation; but it might well also reflect the preference of many historians since the 1960s for subjects with more "social movement" appeal.

As these explorations in social history evolved, several tendencies seemed to divorce them from the larger context of history. One was specialization, the tendency of historians in one field of social history to work independently of others. Such groups organized separate sessions at professional meetings, separate "working groups" within the Social Science History Association, and prepared separate publications, such as the *Journal of Urban History*, the *Journal of Family History*, and *Labor History*. More important, by focusing heavily on the community, social history tended to emphasize smaller contexts of life, somewhat isolated from the larger view. One could easily become preoccupied with a single community, just as a biographer might focus exclusively on an individual person, with a resulting subtle yet powerful influence on one's historical perspective.

Much of this narrowing of focus could well be attributed to the technical aspects of research. For graduate students, one of the most important research considerations is selection of a subject that is manageable within a limited amount of time. A community, much like a personal biography, is well bounded, clearly marked off in space and time. Yet, it is precisely that tendency to place a boundary around one's subject that can lead to a relative blindness to the larger context. Well over a decade before the community study became popular in history, sociologists discussed this limitation in perspective.[14] What about the ties between the community and the larger world, the argument went. Communities were not so isolated as the studies seemed to imply. Few historians, however, were aware of these cautions from sociology.

Social mobility studies gave rise to a special form of this problem. Stephan Thernstrom's first study on Newburyport, Massachusetts, prompted concern regarding his assumptions, in the absence of firm data, about movement away from the community. In the nineteenth century, many community residents clearly present at the beginning of a decade were no longer there at the end; the number exceeded by far those who had died. Where did they go? They may have moved to an adjacent community or much farther away. The question cannot be ignored or guessed about, simply because the data is not available in the census.

Does this not demonstrate a major limitation in mobility studies bounded by a single community? Thernstrom believed that it did not seriously change the results, but others were not so sure.

One study that sought to deal with this problem used pension records to trace Civil War veterans. These records contain considerable information about places of residence, both before enlistment and afterward, throughout one's life. The data indicated that most Civil War veterans who moved had moved merely to an adjacent county; a few went farther away; but only a small number migrated as far as several states away. That illustrates both the limitations of conceptualization that comes from too strong a community focus and, at the same time, reveals some of the difficulties in developing a larger perspective.

Labor history also seems to be undergoing some self-evaluation of this kind. A major trend recently in labor history has been to focus on the working-class community and to elaborate a wide range of elements of community life. Much of this interest has arisen out of a desire to work out the notion of a shared working-class experience. A "sense of class" could involve experiences in the community, as well as at work; hence the growth of interest by labor historians in a wide range of social history subjects: family, women, ethnicity, and religion, all viewed through the medium of the community. That emphasis, however, has tended to steer working-class history away from its central theme, work and the organization of work. The new social history has given far more attention to the working-class *community* than it has to the relationship between workers and machines, the role of working people in the centralization of organization and control in American enterprise. Important historical issues arise from the choices made by those who shaped, organized, and managed the large-scale systems of the industrial economy, from a vantage point far beyond the setting of either work or the community. It appears that fewer labor historians now explore these types of questions as a result of the far greater popularity of a community focus. [15]

It is also worthwhile to examine some of the "roads not taken" in this new field, or taken far less extensively. These, too, have implications for local history. One such road involves the problem of inequality. Some of the first community studies drew important conclusions about the distribution of property ownership, based upon census data, which were as important as those about ethno-cultural patterns in voting. Merle Curti's study of Trempealeau County, Wisconsin, reconstructed patterns of property ownership in one county. [16] Curti's study has led to many other studies, most notably by Lee Soltow. [17] All of them add up to a general description of persistent inequality. If one ranges property owners from ownership of the most to ownership of the least and then divides them into deciles, the top ten percent of owners persistently own a disproportionate amount of land.

This data has had a particularly important implication for rather traditional notions about equality of land ownership on the western frontier, best known from the writings of Frederick Jackson Turner. A study of two counties in southwestern Pennsylvania for the 1790s, for example, indicated that a very large portion of adult males did not even own land, and among the rest there was considerable inequality.[18] Lee Soltow has found similar results for Ohio in 1810.[19] The first reaction to this data was argument that the main point was not inequality within the United States, but the relatively lower degree of inequality here, compared with that in Europe. On that score, the United States displayed "relative equality." Yet, that did not seem to capture the significance of the data: widespread and persistent inequality constituted a major context for American history. These facts were brought into clearer perspective in Soltow's study of Ohio in 1810, when he titled his article "Inequality Admidst Abundance." Inequality, in other words, was a fact that could not be obscured by relative abundance. And it has been given more appropriate attention by a recent attempt to bring together all this data in a book entitled simply *American Inequality*.[20]

This line of argument suggests that the pattern of persistent inequality should shape more of the analytical context of American history. There were slight variations, some toward greater inequality and others toward less, over the course of time, but the over-all setting of persistent inequality remained. Not a community has been studied in detail that does not display such a characteristic. We have come to accept the idea that communities contained a variety of ethnic groups that, over the years, developed either conflict or co-operation, but few studies stress the notion of persistent inequality over long periods of time. Neither do historical exhibits or interpretive programs. The ethnic exhibit at the National Museum of American History in Washington, D. C., for example, focuses on the coming together of ethnic groups into a mass culture, rather than on persistent inequality. To be historically accurate, however, the varied elements of that exhibit should have been placed within the context of inequality.

An excellent theme through which to do this is that of inequalities in consumption—for example, housing and household furnishings, which differ markedly for varied income levels. Inequality in housing was as characteristic of the nineteenth century as it is of the late twentieth. Yet, restoration and reconstruction do not always convey that fact. One example I observed recently was in the Upper Peninsula of Michigan, at Fayette, the iron village being restored by the State of Michigan. A nineteenth-century iron manufacturer laid out the village with a firm sense of inequality. People of different occupations and incomes lived in different places in the village; but while the historic district includes a number of houses of the top entrepreneurial group and of middle-class managers and technicians, it does not include any of the great majority of the people in the village, the workers. The visitor learns about *them* only from exhibits in one of the buildings.

Another road not taken in community studies consists of the larger extra-community context of constant individual movement. People moved out, up, and in, all of which adds up to a general pattern of mobility. The community-focused studies of mobility have emphasized vertical movement. Did people move up? Did success as we often describe it in American history really take place, or is it a myth? The usual method is to measure change in occupation from fathers to sons, such as from blue collar to white collar. Yet, to measure the results of the mobility in terms of some absolute outcome such as "success" or "opportunity" is the least significant potential of mobility studies. Far more important is the larger context of a society in motion. What these investigations have made clear is that any apparently stable social order, whether family, community, or city, is often in motion because of the rapidly changing society around it, because of the impact of large-scale social change on individuals. Some get caught up in these changes, yet others do not. Hence, a resulting social process of differentiation.

Many questions arise from this perspective. Why, for example, in a rural community, do some people move out into more urbanized areas, into the wider world, and others do not? Why, in a particular urban ethnic community, do some of the second generation move out and up, and others do not? Why, among Slavic immigrants—to cite one study—is there a relatively low level of sons of steelworkers leaving the mills to enter high school, while, among the Greeks, even the fathers—let alone the sons—left the mills very rapidly? Such changes indicate a differential response to the individualizing opportunities of the wider world. Whether people simply "succeed" is a somewhat limited context of thought. Far more significant is the process of differentiation that takes place, in which some people get caught up in change, and others do not. Such a differential process can be observed especially in genealogical family reconstruction. If one begins with a set of great-great grandparents and traces descendants through five generations, one can usually observe extensive differentiation. Some of the last generation live in one place, and others in another, while some advance further in education than do others. Why this differentiation?[21]

In the ethnic community, for example, one can trace changes as individuals begin to participate differently in the larger world around them. When many do this, it adds up to patterns of differentiation within the entire ethnic community. The community itself adopts language that reflects these distinctive and separate patterns, such as "shanty Irish" and "lace-curtain Irish." Once a nationality group becomes exposed to the forces of movement around it, it undergoes internal differentiation, so that subcultures begin to emerge. Inequalities develop in income, occupation, or education. This kind of subcultural analysis can provide far more insight about the relationship of the ethnic community to the larger world than is the case when the community is thought of as a more homogeneous entity.

Still a third road not taken involves the analysis of the relationships between the smaller context of life, frequently thought of in terms of the community, and the larger institutional context organized on a larger scale and consisting of larger networks of human interaction. I have already noted the tendency of social history to become involved in smaller, more segmented units of observation and analysis. The two phenomena just mentioned—the larger patterns of inequality and the larger context of differentiation—tend to force one's analysis out into a larger social context; but that can come also from an emphasis on the more formal institutions of government. Different levels of government function not in isolation from, but in close interaction with each other. Each reflects a given range of people, institutions, and public affairs within its geographical scope of jurisdiction, and hence a variety of human impulses come to bear on governmental decisions in those jurisdictions. These hierarchies and networks provide a setting for historical inquiry that can force narrower perspectives in social history out into larger ones.[22]

Those working in more limited community contexts should at least extend the scope of their perspective to statewide networks through state history. That is a much smaller unit than the national government, but one in which it is possible to grasp in one setting a wide range of social, economic, and political impulses. Yet, while social history has generated a considerable number of community studies, it has not led to the reconstruction of the links between local governments and the state or to the use of local and state governments as integrative contexts and focal points for reconstructing patterns of human activity. One can observe these links in fields such as transportation, in which state and local governments have interacted over the years in varying proportions; or in education, in which the state has played an increasingly important role in local affairs; or in social welfare activities involving the care of the unemployable, the handicapped, or the indigent; or in such economic connections as banking, insurance, and commerce, which have linked smaller and larger institutions, often through government. All of these are ways in which the significance of the smaller contexts of life can be identified in terms of their role in the larger networks of which they are a part. And in this larger realm, one can begin to visualize the theme of social history becoming integrated into political history.[23]

One of the curious directions of social history has been a distinctive emphasis on the meaning of the term *social*. Largely because of the intensity of the political movements of the 1960s, that meaning has highlighted the "social problems" of that decade: social problems involving women, blacks, ethnics, labor, the family. Yet, the meaning of *social* in *social history* is much wider than that: it refers to relationships or interactions among people in all of their activities. It is not enough in social history simply to emphasize the primary group, face-to-face settings of the community or the family, the church or common ethnicity. Social history extends to the shared values or interactive networks beyond that smaller scale in the larger arena of the region, the state, the nation, or "society as a whole."

It is precisely this need for a larger focus that is now, I think, beginning to concern social historians. Frequently, I am asked by scholars in family history, women's history, labor history, ethnic history, or the history of race, "What does all this add up to? What is the ultimate objective of research in social history?" The details of the subject are filled out, but the larger significance for American history is not made clear. This limitation is reflected in the impact of social history on textbook writing. Too often, this new research is evident only in expanded factual material, included in a mechanical fashion without significant integration into the larger context. That part of the "new social history" that has been most fully integrated involves politics. Earlier, it was assumed that, in the last third of the nineteenth century, for example, issues such as the tariff, gold and silver, railroad regulation, and the trusts were the main topics to emphasize; but now it is recognized that, when they went to the polls, voters had ethno-cultural concerns foremost in their minds. Yet, ethno-cultural facts also tend to ride piggyback on the larger framework of national economic issues, rather than play an independent role in the text presentation itself.[24]

Let me now extend this emphasis on the interconnection between the community and the larger world more directly into the realm of political history. Through politics, social historians can draw connections between smaller and larger contexts of life. There are several specific types of these connections. To elaborate them will suggest ways in which those concerned with local and community history might keep that larger political connection in mind and incorporate it into their work. It would seem important to convey that larger setting to the public as it visits and observes, as it participates in, and as it reads about local and state history.

There are, first of all, the interactions that occur between the leaders of communities and larger governments such as the state. Communities have not been governmentally isolated. Their governments were created by action of the states, and a constant interaction has taken place between the locality and the state. Often, in the nineteenth century, the main business of the legislature dealt with bills confined to specific localities; even when more general legislation was passed, it often involved some kind of state supervision of local governments. That relationship grew; and, with it, the linkages between representatives from each governmental level. Simply to identify that interaction helps to work out the nature of the relationship and the changes in it. Community studies have identified such people—for example, the lawyer in the local community who becomes the expert in helping local officials understand and cope with the larger maze of state government. In the twentieth century, this function, which anthropologists call "gatekeeping," has extended to relationships between the locality and the federal government. In other words, economic networks such as trade, banking, and transportation, or social contexts such as movement and mobility have counterparts in government—the relationships between smaller and larger institutions, between communities and the formal machinery of the larger state. That can be made concrete by focusing on the people who participated in that interaction as agents of public affairs.

A second feature of this larger setting involves the decline in voting turnout and party commitment and the rise of new types of political action based on shared interest. The decline in party involvement can be traced from the late nineteenth century onward, continuing down to the present; but equally important has been the rise, over the same period of time, of political action based on similar "interest." In the years before

1950, that was confined primairly to economic ties, such as cotton farming, steelworking, banking, or selling groceries. Later, it encompassed other types of common interest, such as hunting and hiking, the activities of elderly people, or the use of electricity—growing more out of the role of people as consumers rather than as producers. That shift in ways of relating to the larger political world constitutes a major aspect of community history. Party commitments were heavily shaped by values sustained through smaller contexts—family, religion, education, the community. When these ties began to weaken, so did ties to party. People began to establish contacts beyond those smaller settings and to link up with others beyond the community, in order to shape forms of action beyond the political party.

Still a third approach to these relationships is to emphasize those affairs that traditionally were carried on at the community level, but which began to be influenced heavily by impulses coming from the state. Initiative in roads and schools, for example, shifted from towns and counties to the state highway commissions and state boards of education, after the late nineteenth century. Banking and insurance came under state supervision, which tended to discipline and constrain community economic institutions. State health and welfare departments reached out to shape and reshape similar activities formerly fashioned largely at the community level. The reorganization of institutions on a scale much larger than the community impacted it significantly and led to differential responses. So far as the community was concerned, each case involved a trade-off of benefits and power. This is a vastly significant process that could well be traced through a community perspective, if one is attuned to the larger context of local affairs.

Finally, one could stress the intrusion into the community on the part of private entrepreneurs who organized economic affairs on a larger scale, but inevitably sought to carry out their activities by using a local site: those who planned the routes for railroad lines in the nineteenth century or selected sites for energy installations, dams, and waste disposal facilities in the last half of the twentieth. In each instance, private corporate ventures needed governmental power and authority to fulfill their objectives. To use local property might require the power of eminent domain, or a revision of local zoning, or state action to override local control. Financial assistance was sought in the form of loans or tax benefits that would permit the location of a new business in a community where it would compete with an existing business. In a considerable number of ways, the private business world, organized on ever-increasing size and scale, has sought to utilize local communities for its own purposes. At times, the community has accepted such action or "siting" as beneficial; but at other times, it has viewed it as harmful. In either case, the power of state and federal governments to facilitate that action has been the focal point of controversy.

In each of these examples just outlined—the personal networks of intergovernmental relationships, the shift from one form of political action to another, the evolution from smaller- to larger-scale systems in government, and the use of state government to intrude into the local community—the connections between the community and the larger world are often difficult to reconstruct. They involve intangible aspects of history. There is little direct data about them in the census records or in governmental archives. The census conveys information about more concrete matters: people, their age, their family relationships, their places of residence, their jobs, their birthplaces, the value of their property, their attendance at school. All these are readily recorded. Hence, the historian tends to write about what is readily available and in the form in which it has been recorded. The kinds of questions raised here, however, about the relationship between society and politics, about the role of the community in the larger world, involve far less tangible factors, about which there is far less information in the historical record. Consequently, one must take up the more difficult task of reconstructing human networks and relationships with indirect evidence.

Yet, it is precisely this kind of historical problem that may well be now coming to the fore. What is the connection between these new aspects of social history and the larger world of public choice? Such connections are inevitably interactive, stressing relationships among people, rather than more tangible characteristics. Yet, they are intensely political. Larger human relationships involve a considerable variety of impulses, of ideas about what is to be preferred, of contention over the distribution of limited governmental resources and power. This is the realm where varied communities and institutions of different objectives and levels of scale, of degrees of cosmopolitan or local outlooks, come into contention. Hence, inquiry within the historical profession raises the question: where does the smaller context of social history fit into the larger context of political history?

We have now come full circle. The new social history first arose from the search for the social roots of politics through the study of voting behavior. Then a more autonomous interest in social history grew rapidly in the 1960s, amid the social ferment of that decade and the discovery of considerable evidence about similar affairs in the past. More recently, questions have arisen about the relationship of these developments with the larger context of history—questions that often take the form of a greater interest in political analysis. Hence the question: what is the relationship between society and politics? To take up this question and follow the larger political world through its intersection with the community could well improve the quality of local and community history. Exhibits and interpretive programs, archival and museum collections, and writing should be increasingly sensitive to such historical questions. To explore such relationships further in state and local history could well enhance the significance of more limited social and community history.

Notes

1. Stephan Thernstrom, *Poverty and Progress: Social Mobility in a Nineteenth Century City* (Cambridge: Harvard University Press, 1964).

2. Sam Bass Warner, Jr., *Streetcar Suburbs: The Process of Growth in Boston, 1870–1900* (Cambridge: Harvard University Press, 1962).

3. Thomas C. Cochran, "The Presidential Synthesis in American History," *American Historical Review* 53 (1948): 748–759.

4. Lee Benson, *The Concept of Jacksonian Democracy: New York as a Test Case* (Princeton: Princeton University Press, 1961).

5. Samuel P. Hays, "History as Human Behavior," *Iowa Journal of History* 58 (1960): 193–206.

6. Paul Kleppner, *The Cross of Culture: A Social Analysis of Midwestern Politics, 1850–1900* (New York: Free Press, 1970).

7. Richard J. Jensen, *The Winning of the Midwest: Social and Political Conflict, 1888–1896* (Chicago: University of Chicago Press, 1971).

8. Frederick C. Luebke, *Immigrants and Politics: The Germans of Nebraska, 1880–1900* (Lincoln: University of Nebraska Press, 1969).

9. Paul Kleppner, et al., *The Evolution of American Electoral Systems* (Westport, Conn.: Greenwood Press, 1981).

10. Paul Kleppner, *The Third Electoral System, 1853–1892: Parties, Voters, and Political Cultures* (Chapel Hill: University of North Carolina Press, 1979).

11. Paul Kleppner and Stephen C. Baker, "The Impact of Voter Registration Requirements on Electoral Turnout, 1900–16," *Journal of Political and Military Sociology* 8 (1980): 205–226.

12. Nora Faires, "Class and Culture: The Development of the German Community in Pittsburgh and Allegheny City, Pennsylvania" (Ph.D. dissertation, University of Pittsburgh, 1981).

13. Susan J. Kleinberg, "Technology's Stepdaughters: The Impact of Industrialization Upon Working Class Women, Pittsburgh, 1865–1890" (Ph.D. dissertation, University of Pittsburgh, 1973).

14. Roland L. Warren, *The Community in America* (Chicago: Rand McNally, 1963).

15. An exception to this tendency is the work of David Montgomery, who has explored the problem of "worker control." See his *Workers' Control in America: Studies in the History of Work, Technology, and Labor Struggles* (New York: Cambridge University Press, 1979).

16. Merle E. Curti, *The Making of an American Community: A Case Study of Democracy in a Frontier County* (Stanford: Stanford University Press, 1959).

17. Lee Soltow, *Men and Wealth in the United States, 1850–1870* (New Haven: Yale University Press, 1975).

18. Robert Eugene Harper, "The Class Structure of Western Pennsylvania in the Late Eighteenth Century" (Ph.D. dissertation, University of Pittsburgh, 1969).

19. Lee Soltow, "Inequality Admidst Abundance: Land Ownership in Early Nineteenth-Century Ohio," *Ohio History* 88 (1979): 133–151.

20. Jeffrey G. Williamson and Peter H. Lindert, *American Inequality: A Macroeconomic History* (New York: Academic Press, 1980).

21. I have explored this approach elsewhere in an attempt to bring together frontier problems in both genealogy and social history. See Samuel P. Hays, "History and Genealogy: Patterns of Change and Prospects for Co-operation," *Prologue* 7 (1975): pp. 39–43, 81–84, 187–191.

22. See a more extended statement of this approach in Samuel P. Hays, "Political Parties and the Community-Society Continuum," in *The American Party Systems: Stages of Political Development*, edited by William N. Chambers and Walter Dean Burnham (New York: Oxford University Press), pp. 152–181.

23. A specific analysis cast in this setting is Samuel P. Hays, "The Structure of Environmental Politics Since World War II," *Journal of Social History* 14 (1981): 719–738.

24. See, for example, Robert Kelley, *The Shaping of the American Past* (Englewood Cliffs: Prentice Hall, 1982). For a more integrative approach, see John G. Clark, *Three Generations in Twentieth-Century America: Family, Community and Nation* (Homewood, Ill.: Dorsey Press, 1977).

Suggestions for Additional Reading

Benson, Lee. *The Concept of Jacksonian Democracy: New York as a Test Case*. Princeton: Princeton University Press, 1961.

Pioneering monograph in the "new political history" demonstrating the use of social science methodology and theory in the analysis of popular voting behavior.

Cochran, Thomas C. "The Presidential Synthesis in American History." *American Historical Review* 53 (1948): 748–759.

Early critique of conventional political history; emphasizes the need for incorporating social science concepts and methodology and shifting the focus away from national politics and the presidency.

Hays, Samuel P. "History as Human Behavior." *Iowa Journal of History* 58 (1960): 193–206.

Important early statement of the value of a behavioral approach in political analysis.

Hays, Samuel P. "The Social Analysis of American Political History, 1880–1920." *Political Science Quarterly* 80 (1965): 373–394.

Essay arguing for a "social analysis of politics."

Hays, Samuel P. "The Structure of Environmental Politics Since World War II." *Journal of Social History* 14 (1981): 719–738.

Example of analysis linking society and politics.

Hays, Samuel P. "Political Parties and the Community-Society Continuum." In *The American Party Systems: Stages of Political Development*, edited by William N. Chambers and Walter Dean Burnham, 152–181. New York: Oxford University Press, 1967.

Extended statement on the value of politics in broadening the analytic perspectives of social history research.

Jensen, Richard J. *The Winning of the Midwest: Social and Political Conflict, 1886–1896*. Chicago: University of Chicago Press, 1971.

Notable example of ethnocultural analysis of voting behavior.

Kleppner, Paul. *The Cross of Culture: A Social Analysis of Midwestern Politics, 1850–1900*. New York: Free Press, 1970.

Intensive study of voting behavior, focusing on the role of religion, ethnicity, and personal value systems.

Kleppner, Paul. *The Third Electoral System, 1853–1892: Parties, Voters, and Political Cultures*. Chapel Hill: University of North Carolina Press, 1979.

Expansion and elaboration of Kleppner's earlier analysis of voting behavior in the Midwest.

Kleppner, Paul, et al. *The Evolution of American Electoral Systems*. Westport, Conn.: Greenwood Press, 1981.

Recent volume on the American party systems.

Luebke, Frederick C. *Immigrants and Politics: The Germans of Nebraska, 1880–1900*. Lincoln: University of Nebraska Press, 1969.

Another fine example of the "ethnocultural school."

Soltow, Lee. "Inequality Amidst Abundance: Land Ownership in Early Nineteenth-Century Ohio." *Ohio History* 88 (1979): 133–151.

Essay examining the problem of economic inequality in Ohio in 1810.

Soltow, Lee. *Men and Wealth in the United States, 1850–1870*. New Haven: Yale University Press, 1975.

Careful analysis of the evolution of wealth distribution, focusing on the mid-nineteenth century but actually providing perspective on the period from 1790 to the 1960s.

Williamson, Jeffrey G., and Peter H. Lindert. *American Inequality: A Macroeconomic History*. New York: Academic Press, 1980.

Recent volume on the problem of inequality in American society.

Costumed hostesses and a log cabin from "Ye Olden Times" provided visitors to Philadelphia's Centennial Exposition of 1876 with a uniquely Victorian interpretation of life in colonial America.

9

Things Unspoken: Learning Social History from Artifacts

Barbara G. Carson
Cary Carson

ALL THE EXCITEMENT stirred up by the bright and brassy new historians has diverted attention from two obligations that a people can reasonably expect the keepers of its collective memory to fulfill. We indulge the awesome cheek of those who preach that God calls all creation social history, because their pretense holds promise of a unifying logic to make sense of an incoherent past and an inchoate present. That logic is vital. Human society depends for its very existence on a common sense of who we are and where we have come from. Our conduct as individuals and collectively as a nation is regulated by a pervasive, generalized, historical vision. In ordinary times, it validates and reinforces our conformity to accepted values and established norms. Quite simply, we live according to a self-made mythology whose authorship we disguise from ourselves by calling it history. Only by acting *as if* the world made sense can we form ourselves into orderly communities and call our neighbors fellow men and women. The trouble comes when we perceive a misalignment between everyday experience and our common understanding of the past. When that happens, we scramble around to invent some other version of our history that better fits our altered circumstances. Proponents of the new social history believe they have discovered an improved formula for understanding the global village that came into being in the sixties and seventies. They deserve a hearing from us all—historians and nonhistorians alike—because, just possibly, they might be right. At the very least, we should reserve judgment until we see if they really can reassemble the separate pieces of the past into a convincing cosmography and then—in performance of their second duty as historians—can impart that vision to the public at large.

Seminars like those sponsored by the American Association for State and Local History, from which the essays in this book took their inspiration, represent an encouraging sign that newer ways of historical thinking are beginning to find a wider audience. Conferences and popular publications put scholars in touch with those other professional historians whose museums and historical societies reach the general public directly. A line of communications is thereby opened, and a conversation started. But, if one takes the trouble to eavesdrop on those exchanges, often what one hears still sounds like Dial-a-Professor. Even the contributors to this volume speak the patois of their separate specialties as experts on the American family, on women, on urban and rural history, on ethnic groups, and so on, through the familiar academic subsets of human knowledge. From a tender age, graduate student historians learn to carve the past into pieces small enough to master in a lifetime of research. That is right and natural. Reliable scholarship stands on well-laid footings. But who superintends the works as a whole, while the craftsmen labor in the builders' trenches? Historians ought to; they have the best credentials; but often they are not ready or willing, and the initiative passes to others less qualified.

The conversation lately begun between academic social historians and their opposite numbers in museums and historical agencies may accomplish more than just spreading the good word. It may also hold the secret to the problem of adding up the sum of the new social history's parts. This suggestion will surprise both parties—the research historians, because they are the accustomed explorers and first discoverers; and the teachers and museum interpreters, because their calling as instructors and popularizers leaves them little time for original speculative thinking. No one should expect the leopards to exchange their spots. Even so, there is reason to believe that a synthesis of recent scholarship could occur outside the university, for the simple reason that the new model social history shows a remarkable affinity for the spatial, tangible, real worlds that past ages have sloughed off and left behind as the artifacts we preserve at historic sites and collect in museums. The definition of social history that Peter Stearns offers in this book's introductory essay—"*the ordinary activities of ordinary people*"—needs only props and stage directions to bring to life the central events in the new historians' *tableau vivant*. Births, christenings, schooling, courtship, weddings, housework, farm work, office work, no work, leisure, play, holidays, social gatherings, family reunions, church attendance, sporting events, riots, crimes, broken marriages, illnesses, deaths, funerals, bereavements—all were acted out in real, three-dimensional settings. All can be vividly recalled—indeed, can only be vividly recalled—when those historical settings are evoked. In that line, historians who have a knowledge of material life—history's scene-setters—have a clear advantage over those who have not.

Bookish scholars will concede the point, but not the game. They will maintain, with good reason, that reconstructions of the past—whether as museum settings, gallery exhibits, films, or even finely drawn word pictures—can illustrate only the current state of knowledge derived mainly from written-record sources. They are absolutely right. Yet, lest we try to run before we learn to walk, let us remember that our immediate aim is not to reckon up a greater sum than social history's separate parts but, for now, merely to add them all together. A prolific monographic scholarship of twenty years must somehow now be reassembled into the integrated experience that real life always is (and was) and into the comprehensive account of it that the new social history aspires to be. Reconstructed physical settings, by themselves hollow and meaningless, are no substitute for the human activities that once took place in them. Yet, if well done, they can work wonderfully to concentrate the mind on the complex connections that comprised the fullness of family and community life. Like the scene of a crime meticulously recorded by police photographers before a shred of evidence is disturbed, convincingly reconstructed historical settings are charged with a kinetic energy of events lately transpired and are replete with clues that skillful interpreters can use to conjure up the human dramas that appear to have just occurred. If the aim is to rewrite American history as community history and to reach the public for whom it is intended, academic social historians can do worse than make common cause with students of material culture.

The case for collaboration is easier to state than to demonstrate. It requires knowledge of a subject little explored even by museum educators, namely, the ways that people learn history when they meet the past face to face. Whole libraries are filled with technical literature on historical architecture and decorative arts and on the development of historic sites and the furnishing of period rooms.[1] A smaller number of books and articles offer instruction in the gentle art of interpreting the historical scene, but pay very little attention to the actual learning process that either the scene or its interpretation may set in motion.[2] Getting closer to the subject, a few psychologists have begun to study the motivations of museum visitors and the effectiveness of various exhibition tech-

niques in attracting attention, holding interest, and conveying information.[3] Virtually no one has squarely addressed the questions that ought to
be foremost in the minds of those who teach or seek to learn history
outside the formal classroom: How, it is necessary to ask, do adults size
up history incarnate? How does the mind's eye "read" historical artifacts,
singly and when assembled into habitats? A glance records a multitude of
images that our brains instantaneously untangle, evaluate, edit, and present to our consciousness as maybe two or three dominant impressions—all long before a guide or interpreter has had time to say, "Good
morning. Please stay on the gravel paths." Our ultimate design in writing
this essay is to suggest ways in which artifacts can be used to acquaint the
general public with the ideas that animate the new social history. To
entertain the least hope of success, we must recognize at the outset that
visual learning about the past obeys rules that apply to instruction in
history—new or old.

Two points need clarification to start with—one about our readers and
the other to explain our flexible definition of the term *reconstructed historical setting*. We have been careful to address both teachers and learners in
what we say here. The line between them is hard to draw when dealing
with two such generally unfamiliar subjects as a newfangled history and
the psychology of learning by looking. Unquestionably, exhibit planners,
museum interpreters, and classroom teachers of social history have professional reasons to become better acquainted with the didactic properties of artifacts, sites, and settings. So do students. We would like to
think that we are also writing for a portion of that enormous audience of
some seventy-five million Americans who visit history museums every
year. Speaking frankly to them, we have to acknowledge that, until many
more professional museum teachers catch on to the new trends in social
history, intelligent lay visitors to museums and historic sites will have to
exercise their own initiative to elicit the information necessary to construct a fuller, rounder picture of the past. Some simple guidelines for
learning social history from artifacts are described later in the essay, as
much for these do-it-yourself historians as for professional site planners
and museum interpreters.

We also prefer a broad definition of the historical scene, one that rules
in, not out, the many different physical forms the past assumes. Historic
sites, historic houses, restored and reconstructed towns and villages,
and—on a smaller scale—period rooms and period settings are only the
most complete, self-conscious, and, at best, authentic of our historical
re-creations. We are also presented with other appearances of the past in
films, illustrations, stage plays, works of fiction, and, occasionally, even

history books. All have a similar purpose. They use artifacts, pictures of artifacts, or descriptions of artifacts to set a scene that puts viewers or readers in a sufficiently believing frame of mind to swallow whatever comes next—the message, the pitch, the interpretation. Consequently, much of what we say here about elaborately reconstructed historical settings will apply in varying degrees to the other encounters we have with history embodied in material form.

Where so much is learned visually before formal instruction ever begins, it is surprising that history's set designers—its curators and museum educators, mainly—have given so little forethought to the properties that make or do not make historic sites and period rooms effective teachers. An illustration from Colonial Williamsburg provides only an extreme case of the myopia that afflicts museums generally.

Several years ago, Williamsburg decided to refurnish and reinterpret the Governor's Palace, a favorite exhibition building with visitors since it was reconstructed and first opened to the public in 1934. Its refurbishment, forty years later, enlisted the skills and energies of about forty-five curators, conservators, architects and architectural historians, social and institutional historians, archaeologists, and interpretive specialists of one kind or another. All told, they devoted tens of thousands of hours to research and preparation. The vast body of knowledge they accumulated they then subjected to a series of drastic compressions, first into a digest made to fit the 150 hours given to training tour guides, then into a 45-minute abridgement adapted to the tour itself, and, finally, into the several 3- or 4-minute segments that interpreters spend at each station in the course of a tour. If visitors were to hang on every precious word that guides utter, they would hear a total of perhaps two thousand words, the equivalent of eight to ten printed pages. In fact, tests show that they listen to only half of everything a hostess says. Yet, surveys confirm that visitors overwhelmingly find the Palace tour richly rewarding and, more to the point, actually improve their knowledge of the historical subjects addressed on the tour by a factor of two or three. The conclusion is inescapable: where so much information must necessarily be distilled into a severely abbreviated oral presentation and where only half of that is heard anyway, yet, where learners receive substantial instruction notwithstanding, they are obviously picking up a great deal from what they see and from what they say to one another about it as they walk from room to room. Tests conducted before the Palace was refurnished established these learning patterns conclusively. Yet—and this is our point—*never once was that knowledge applied to planning the new exhibit.* The curators' guiding aim was to furnish and arrange each room with the greatest possible fidelity to a detailed household inventory compiled after Governor Botetourt's death in 1770. When the matter was considered at all, interpretive planners simply assumed that authentically re-created interiors would make the best social history classrooms. Fortunately, that turned out to be a fair assumption; but those who participated in planning the Palace, like exhibit designers almost everywhere, gave scarcely any thought to understanding how learning would take place in the visually exciting social spaces they created.

How does it? And, to anticipate a later question, how can such knowledge be used to design an interplay between artifacts and oral or written interpretations that leads to exploration of new social history themes? Here psychologists can get us started, especially those who have experimented in recent years with what are called naturalistic surveys. These take various forms, but one way or another, all record people's spontaneous behavior and evaluate it in relation to the context in which it occurs. Robert Wolf of the Department of Psychological Studies at the Smithsonian Institution and Robert Birney at Colonial Williamsburg have employed naturalistic evaluation methods to study visitor behavior specifically in history museums.[4] They and their associates unobtrusively eavesdrop on visitors and record verbatim their informal remarks; in addition, they sometimes conduct post-tour interviews. These data are then carefully studied for patterns that indicate the ways in which people typically perceive artifacts and by what means they unconsciously organize their learning experience in museum settings.

The almost universal initial reaction to exhibits of any kind is an attempt by visitors to identify the artifacts or scenes they encounter, usually by trying to stick names on them.[5] "Oh, this must be the butler's pantry." "Look, Bill, see the chandelier." Looking and naming accounted for 43 percent of the tabulated responses in the Governor's Palace survey. Frequently, members of parties touring together help each other make these identifications. Parents characteristically call certain objects to children's notice and relate them to their experience by giving them familiar names. "Sarah, see that sheep? That's a colonial lawnmower." If exhibits are accompanied by labels, visitors almost invariably identify artifacts verbally first, then read the labels to double-check their answers. Observers studying visitor participation in three special "discovery corners" in the National Museum of American History reported that the single most sought-after piece of information about objects that visitors were allowed to touch was the name of each, which, if the least bit technical or unfamiliar, they automatically translated into the vernacular. *Muskets* became *guns* that shot *bullets*, not *balls*. Common names smooth the way to a common understanding.

Once objects have been identified, many visitors are curious to know how they worked. "Seeing how it works is important" is a statement that recurs many times in the Smithsonian surveys. "Most kids don't know how things work," parents are sure. Many adults do not know, either. All ages, therefore, welcome diagrams and demonstrations that explain the operation of mechanical equipment. "Now I begin to understand how a telephone works," says one pleased respondent; "it has an electromagnet." Another tries on an artificial arm: "At first I wasn't sure of the muscle control, but I've started to get the hang of it." Often, the mere act of identifying objects is enough to lead people to accurate conclusions about their use and the original function of the settings they furnish. "Now is this the warming room?" one woman asks a friend, as she pokes her head into an alcove in the Governor's Palace. "Yes," replies the other, pointing to a plate warmer, "after they brought [the food] over here, they warmed it." First woman: "For crying out loud!" When such questions and comments about the functions of artifacts are added to the looking and naming responses recorded in the Palace survey, the number of conversational exchanges that served to orient visitors to the historical surroundings approaches 70 percent.

The psychologists who conducted these surveys do not come right out and say so, but what is really going on in these initial engagements between visitors and museum exhibits is fairly easy to guess. Naming provides access to each person's memory system. Names, functions, dates ("How old is that thing?"), and provenances are the co-ordinates people use to locate the mental pictures of the past that we all carry around in our heads. Images called up from this repository of everybody's personal material culture are the templates against which we test the familiarity of every new appearance of history we come across. Every time we are presented with a scene from the past, three-dimensional or otherwise, we ask ourselves how well it squares with our accumulated preconceptions. Recognition gives us a sense of control. Hence, every artifact is evaluated on what we take to be its "rightness" to the setting it occupies or to which it is restored, in our mind's eye.

Learning about history starts, then, with a blunt question about its honesty: Is this thing really what it pretends to be? A suspicion of being fooled explains museum visitors' keen interest in realism. "It's all so real," exclaims a woman interviewed about a bicentennial exhibit at the National Museum of Natural History. "It looks as if the family had just left the cabin." "Here you can *see* history," explains someone else,"—the way things look—the way it must have been. Seeing it makes you believe it happened." Although wary by nature, people want so badly to accept what they see that they will unconsciously edit out anachronisms. "Hey, guys, look at this," calls out one of a group of boys touring an ecology exhibit. "They got real trees in here, and they're made out of rubber!" "Original" pieces of furniture are the hard currency of historic house museums. Without them, visitors will be somewhat appeased by "exact copies," but woe unto the restoration that gets a reputation for showing "mostly repros." On the other hand, where visitors are told that reproductions have been used to enhance realism by filling in a historical setting with things otherwise unavailable, they willingly place their trust in the semblance of realism. The late James Short of Colonial Williamsburg always maintained that believability was what most people really meant when they talked of authenticity. "When it's real, you can relate to it," summed up a respondent to the Smithsonian survey. When it is not, doubt creeps in.

A split second is all the time the brain needs to run through the steps that bring the history learner to the most critical moment in the visual learning process, the point of passing judgment. The artifact, habitat, illustration—whatever it is—has been observed, identified, named, and its veracity put to the test. The time has come to find the thing either credible or dubious. In practice, as the Williamsburg surveys show, these verdicts are seldom expressed as conscious choices. Most people, if they make any verbal statement at all, indicate acceptance of what they see by "liking" it or "wanting" it or otherwise assimilating it by letting something familiar or personal vouch for its authenticity. "The governor must have been related to my aunt. She puts slipcovers on everything." Disbelief is usually expressed in exclamations of surprise or by asking questions that challenge the offending object. "I didn't know they had Venetian blinds back then!" "I still can't believe they had such high ceilings. How did they ever heat the place?"

Teachers and museum interpreters must never forget that visitors pass these judgments on every new scene they are shown and on every artifact that catches their notice. They must learn to look for the signs that will tell them when people accept the evidence of their eyes and those other signs that should alert them to doubtfulness or stark incredulity. Depending upon which it is, practiced interpreters will adopt one of two quite different teaching strategies, for both responses offer learning opportunities, each of a different kind. Where history's manifestations live up to visitors' expectations, they are disposed to become further involved in the scene and its meaning. Guides (or, for that matter, labels or mechanical interpretive devices) need only confirm the rightness of these initial impressions before going on to select elements from the scene to use in developing the all-important ideas and themes. Visitors to the cliff dwellers' settlements at Mesa Verde, Colorado, for example, are encouraged at Spruce Tree House to climb down through a small hole in one of the forecourts into a dimly lit, subterranean kiva where the menfolk clubbed together for recreation and ritual. The stone seat around the circular walls, the shaft of heavy, yellow light from the hatch overhead, the muffled footsteps and sounds of "village life" above, and even the indistinct figures of fellow tourists climbing up and down the wooden ladder work such a powerful effect on the senses that the Park Service ranger, her voice raised hardly above a whisper, need only speak three or four sentences to flood the space with the ambience of men and boys sharing a special, secret, magical place that gave their fellowship a oneness with ancient traditions and living community. A very different, but equally compelling example can be found in John Demos's superb little book on family life in Plymouth Colony.[6] Three opening chapters that describe "The Physical Setting" use mere words printed on pages of paper to build and furnish in the reader's imagination Pilgrim houses so realistic that no one can help listening sympathetically to the author's views on the subjects that his book is really about, child-rearing and family life. The kiva interpretation is almost wholly subjective; the book, just the opposite. Yet both make effective use of highly believable historical re-creations as an inducement to learning more about two very unfamiliar cultures.

A different strategy is needed to deal with the skeptic, usually a person who finds that, try as he might, he just cannot believe his eyes. His impediment to learning must be addressed at once, and his doubts allayed, if possible. As long as he harbors misgivings, everything he sees or hears will be compromised. A discordant anachronism, real or perceived, "not only kills the atmosphere," explains a perceptive interpreter at a historic house museum in Leadville, Colorado, "but it does something far more destructive. It can be something very minor, like plastic buttons or zippers [on a costume], but it forces the visitor to sort out the real from the fake."[7] These are booby traps that teachers and interpreters must learn to recognize and disarm, sometimes turning them to their own advantage. Tours of the Governor's Palace at Williamsburg reach a visual climax in a large, ornate ballroom added to the building in the 1750s. The recent renovation greatly enriched this lavish scene of official entertainment by making some spectacular additions: Prussian blue wallpaper with gilt borders, three matched chandeliers, a suite of cherry chairs and settees, and brightly painted coats of arms over the doors. The dazzling scene literally takes away the breath of many visitors—until their eyes fall on a big, black, coal-burning, cast iron, pot-bellied stove standing a good five or six feet away from the wall. A closer look reveals that it is not really a pot belly the likes of which most people have ever seen before. But there is no denying its enormous size, its ungainly stovepipe vented out a nearby window, trapper-cabin-style, and its wholly unexpected presence in the polite company of the room's eighteenth-century fittings. Hostesses know that nothing else will be heard until they explain that Lord Botetourt purchased three "elegant warming Machines" from a London foundry and installed one in his ballroom just as the reproduction shows. Once that much has been said, by way of background, the stove becomes an invaluable asset to interpreters who have learned how to use its commanding presence to start people thinking—first, about the problem of heating such a cavernous interior, and then why almost 40 percent of the total living area in the Palace was reserved for a special-purpose ballroom and supper-room. The visitors' train of thought can lead easily from there to the art of dancing, which, they are sometimes told, assumed a formalized and sophisticated social organization in the eighteenth century. The passion for dancing gave rise to the fashionable practice of installing assembly rooms in official residences, private homes, and even inns and taverns, where genteel social gatherings were often organized by subscription. In so many words, the Palace stove and its heating capacity can open a subject as broad as the commercialization of leisure in the eighteenth century.

With true believers at last firmly in tow, the interpreter (or interpretive exhibit) is ready to turn the visitors' faith to the task of teaching history. At this stage, we are still talking about any kind of history; but, as our chief interest is *community history*, what can we say about using historical artifacts as points of departure for excursions into the worlds best known to social historians? The answer to that depends on the answers to two other questions: Out of everything that social history now embraces, what is most worth learning and, consequently, most worth teaching? Second, what aspects of social history are most teachable in three-dimensional historical settings?

Leaving aside for the moment whether or not "history from the bottom up" describes ends or means, we can say with certainty that social historians' new-found interest in the common folk and their commonplace activities legitimizes the vast array of everyday artifacts that bulk large in museum and historical society collections. There is only one Liberty Bell; but church bells, school bells, farm bells, cow bells, and Southern belles abound. Such curios and relics have long been the stuff of "pots-and-pans history," playthings for antiquaries. Now, by scrutinizing the mundane events of everyday life for patterns of behavior that reveal a people's basic living conditions and cultural values, social historians have invested ordinary artifacts with new meaning. If such things serve scholars only rarely as primary evidence, many more qualify as props that teachers and interpreters can use to re-create and sometimes even re-enact the activities in which the artifacts once were instrumental. Work, play, eating, sleeping, dressing, socializing, traveling—all involved the use of objects. Indeed, beginning in the seventeenth century, the lives of ordinary people increasingly came to be governed by a system of manners and social conventions that required a growing assortment of personal and household artifacts to mediate human relationships. This is the history of material life, a subject no less central to the study of American society than family history or women's history, although historians have hardly begun to explore it.[9] This is not the place for that, either; our aim is to learn how artifacts can elucidate social history themes. For that, it is enough to remember that antique structures, furnishings, clothing, and machines and tools can be put to work again to recall the tasks, activities, and rituals that originally employed them. Visitors to historic sites and outdoor museums expect to see the tools of many trades reused in craft and cooking demonstrations, farm work, and small-scale manufacturing. Some museums now employ actor-interpreters to bring back to life the still wider spectrum of social customs and domestic routines for which teapots, telephones, and parlor organs were essential equipment no less than a plowman's share or a craftsman's hammer.[10] Where careful planning has gone into such demonstrations and reenactments, audiences are led by easy stages from what they can touch—the artifacts—to what they can see—the artifacts in use—to what they can only grasp intellectually— the reasons for doing whatever it was that the men and women portrayed were doing at that particular time and place in history. A young woman hulls peas in the open doorway of a doctor's kitchen at Conner Prairie, an Indiana pioneer village re-created to the year 1836. She explains to passersby that she and other immigrant farm girls get jobs in town as housemaids, to learn English and perfect the skills they need to become good wives and mothers. Her artifacts—the homespun dress and apron she wears and the earthenware bowl that catches the peas—are typical social history props. Their utterly prosaic appearance is the reason that teaching the new-style history need not be hindered for want of the icons that only a few great museums can own. Nor should it be unduly hampered by the bias of most museum collections toward things uncommonly beautiful, expensive, and rare. Prints, drawings, photographs, advertisements, catalogues, and artifacts recovered by archaeologists can restore the appearance of daily life to virtually every period of American history, every region, and, yes, even every enshrined birthplace of a patriot, president, or Confederate general. Given their priorities, social historians have reason to rejoice in the truth of the old folk saying that the great and the small put on their pants pretty much the same way, one leg at a time.

Yet, therein also lies a serious problem when it comes to disseminating social history to the public. Too often, its practitioners appear to glory in the inglorious and relish the decline and fall of history's textbook heroes. "History from the bottom up" seldom gets up very far. Although—fortunately—nothing came of a proposal we remember a few years ago to declare a moratorium on the study of all prominent white males in American history, one often hears it said that social history deals with ordinary people *rather than* the elite. That reputation does it no good, because as long as it comes off sounding radical chic, social history stands no chance of general acceptance. Moreover, it does not do justice to its purpose. Historians must not suppose that they can rest content when they have finally restored to their rightful places in history's pages all the blacks, women, Hispanics, Native Americans, homosexuals, and poor white trash that were left out in the earlier editions. Such folk most certainly belong there, but not only or even chiefly because every people deserves a chance to tell and hear told its own part in the American story. A full cast of characters is needed most importantly, because social history has a higher calling as community history. Known more precisely as the history of society, its practice requires paying primary attention to the complex web of connections that every person forms freely or otherwise with his fellow men and women in the cause of raising families, earning livings, making laws, worshipping gods, and whatever else cannot be done alone. Social history worth its salt deals with ordinary people *as well as*, not rather than, the elite, and with everyday activities *no less than* world-class events. Everyone participates in the life of some community, be it a single family, a neighborhood, a fraternal lodge, or the affairs of whole cities, states, or nations. Ultimately, social historians must present us with group portraits of these manifold human associations, painted in ways that help us to understand and appreciate that the greatness of mankind is the ingenuity that men and women *can* exercise in pursuing peacefully (if not harmoniously) common courses of action toward common goals.

Anthropologists, sociologists, and now—increasingly—social historians contend that a community's physical form is basic to its self-identification.[11] Communities are *places*, usually relatively small places. Sometimes their limits are as clearly defined as the walls of a house or the bounds of a town. Other times, community space is less seen than felt, its outer limits determined by the inhabitants' common way of life and common actions. These, too, we have seen, often require special structures, tools, or utensils, but their functions go only so far to determine their appearance. Objects of similar purpose have assumed a multiplicity of forms from place to place and from one time to another. Consciously or—more often—unconsciously, those who make and build the things that a community provides for itself design them in accordance with the ethos of the place. Therein lies the essence of vernacular culture. Folk traditions remain vital and unalloyed where a people's everyday associations are still predominantly local. Connections with a wider world are few and tenuous, and, consequently, outside influences slight. Of course, no early American community existed in perfect isolation. Even where familial ties and familiar associations ran strongest, ministers, office-holders, soldiers, storekeepers, market farmers, and others trafficked with larger, external social, political, and economic networks. Often the production of agricultural surpluses, sold abroad, opened a way for foreign influences to flow back into tightly knit communities. That happened not because exotic customs, once introduced, proved irresistible. On the contrary, vigorous folk communities characteristically shrugged off the "furrin ways" they had no need for. Indeed, the confrontation between them-folks and we-uns was the recurring dynamic that marked and maintained the boundaries between one community and its neighbors. Folk culture conservatism was impenetrable to everything except forces of change that worked slowly from the inside out. Newer needs came to replace old ones, as, for example, farmers with cash crops to sell perceived that their business dealings would profit from a certain degree of accommodation to styles and customs practiced by their business associates in foreign parts. Back home, the prominence they enjoyed as a consequence of their wealth or reputation outweighed the peculiar cut of their coats or their sudden, unnatural fondness for baths. Their eccentricities were tolerated, forgiven, and finally copied by others who hankered after similar social visibility. Little by little, inward-looking communities turned outward, and their horizons grew wider.

Artifacts and the things artifacts can do, being highly portable and reproducible, have often been important agents of such cultural change. Usually, however, a traditional material culture is modified as little as can be got away with; folk builders and makers adopt only such design alternatives as need requires. Consequently, a great many artifacts contain trace elements of both a community's internal and external associations. Historians, intent on re-creating a semblance of community life, can extract from artifacts' split personalities certain elements that define a folk culture's homogeneous self and others that display its extroverted alter ego.

Take, for example, an ordinary piece of eighteenth-century storage furniture. A Philadelphia chest of drawers in the collections of the Winterthur Museum will do admirably.[12] The one we have in mind is mahogany and has a lock on each of its four graduated drawers. In the colonial period—and well into more recent times—locks were commonly installed on the lids of chests and trunks and on the drawers and doors of desks, secretaries, clothes presses, jewel cases, cupboards, and spice cabinets.[13] They indicate the user's concern for the security of whatever he or she kept inside. To us, the old-fashioned habit of locking furniture seems curiously redundant. After all, if people did not lock their houses, what is one to make of all the evidence of antique door locks? Today, we bolt our doors, activate alarm systems, and rest reasonably assured that we have secured our property against intruders by creating a barrier around the periphery of our private space. When we go out, no one remains at home to wash clothes, cook meals, care for children, await deliveries, or fetch in water and firewood. Not so many years ago, these tasks required someone's almost constant attention. Even modest households employed domestics. Although such people were inmates, they were not, strictly speaking, family, and often they were not entirely trusted. Yet, to perform their duties, they needed free access to most of the house. A peripheral security system was pointless in their case. Instead, each drawer and cupboard had to be separately secured. Each could be unlocked only by the mistress or housekeeper or someone in authority who kept the keys. Thus, a thoughtful interpreter can use something as simple as a lock and key to conjure up a vanished social system of masters and servants, the work routine of a staff of (usually female) domestics, and even something as intangible as the ambivalent trusting-yet-distrustful relationship between workers and supervisors.

The same piece of furniture has other stories to tell, too, tales from places far away from Philadelphia. Its carcass of West Indian mahogany testifies to its maker's ties with an established network of timber merchants, importers, sea captains, agents, and entrepreneurs. Likewise, the brass drawer pulls and escutcheons on the chest, which are identical to illustrations in a pattern book owned by a Philadelphia merchant, lead back through who knows how many hands to a brass foundry in England. Even more expressive of its maker's and owner's involvement in a larger culture is the fashionable appearance of its serpentine front and fluted corners. Although it is unmistakably the product of a Philadelphia cabinet shop, its lines mark it as the property of someone whose educated tastes would open doors far beyond the Schuylkill. Comparable latent elements in almost every artifact will respond similarly to the summons of knowledgeable students, interpreters, teachers, and even laymen who are willing to question what they see.

We have now arrived, in a roundabout way, at an answer to our question about social history's real worth. At best, it explores communal experiences. We have seen, too, that becoming acquainted with the history of society is made easier by paying attention to the physical characteristics that gave historical communities spatial definition and cultural identity. Because artifacts and man-made environments are the tools everyone used to engage in everyday activities, today they can be reused to reveal, once again, the interdependencies and working relationships through which men and women practiced the art of living.

They can be. That does not mean that they often are. Social history is hard to put into exhibit cases, and human relationships pale to invisibility alongside the aggressively exhibitionist artifacts that equip work-places and furnish period rooms. Interpreters have only seconds or, at most, minutes to say their piece. Museum visitors do not know what to sample first in the riot of visual delights that tempt their eyes. Therefore both do what psychologists tell us comes most naturally: they pick out a few conspicuous things and give them names or identify the materials from which they are made. This course of least resistance leads directly to the junkyard of "old social history," unless teachers and learners make an effort at imagination. Not a big effort. Nor one that requires much specialized knowledge. Far more useful is a set of simple operating procedures that can be carried in the head and learned so thoroughly that their use becomes second nature.

From our own experience as teachers, as planners and interpreters of museums we have worked for, and as visitors to others, we have developed, over a period of years, a handy sort of catechism that can be used to ferret out the social history inherent in many different kinds of reconstructed historical settings. We make no claims for its originality, for we have seen it unintentionally employed by a few exceptionally able interpreters and in some unusually successful exhibits. So simple that any intelligent museum visitor can master its application with a little practice, it involves nothing more difficult than addressing four questions to the assemblage of artifacts that comprise a historical scene. The questions start with our desire to identify and name what we see in front of us: *What was this place?* From that, they follow in logical sequence: *What activities normally occurred here? Who performed them? How did those people work together to accomplish their tasks or make the activities happen?* From inanimate things, attention turns to people and their relationships. By Socratic inquiry, aimless gawking becomes a purposeful search for particular artifacts that can answer particular questions. Most important, the mind is spurred on beyond mere looking and naming to contemplate the social bonds that formed the basic building blocks of community life.

The first two questions can apply to single artifacts almost as readily as they can to artifacts brought together into functional groups. Objects removed from their social or occupational contexts and exhibited in conventional art museum-style limbos can still answer questions of identification and function—what was this thing, and what was it used for? To inquire further requires somehow reconstructing the habitats in which single artifacts were originally parts of a working whole. Where the designers of gallery exhibits have not obliged by re-creating miniature or substitute contexts in models, drawings, photographs, or films, do-it-yourself historians must as a last resort call up from memory the mental pictures of the past that most of us store in our minds like paintings stored in a study collection. Once before us, these images can be peopled and the figures animated to disclose dynamic social relationships. The result will be, of course, as true or as flawed as the information we bring to bear. Image-making is a poor substitute for the genuine article. Unquestionably, the exercise is made easier and more reliable when curators, designers, and historians have used their professional skills to set the scene beforehand.[14] Let us, therefore, illustrate the application of our four-part catechism by reference to a carefully researched, fully re-created, three-dimensional historical setting.

Imagine an eighteenth-century plantation. Make it a Chesapeake plantation, perhaps a very large one, such as George Washington's Mount Vernon or George Mason's Gunston Hall, or, better yet, something smaller and more typical of a lesser planter—a slave owner and a gentleman, to be sure, but not one of Virginia's fabled pashas. The National Colonial Historical Farm outside Washington, D.C., or the Washington birthplace at Wakefield, Virginia, are historic sites more in scale with the experience of larger numbers of eighteenth-century Marylanders and Virginians.

Your visit to this plantation has brought you to the kitchen, a one- or two-room frame building some little distance from the house. Stepping inside and seeing immediately a large fireplace and an array of cooking utensils, you correctly conclude that here was a kitchen where food was prepared for more people than could possibly have occupied the building. Who were they? Looking around for answers, you notice that shelves and a plate rack mounted along the wall hold several large pewter serving pieces, but there seem to be no dinner plates except some battered wooden trenchers. Further investigation reveals the absence of table knives and forks and fine glassware of any kind. Clearly, the cooked food was carried away on the pewter platters, presumably to the nearby house, and there dished out on tablewares considered too valuable to be stored in the kitchen. Already, you can infer something about the people who staffed this outbuilding and their perceived inferiority. Obviously, there was a cook, and probably a cook's assistant to keep the hand-cranked spit turning before the fire. The scene implies the presence of others as well—someone to run hot food to the dining room and someone to keep the water buckets filled and the firewood replenished. A table, placed out of the way in one corner and set with trenchers and cast-off spoons, suggests that the kitchen also doubled as a mess hall for slaves detailed to the house, the garden, and the stable. In fairly short order, your questions and answers have uncovered a variety of relationships among just the half dozen or so black users of this space. A pecking order is evident, even among slaves, with the skilled cook exercising a manager's authority over assistants and helpers. Yet, at mealtimes, and probably in idle moments between chores, domestics, stable hands, dairy maids, and gardeners dropped by the kitchen and involved the cooks in exchanges of an informal, familiar, even familial kind. Besides stools and one up-ended crate set round the table, two old, mended chairs show heavy wear on the back legs and front stretchers where loungers, engrossed in conversation, tipped them back against the wall and propped up their feet. The scene that your discerning eye has re-created can easily set you thinking (especially with help from a guide or a few interpretive labels) about the vital support that friends, kinfolk, and workmates gave to one another in this slave society and the important role they played in raising children. Both were African traditions that fortified individuals and families in the ordeal of slavery.

Who else used this kitchen? Three shawls hang on pegs beside the door, two of coarse homespun, mended here and there, the other of a finer material. The third peg also holds a ring of keys. Careful curatorial scene-setting has thus defined the gender of the cook and her female assistant and also implies another level of supervision provided by the planter's wife or the housekeeper. The keys recall the padlock you saw on the meathouse outside, which the mistress opened every day on her morning rounds. Here in the kitchen, a six-board chest and a large cupboard, both fitted with locks, remind you that, despite the daily collaboration between cook and mistress and despite the kitchen's extensive use by slaves and servants, their white masters maintained off-limits areas within their work and living spaces. The distrust manifested by locks and keys was no matter of mere caution or practicality; it sprang ultimately from the racism that shot the eighteenth century through and through. Even that has left its artifacts in this kitchen: an iron pot simmers in one corner of the hearth, behind the frying pans, spits, trivets, gridirons,

Dutch ovens, stew pots, sauce pans, patty pans, and other paraphernalia needed to prepare the planter's mid-day meal. The single pot contains slave fare: hominy, most days; sometimes, boiled meat; occasionally, the "heads and plucks" of chickens—in short, cooked slops for those whom many planters regarded as their walking, talking animals.

The question-and-answer approach can be adjusted to the different ways people engage in the learning process. For those who prefer to sample information a little at a time, pausing to digest it, then returning for more until they have mastered as much of a subject as they care to know, a line of questioning that leads from objects to uses to users to relationships provides a simple strategy for orderly, efficient learning. Others choose to experience information all at once, directly and immediately. Social history can be taught to them by applying the inquiry method somewhat differently. Such people move easily—too easily—between past and present. The instant they heft an axe or shoulder a musket, they assume a role that automatically tells them where they are, what they are doing, whose personna they have put on, and who else might have been involved. The trick for interpreters is helping them distinguish historical reality from their personal reactions to the experience they are engaged in. Interpreters wise enough to know that participatory learners usually absorb more by feeling than reasoning can still give direction to social history learning experiences by asking the what-how-who-and-why questions in ways that test those feelings against historians' understanding of the facts. Visitors invited to taste cornmeal mush from the stew pot in our last illustration might be asked, "If you were a slave and ate 'pone, day in and day out, after working so hard every morning to roast meats and bake pies for the planter, how might you feel toward your master? How would you feel about yourself?" Questions like that, deliberately contrasting the past and the present and containing such historical information as learners need to draw valid conclusions, can discipline undiscriminating imaginations and thereby inculcate an appreciation for the significant differences between now and times gone by.

The past in physical form is often less successful at conveying other aspects of social history. Contrasts and differences imply change; yet, museums, like all other visual representations of the past that reflect the surface world, seem ill-equipped to penetrate the deeper, longer-lasting, latent events that contemporaries only dimly perceived or were wholly unaware of, however much they struggled with the consequences. These days, social historians understand that long-term shifts in sex ratios, birth and death rates, wealth distributions, patterns of landholding, labor supplies, and standards of living underlay and profoundly shaped the course of those more visible events that contemporaries were conscious of and tried to influence.[15] Social history that fails to take these fundamental conditions into account can only explain historical change superficially. The problem for museums is not that latent events left behind no artifacts—they did; but when restored to their appropriate historical settings, the artifacts document only a single instant, an episode, a millisecond in the much longer, slower, never-ending transformations of human history. Of necessity, most outdoor museums and historic sites portray particular places at particular times. The questions we can direct at their re-created historical scenes, no matter how incisive, illuminate the state of things at one moment only—1627, at the Pilgrim's Plimoth Plantation; 1824, at Fort Snelling on the Mississippi River; the third quarter of the eighteenth century, at Colonial Williamsburg; one winter, at Valley Forge; and a single engagement, at Antietam.

To gain perspective on a deeper order of events, social historians who teach with artifacts are increasingly experimenting with historical settings that do funny things with chronology.[16] Some skip blithely over decades or whole centuries to bring together, side by side, deliberately contrasting historical scenes that make plain the extent of changes that have taken place in the intervals. Long the organizing rationale of museums that display the decorative arts in a chronological sequence of period rooms, the time-line has become the most widely used approach to history exhibits of the gallery type. Now a few outdoor museums are trying it, too. Living History Farms, outside Des Moines, Iowa, makes near neighbors of an 1850s farmstead, another of 1900, and a futuristic "Farm of Today and Tomorrow"—their juxtaposition intended to demonstrate to visitors how technology, transportation systems, density of settlement, and market networks all contributed to the development of Midwestern agricultural economies. Visitors to another open-air museum, Upper Canada Village, approach a substantial Victorian farmhouse along a lane that first leads past the overgrown ruins of a pioneer's shanty. Then comes the settler's old log house, the windows now boarded up and the structure reused as a poultry coop. A little farther along, one sees, across a mature apple orchard, a still larger log dwelling, typical of those built a generation after settlement but subsequently given over to housing a family of immigrant hired hands when the prosperous grandson of the original settler built the big stone house. The whole scene is set in the year 1860, but, by carefully creating the illusion of time gone by, the museum invites visitors to think about the process of homesteading over two or three generations. The magic of time-lapse history can work, even in a single building. "The Time Machine" is the name given to the exhibit planned for the new Hall of Everyday Life at the Smithsonian Institution's National Museum of American History. The skeleton of a seventeenth-century house from Ipswich, Massachusetts, joined to another newly built in 1752, renovated and modernized in the ensuing centuries, may be installed (according to one scheme) complete with aluminum siding and a second-hand Nash Rambler parked out front. An audio-visual presentation will fill the house with sights and sounds that, in the words of its designers, treat "the passage of time itself—soundless, invisible, yet profound in the ceaseless changes unrolled in its train."[17]

So museums *can* show the transformation of society and, by setting up comparisons, *can* encourage visitors to inquire after the reasons for the differences that they observe. To the four questions that museum visitors have learned to address to any one historical scene, they must add a fifth and a sixth question, to analyze contrasting settings: *How have people's circumstances and relationships with one another changed from one period to the next? As a consequence of what?* Artifacts, being able to communicate only in their respective present tenses, are powerless to answer the last question. The basic social history explanations that string events and momentary occasions together into one unbroken continuum must be forthcoming from knowledgeable interpreters, interpretive exhibits, or history learners themselves.

To see history whole and to understand its mainsprings are the highest aspirations that social historians can have. They labor for the day when the popular mind embraces their account of the past and, so doing, puts aside the older, outmoded historical schema that explained the present simply as progress from an inferior but improving past. In the American context, progressive history has focused most intensively on the nation's political life, where the themes that seemed to address the essence of the American experience were those that told the story of our longing for individual liberty and justice and our struggle for independence and self-government. Modern scholarship has not invalidated these ligaments in the narrative that describes the growth of democratic institutions, but it does deny their importance as the organizing themes best able to explain how our society has evolved the way it has. In rejecting the old order of explanation—a mythology whose power to inspire belief is waning—historians are only responding to the public they serve. Little by little, in that mysterious way that a people reassesses its past in relation to itself, we are increasingly coming to sense that Western history has owed at least as much to universal human instincts for interdependence as it has to the drive for independence. Social historians have a clear calling to put that story together into a single, coherent, general account that explains how the fragile social contract of modern civilization has been formed out of innumerable earlier states. Scholars have recently made remarkable progress in understanding critical aspects of the story; but most are still too engrossed in technical studies to attempt a synthesis of sufficiently epic proportions to capture the popular imagination and become the new working mythology that helps us see deeply into our own times and affairs. Academic historians cannot expect the world to wait for their sober conclusions, especially considering that their advice is offered gratuitously. Second-best will have to be some method of showing to the general public the work in progress, an acceptable expedient in view of the fact that it is more important to communicate social history's perspective on the past than to know all the answers to the questions it poses.

The challenge for historians, it seems to us, is the challenge of effecting a general re-education in historical thinking. In that great work, academicians need to join forces with colleagues who already reach public audiences, whose stock and trade are the "little communities" implicit in every re-created historical setting, and who specialize in the art of nonverbal or only partly-verbal communication. Students, teachers, and interpreters of material culture are somehow freer to narrate the history that is all around us and the history of which each of us is part.

Notes

1. Many works could be cited. A useful starting point is Frederick L. Rath, Jr., and Merrilyn Rogers O'Connell, *A Bibliography on Historical Organization Practices*, 3rd edition, 6 vols. (Nashville: American Association for State and Local History, 1975–1982).

2. Freeman Tilden, *Interpreting Our Heritage* (Chapel Hill: University of North Carolina Press, 1957); William T. Alderson and Shirley Payne Lowe, *Interpretation of Historic Sites* (Nashville: American Association for State and Local History, 1976); Grant W. Sharpe, editor, *Interpreting the Environment* (New York: John Wiley and Son, 1976); Edward P. Alexander, *Museums in Motion: An Introduction to the History and Functions of Museums* (Nashville: American Association for State and Local History, 1979); William Lewis, *Interpreting for Park Visitors* (Philadelphia: Acorn Press, 1980).

3. Chandler G. Screven, *The Measurement and Facilitation of Learning in the Museum Environment: An Experimental Analysis* (Washington, D.C.: Smithsonian Institution Press, 1974). Others are conveniently collected in Chandler G. Screven, "A Bibliography on Visitor Education Research," *Museum News* 57 (March/April, 1979): 56–59, 86–88; and Robert L. Wolf, et al., *New Perspectives on Evaluating Museum Environments: An Annotated Bibliography* (Washington, D.C.: Department of Psychological Studies, Office of Museum Programs, Smithsonian Institution, 1979). See also the section on "Adults as Learners" in *Museums, Adults, and the Humanities. A Guide for Educational Programming*, edited by Zipporah W. Collins (Washington, D.C.: American Association of Museums, 1981).

4. Robert L. Wolf, Mary Ellen Munley, and Barbara L. Tymitz, *The Pause that Refreshes: A Study of Visitor Reactions to the Discovery Corners in the National Museum of History and Technology, Smithsonian Institution* (Washington, D.C.: Department of Psychological Studies, Office of Museum Programs, Smithsonian Institution, 1979); Robert L. Wolf and Barbara L. Tymitz, "East Side, West Side, Straight Down the Middle": A Study of Visitor Perceptions of "Our Changing Land," the Bicentennial Exhibit, National Museum of Natural History, Smithsonian Institution (Washington, D.C.: Department of Psychological Studies, Office of Museum Programs, Smithsonian Institution, 1979); Robert C. Birney, "An Evaluation of Visitors' Experience at the Governor's Palace, Colonial Williamsburg, Virginia," *Academic Psychology Bulletin* 4 (1982): 135–141; results of a follow-up survey to be published in the same journal. For similar studies at Sturbridge Village, see D. Geoffrey Hayward, *Evaluation of Interpretive Changes in the Fitch Home, 1979–1980, Old Sturbridge Village* (Amherst, Mass.: Environmental and Behavioral Research Center, University of Massachusetts, 1981).

5. The following visitors' comments are taken from the surveys cited in footnote 4, from Kristin Fischer, "Governor's Palace Study, Part V" (Colonial Williamsburg Foundation, 1980, typescript report), and from the authors' own observations.

6. John Demos, *A Little Commonwealth: Family Life in Plymouth Colony* (New York: Oxford University Press, 1970).

7. Staff of Colorado State Museum, *Interpreting Healy House: An Interview* (Nashville: American Association for State and Local History, 1974), pp. 14–15.

8. For artifacts used as primary sources for historical research, see Cary Carson, "Doing History with Material Culture," in *Material Culture and the Study of American Life*, edited by Ian M. G. Quimby, (New York: W. W. Norton & Company, Inc., 1978), pp. 41–64.

9. Carol Shammas, "The Domestic Environment in Early Modern England and America," *Journal of Social History* 14 (1980): 3–24; Cary Carson and Lorena S. Walsh, "The Material Life of the Early American Housewife" (Paper presented to the Conference on Women in Early America, Colonial Williamsburg Foundation and the Institute for Early American History and Culture, November 1981).

10. James Deetz, "The Reality of the Pilgrim Fathers," *Natural History* 78 (1969): 32–45; Shomer Zwelling, "Social History Hits the Streets: Williamsburg Characters Come to Life," *History News* 35 (January 1980): 10–12.

11. Darrett B. Rutman, "The Social Web: A Prospectus for the Study of the Early American Community," in *Insights and Parallels: Problems and Issues of American Social History*, edited by William L. O'Neill (Minneapolis: Burgess Publishing Company, 1973), pp. 57–89.

12. Accession no. 59.631, Winterthur Museum, Winterthur, Delaware. Illustrated in Joseph Downs, *American Furniture, Queen Anne and Chippendale Periods* (New York: Macmillan Co., 1952), no. 178. The brasses are discussed and illustrated with the chest in Charles F. Hammel, "Samuel Rowland Fisher's Catalogue of English Hardware," *Winterthur Portfolio* 1 (1964): 188–197.

13. In pockets of rural Connecticut, sideboards have long been called "lockers," in explicit recognition of their use in keeping valuable dining room utensils safe (information from Kevin Sweeney, administrator-curator, Webb-Deane-Stevens Museum, Wethersfield, Connecticut).

14. It should go without saying that these scenes are always abstractions that can only approximate the "truth," no matter how complete their documentation. Darwin P. Kelsey discusses their limitations intelligently in "Historical Farms as Models of the Past," *Association for Living Historical Farms and Agricultural Museums Annual Proceedings* (1975), pp. 33–38.

15. For a perceptive summary view of social history's current state and future prospects, see Bernard Bailyn, "The Challenge of Modern Historiography," *American Historical Review* 87 (1982): 1–24.

16. Cary Carson, "Living Museums of Everyman's History," *Harvard Magazine* 83 (July–August 1981): 22–32.

17. Richard Rabinowitz, et al., *Sixteen Elm Street: The Time Machine. A Shooting Script for a Multi-Media Presentation at the National Museum of American History* (Washington, D.C.: American History Workshop for the Smithsonian Institution, 1982), p. iii.

Suggestions for Additional Reading

We have used the footnotes to indicate further readings related to specific points raised in the essays. Here, we offer a few more general suggestions.

Deetz, James. *In Small Things Forgotten: The Archeology of Early American Life.* Garden City: Anchor Books, 1977.

> Although not mentioned as such, the ideas implicit in the new social history permeate Deetz's analysis of architecture and artifacts. His work has been influential in the interpretive programs at Plimoth Plantation.

Ettema, Michael J. "History, Nostalgia, and American Furniture." *Winterthur Portfolio* 17 (1982): 135–144.

> A review essay of three furniture studies gives the author a chance to spell out the distinction between antiquarian, object-oriented explorations of the past and problem-solving, thematic history.

Jackson, J. B. "The Westward-Moving House." In *Landscapes,* pp. 10– 42. Amherst: University of Massachusetts Press, 1970.

> This fictional account of three generations of Americans and their attitudes toward land, houses, personal possessions, and earning a living and their sense of self in relation to their communities suggests ways in which historical sites might use individual cases to represent broader social concerns.

Quimby, Ian M. G., editor. *Material Culture and the Study of American Life.* Published for the Henry Francis duPont Winterthur Museum, Winterthur, Delaware, by W. W. Norton & Company, Inc., New York, 1978.

Schlereth, Thomas J. *Artifacts and the American Past.* Nashville: American Association for State and Local History, 1980.

Schlereth, Thomas J., editor. *Material Culture Studies in America.* Nashville: American Association for State and Local History, 1982.

> Many of the essays in Schlereth's works show how others approach the problem.

The Contributors

DAVID BRODY is Professor of History at the University of California at Davis. He received his Ph.D. in history at Harvard University in 1958. A pioneering figure in the new labor history, Professor Brody is author of *Steelworkers in America: The Nonunion Era* (1960); *The Butcher Workmen: A Study of Unionization* (1964); *Labor in Crisis: The Steel Strike of 1919* (1965); *Industrial America in the Twentieth Century* (1967); and *Workers in Industrial America: Essays on the 20th-Century Struggle* (1980). He is also author of two major overviews of the field: "The Old Labor History and the New: In Search of an American Working Class," *Labor History* (1979) and "Labor History in the 1970s: Toward a History of the American Worker," in *The Past Before Us: Contemporary Historical Writing in the United States* (1980), edited by Michael Kammen for the American Historical Association.

BARBARA G. CARSON is Assistant Professorial Lecturer in American Studies at George Washington University. She earned an M.A. in 1965 from the Henry Francis duPont Winterthur Museum Program in Early American History and Culture at the University of Delaware. Prior to assuming her current position, Ms. Carson taught at St. Mary's College of Maryland and the Radcliffe Institute, held research positions at St. Mary's City, Maryland, and Plimoth Plantation, and served as assistant curator, Collection of Historical Scientific Instruments, Harvard University. She has appeared on the programs of the Southern Historical Association and the Antiques Forum at Colonial Williamsburg and has lectured at the Summer Institute of the Museum of Early Southern Decorative Arts, the Decorative Arts Seminar at the Yale University Art Gallery, the Summer Institute at the Winterthur Museum, and AASLH's workshop series on Interpreting the Humanities through Exhibit Design.

CARY CARSON is Director of Research at the Colonial Williamsburg Foundation. He holds an M.A. from the Henry Francis duPont Winterthur Museum Program in Early American History and Culture (1965) and a Ph.D. in history from Harvard University (1974). Prior to coming to Williamsburg in 1976, Dr. Carson was Co-ordinator of Research at St. Mary's City, Maryland, and Research Associate at the Smithsonian Institution. He has also taught at Yale University, Carleton College, the College of William and Mary, and St. Mary's College of Maryland. Currently he serves on the editorial board of the *Winterthur Portfolio*. His publications include "Doing History with Material Culture," published in 1978 in Winterthur's *Material Culture and the Study of American Life*; "Living Museums of Everyman's History," *Harvard Magazine* (1981); and articles in *Winterthur Portfolio*, *History News*, the *Maryland Historical Magazine*, *Vernacular Architecture*, and other journals.

KATHLEEN NEILS CONZEN is Associate Professor of American Urban History at the University of Chicago. She received her Ph.D. in history from the University of Wisconsin in 1972. Professor Conzen serves on the editorial board of the *Journal of Urban History* and has participated in the programs of the American Historical Association, the Organization of American Historians, the Association of American Geographers, the Berkshire Conference on the History of Women, and numerous other professional organizations and conferences. Her publications in the field of urban history include *Immigrant Milwaukee, 1836–1860: Accommodation and Community in a Frontier City* (1976) and "Community Studies, Urban History, and American Local History," in *The Past Before Us: Contemporary Historical Writing in the United States*, edited by Michael Kammen for the American Historical Association (1980).

SAMUEL P. HAYS is Distinguished Service Professor of History at the University of Pittsburgh. He holds the Ph.D. from Harvard University (1953). Professor Hays was an influential figure in the emergence of the "new political history" in the 1960s and has published numerous studies that reflect his interest in the "social analysis of political life," including his latest book, *American Political History as Social Analysis* (1980). Other publications include *The Response to Industrialism* (1957); *Conservation and the Gospel of Efficiency: The Progressive Conservation Movement* (1958); "History as Human Behavior," *Iowa Journal of History* (1960); "The Politics of Reform in Municipal Government in the Progressive Era," *Pacific Northwest Quarterly* (1964); "The Social Analysis of American Political History, 1880–1920," *Political Science Quarterly* (1965); "Historical Social Research: Concept, Method and Technique," *Journal of Interdisciplinary History* (1974); and "The Changing Political Structure of the City in Industrial America," *Journal of Urban History* (1974).

ELIZABETH H. PLECK is Research Associate at the Center for Research on Women, Wellesley College, and visiting Associate Professor at Wellesley College and the Massachusetts Institute of Technology. She received her Ph.D. in the History of American Civilization at Brandeis University in 1973. She currently serves on the executive board of the Social Science History Association and the nominating committee of the American Historical Association and is editor of the Series in American Social History published by the State University of New York Press. Dr. Pleck is author of *Black Migration and Poverty: Boston, 1865–1900* (1979); editor with Nancy F. Cott of *A Heritage of Her Own: Toward a New Social History of American Women* (1979); and editor with Joseph N. Pleck of *The American Man* (1980). Other publications include "Two Worlds in One: Work and Family," *Journal of Social History* (1976); and "The Two-Parent Household: Black Family Structure in Late Nineteenth-Century Boston," *Journal of Social History* (1972). She has also appeared on the programs of the Organization of American Historians, the American Studies Association, the Social Science History Association, the American Historical Association, the Berkshire Conference on the History of Women, and other professional organizations and conferences.

HOWARD N. RABINOWITZ is Associate Professor of History at the University of New Mexico. He received his Ph.D. in history from the University of Chicago in 1973. Professor Rabinowitz is editor of *Southern Black Leaders of the Reconstruction Era* (1982) and author of *Race Relations in the Urban South, 1865–1890* (1978) and numerous articles in the *Journal of American History*, the *Journal of Urban History*, the *Journal of Southern History*, *American Jewish History*, *American Studies*, and other scholarly journals. He also serves on the board of editors of the *Journal of Southern History* and has appeared on the programs of the Organization of American Historians, the Southern Historical Association, the Association for the Study of Afro-American Life and History, and other professional organizations.

PETER N. STEARNS is Heinz Professor of History at Carnegie-Mellon University. He holds the Ph.D. from Harvard University (1963). Professor Stearns's research interests span both European and American history, and he is author of numerous surveys and monographs in social history, including *European Society in Upheaval: A Social History Since 1750* (1967), *Lives of Labor: Work in Maturing Industrial Society* (1975), and *Be a Man! Males in Modern Society* (1979). He is founder and editor of the *Journal of Social History* and has contributed articles to the *Journal of Interdisciplinary History*, the *American Historical Review*, the *Journal of Family History*, and other journals. He also serves as co-director of Carnegie-Mellon's new program in applied history and co-directs the N.E.H.-funded Project on Social History, which is preparing social history materials for use in secondary-school classrooms.

ROBERT P. SWIERENGA is Professor of History at Kent State University. He received his Ph.D. at the University of Iowa in 1965. He is co-editor of *Social Science History* and serves on the editorial boards of *Agricultural History* and *Fides et Historia*. Professor Swierenga's publications include *Acres for Cents: Delinquent Tax Auctions in Frontier Iowa* (1976); *Pioneers and Profits: Land Speculation on the Iowa Frontier* (1968); *Quantification in American History, Theory and Research* (1970); *Beyond the Civil War Synthesis: Political Essays of the Civil War Era* (1975); and articles in the *Journal of American History*, the *Journal of Economic History*,

Agricultural History, the *Journal of Social History,* and other scholarly journals. He has also appeared on the programs of the Organization of American Historians and other organizations and has spoken at numerous conferences on rural history, ethnic history, and quantification.

MARIS A. VINOVSKIS is Professor of History at the University of Michigan. He received the Ph.D. in history at Harvard University in 1975 and is considered a leading specialist in family history and historical demography. He is on the editorial board of the *Journal of Family History.* His publications include *Fertility in Massachusetts from the Revolution to the Civil War* (1981); *Studies in American Historical Demography* (1979); "From Household Size to the Life Course: Some Observations on Recent Trends in Family History," in the *American Behavioral Scientist* (1977); and "Recent Trends in American Historical Demography: Some Methodological and Conceptual Considerations," in the *Annual Review of Sociology* (1978). Professor Vinovskis is also co-author with Carl F. Kaestle of *Education and Social Change in Nineteenth-Century Massachusetts* (1980) and co-editor with Tamara K. Hareven of *Family and Population in Nineteenth-Century America* (1978). He earlier served as deputy staff director, U.S. House Select Committee on Population and has appeared on the programs of numerous professional organizations and conferences.

Index

Acculturation. *See* Assimilation
Achenbaum, Andrew, 130
Adolescence: concept of, 126–127; ethnic differences in, 127; and transition from school to work-place, 127–128; gender differences in, 127–128; and childbearing, 128
Agriculture. *See* Rural history; rural life
Annales. See French social history
Aries, Philippe, 123
Artifacts: and new social history, 8–9, 182–184, 201; and urban history, 80; and problem of inequality, 169–170; use of in interpretation, 182–190, 191–192, 193–196, 198, 200; how visitors learn from, 183–190, 195–196, 198, 200; as expression of culture, 193–195; model for learning from, 195–200
Assimilation: models, 24–28; and melting pot, 25–26; and doctrine of Anglo-conformity, 26–27; and cultural pluralism, 27–28; and alienation or persistence, 29, 31–33, 98–101; structural, 32; and Mann's typology of ethnic identity, 40; and Higham's concept of pluralistic integration, 41–42

Bailyn, Bernard, 155
Baltimore Neighborhood Heritage Project, 153
Barton, Josef: on migration patterns, 29–30; on social mobility, 34–35; on ethnic family life, 36; mentioned, 38
Beauvoir. *See* de Beauvoir

Becker, Gary, 143
Beecher, Catherine, 53, 59
Benson, Lee, 162
Benson, Mary, 58
Berkner, Lutz, 117
Bernard, Jessie, 56
Bernard, Richard, 97
Bernstein, Irving, 146
Biographies: of women, 53
Birney, Robert, 186
Blacks: slavery of, 25, 32–33; migration patterns of, 31; and community formation, 31–33; social mobility of, 34–35, 38; family size of, 35; and assimilation, 40–41; in Pittsburgh, 148
Blassingame, John, 25, 32
Bloch, Marc, 104–105
Bodnar, John, 39
Bogue, Allan, 95–96
Borchert, James, 32–33
Bower, Ames Sheldon, 61
Boyer, Paul, 53
Braudel, Fernand, 105
Braverman, Harry, 151
Brecher, Jeremy, 150
Briggs, John: and studies of Italian immigrants, 24, 30, 33, 35, 39
Brody, David, 142–143, 144–145
Brownell, Blaine, 79
Burton, Vernon, 104

Calhoun, Arthur, 115–116
Camarillo, Albert, 30, 31, 39
Castillo. *See* Griswold del Castillo

209

adolescence, 127; and working-class culture, 147–148, 155; and inequality, 169. *See also* names of specific groups
Extended family. *See* Family

Faires, Nora, 166
Family: and household size, extended or nuclear, 12, 35, 116–117; and ethnicity, 35–36, 148; and women, 55–56, 57; in rural life, 102–103; and new social history, 115, 116; antecedents of, 115–116; and quantification, 116; influence of social science on study of, 116; and concept of generations, 117; cycles, 117–118; Duvall's eight-stage model of, 117–118; life-course analysis of, 118–120; and childbearing, 120–123; and early child development, 123–126; and adolescence, 126–128; and old age, 128–131; dissemination of research on, 131
Farmers. *See* Rural history; Rural life
Father: redefinition of in early America, 124–125
Feminism: and absence of women from history, 51; as part of women's history, 57, 60–61
Fertility. *See* Childbearing
Films: as stories of plain people, 152–153; in historical re-creations, 196
Fine, Sidney, 146
Fischer, David, 130
Foner, Philip, 149
Fort Snelling, 199
Fox, Dixon Ryan, 23
Fragmentation: as problem of social history, 14–15
French Canadians: marriage patterns of, 36; and ethnocultural tensions, 147
French social history, 5, 10, 24, 104–105, 108, 116, 120
Frontier, 94–95, 146, 169. *See also* Turner, Frederick Jackson

Gage, Matilda, 52
Garcia, Mario, 31, 32, 33
Gates, Paul W., 95
Gender: as social category, 54–55. *See also* Women
Genovese, Eugene, 32
Geographical mobility, 74–76, 167–168
Germans: marriage patterns of, 36; social mobility of, 75; as farmers in Texas, 98–100; religious values of, 101; and politics, 162–163, 164–165; subcultures of, 166

German scholars, 140
German social history, 10
Goldfield, David, 79
Gordon, Milton: on structural assimilation, 32; mentioned, 27, 40
Greeks, 170
Green, Carol Hurd, 53
Greven, Philip, 115, 116, 117
Griswold del Castillo, Richard, 28, 31, 39
Gutman, Herbert: and study of slavery, 32, 35; and labor history, 143–144; as exponent of Thompson approach, 147

Hale, Sarah, 52
Handlin, Oscar: as forerunner of new social history, 25; on immigrant alienation, 29–30, 31, 33; and the "new urban history," 78; as teacher of historians, 143, 144; mentioned, 33, 39
Hareven, Tamara: and studies of French Canadians, 36; and redefinition of family cycles, 118; and study of Amoskeag mills, 147–149
Harrison, Brian, 146
Hays, Samuel P.: and study of social change, 78; and rural studies, 96; and local studies, 104
Heer, David, 36
Henretta, James, 103
Herberg, Will, 36
Higham, John, 41–42
Hinding, Andrea, 61
Hispanics. *See* Mexican Americans
Historical geographers, 97–98
Historical setting. *See* Artifacts; Interpretation
History Workshop, 3–4
Hobsbawm, Eric, 146, 149
Hofstadter, Richard, 92, 144
Homosexuals, 192
Household size. *See* Family

Immigration. *See* Ethnicity; names of specific groups
Indians. *See* Native Americans
Industrialization: and effect on families, 121
Inequality: as problem in local history, 168; in consumption, 169–170
Institutional perspective: in urban history, 77–78; in labor history, 139–142; on social history, 171
Intermarriage: of ethnics, 36; in rural society, 97